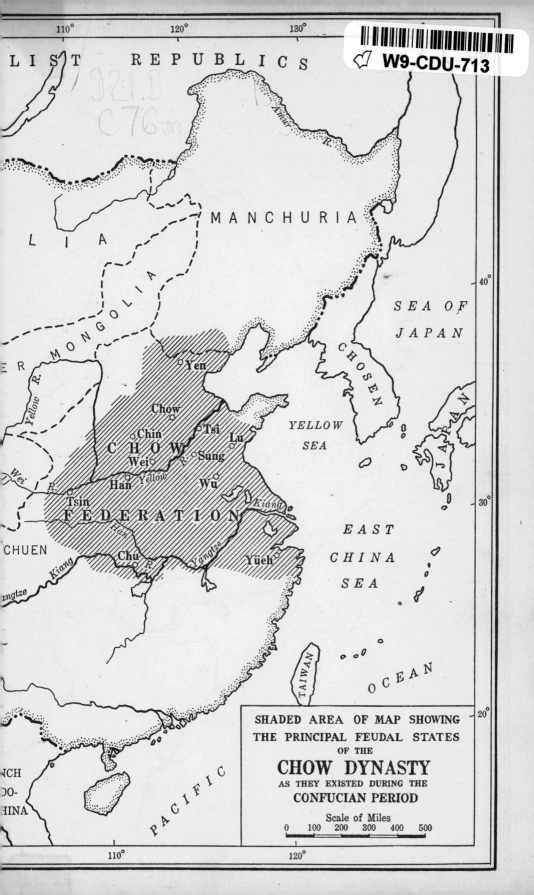

SHADED AREA OF MAP SHOWING
THE PRINCIPAL FEUDAL STATES
OF THE

CHOW DYNASTY

AS THEY EXISTED DURING THE
CONFUCIAN PERIOD

Scale of Miles

0   100   200   300   400   500

MASTER KUNG

Master Kung was always followed by his youthful though grey-headed disciple Yen Yuan.

MASTER KUNG

THE STORY OF CONFUCIUS

by

CARL CROW

Illustrated

HARPER & BROTHERS PUBLISHERS

New York and London

To

STANLEY WENT

but for whose encouragement this book
would never have been written.

CONTENTS

CONTENTS—*continued*

CONTENTS—*continued*

LIST OF ILLUSTRATIONS

PREFACE

ALL the world has heard of the great Chinese sage Confucius but few know of Master Kung though the two characters are embodied in the same person. Master Kung is the sincere, lovable, entirely human scholar and gentleman who was born in the sixth century before Christ, lived a blameless life, suffered more disillusionments and disappointments than usually fall to the lot of men and died feeling that his life had been a failure. Confucius was the creation of generations of later scholars who deified the man, interpreted his acts and sayings by methods which would justify this deification and so created an intellectual Frankenstein monster, a fleshless creature conceived and born between the covers of a text-book.

The story of the life of Master Kung as told in the following pages does not represent any new discoveries regarding the facts of his life but is the first attempt to put all the known or generally accepted facts into a chronological order against the historical and social background of the period. The two main sources of information which have been drawn on are available to any student in translated form. One is found in the great historical works of the Chinese historian Sze Ma Chien, who was born a few centuries after the death of the sage. The other authority is the monumental work known as *The Chinese Classics* translated by the Aberdeen Missionary, James Legge, who came to China to 'convert the heathen' and remained to give to English readers their first authentic information regarding Chinese literature and culture.

Orthodox Confucian scholars may find in this book some reasons for disagreement, but if they do it will most probably be because Master Kung the man and the deified Confucius are different entities who must be looked upon from different points of view. There are a great many different versions as to various incidents in his life and when it has been necessary to make a choice I have tried to select the one which appeared to be most generally accepted by the

Chinese themselves. My most sincere hope is that in presenting him as a man I have not failed to depict the true greatness of his character, a greatness which has in every way justified the adulation in which his countrymen have held him throughout the centuries and will continue to hold him so long as there is a Chinese race.

A NOTE ON THE ILLUSTRATIONS

THE illustrations in this volume are selections from copies of pictures depicting the life of the sage which are engraved on more than 100 stone tablets in the great Confucian Temple at Chufu (Zigzag Hill) in Shantung. The original pictures are attributed to a famous artist of the T'ang dynasty (about A.D. 700) and were probably copied and improved upon many times by succeeding generations of artists before being engraved on stone and placed in the Chufu temple a few centuries ago. It was during the T'ang dynasty that pictorial art had its first great development. In their original form the reproductions in this book probably constituted the first attempts to illustrate historical events by means of pictures. Every generation of artists from the time these pictures were originally produced has copied them and they have been reproduced by dozens of publishers. Albums containing lithographed or wood block copies of these drawings are sold to pilgrims who visit the birthplace of the sage and are to be found in homes and libraries all over China. Similar pictures painted in colours on silk by famous artists are among the prized possessions of wealthy art collectors and have been considered as appropriate presents to give to emperors. Whether in the form of rough wood block reproductions or the work of famous artists, the incidents depicted are always the same and the composition of the pictures differs only in minor details. It is interesting to note that while these pictures of the life of the great sage are found everywhere, there are no images of him.

The first thing about the illustrations that strikes one's attention is the fact that the costumes depicted have but little resemblance to the Chinese costumes of to-day but are very similar to the Japanese kimona. There was during the time of Master Kung no contact between the Japanese and Chinese, the two people being entirely unknown to each other; but a few centuries later, before the styles of Chinese dress had changed, there was an active, though mainly piratical, trade between the two countries. The island visitors found China enjoying a very advanced state of civilisation and they absorbed and adopted the customs and the culture of their continental neighbour almost as readily and as completely as they absorbed Western ideas during the last century. Chinese fashions in dress changed but the Japanese fashions did not, with the result that the Japanese national dress of to-day appears to be an almost exact duplicate of the dress worn by Master Kung about 2,500 years ago.

The heavy two-wheeled cart which appears in so many of the pictures is exactly the same as the cart which is a familiar sight in all parts of North China to-day and has not been changed since Master Kung rode in them, though the carts are now usually drawn by mules instead of oxen. The agricultural implements, the grain measures and the musical instruments are the same as to-day and are generally believed to be identical with those used at that time. In other points the pictures do not display such historical accuracy. In some of them Master Kung is shown using a camel's hair writing brush and tablets of paper but brush and paper were not invented until several centuries later and all writing consisted of characters incised on wooden tablets. Readers who take the trouble to check the illustrations with the text will doubtless be surprised to note that on page 65 Master Kung is depicted as a bearded adult. He was at that time less than twenty years old but the artist viewed him retrospectively as a sage and depicted him as one. Many famous painters have taken a similar liberty or have been equally careless with historical facts. The next illustration on page 69 depicts him as keeper of the herds, a position he held a few years later and here he is shown as a beardless youth. Just why this should be I do not pretend to say, but there was undoubtedly some significance to this change in the method of depicting him following different avocations as artists of many succeeding generations have followed the same convention.

While the Chinese artist may be careless regarding the historical treatment of subjects he does not allow the limitations of space or perspective to interfere with the complete and graphic presentation of the story he is depicting. In any scene showing events which have a remote connection with warfare, battle flags are to be seen flying in the background even though the battlefield may be many miles distant. Sometimes the inclusion of a thin line of clouds separating the foreground from the background indicates that the two scenes may be very remote from each other. The screen before which Master Kung is seated in many of the rural scenes is, of course, only a device of the artist to draw attention to the central character in the picture and to invest him with surroundings of a dignity appropriate to his rank. It would never occur to any Chinese to question the propriety of this procedure.

MASTER KUNG

CHAPTER I

*The remarkable circumstance concerning the birth
of the son of an old soldier who was destined to
influence the lives of untold millions of his fellow-
countrymen and to gain a fame which has flourished
throughout the centuries.*

HAVING reached the ripe age of seventy Kung the Tall who was
living in what is now the province of Shantung in Northern
China drew up a well considered balance sheet of his earthly
accounts, putting on the credit side all the accomplishments in
which he took pride and on the debit side all the worthy desires
and ambitions which the passing years had left unfulfilled. The
strong old man did not know that the final reckoning of his earthly
affairs would come as soon as it did, but he was aware that it could
not be long delayed. He came of a long lived family and, for his
age, he was remarkably strong and vigorous, but after seventy the
years travel faster, and of his many recorded generations of ancestors
few had outlived the span of life which he had attained. The passing years had washed out the passions of youth, the vanities of
middle age, and most of the delusions which had remained for the
autumn of his life. As is usually the case with men who at the age
of seventy have encompassed their allotted span and are prepared
to die, most of the entries in the book had been completed, sum-
marised and assessed. But until a man breathes his last he invariably thinks and believes that he can by one more journal entry or
another alter the debit or credit balance. Kung the Tall considered
the matter carefully and, like numerous others of his age who lived
before, and many more who have lived after him, was but moder-
ately satisfied with the summary and analysis of accomplishments
he had drawn up.

While the individual items included on the credit side of his account were few in number, on the whole the reckoning thus far was fairly satisfactory. Though the land of his birth, now known as ancient China, was the home of illustrious families, none in that country came of a more distinguished or more aristocratic lineage. The roots of his family tree went back to emperors of such a remote period that their very existence was cast into doubt by prying and suspicious students born a thousand years later, and have been the subject of scholarly controversy for many centuries. But Kung the Tall's pride of ancestry did not rest entirely on this ancient relationship. It had only a slightly less brilliant but more secure foundation in the fact that he was a blood relative, a direct descendant, of one of the great Dukes of Chow who had ruled the country for more than five centuries. But for the fact that an ancestor had voluntarily surrendered his rights to a brother of superior talent his family would have been rulers of the feudal state of Sung. There could be no doubt as to the authenticity of this ancestry; and with the Kings of Chow had begun the authentic history of the country which foreigners were later, in error, to call China. Before the advent of the Kings of Chow, legend alone had provided traditions. On the secure foundation of this historical ancestry his family was among the best. His own humble career, while it had added but little to the honour of the family name, had certainly not detracted from it. He had led a good, useful and respectable life, there was no scandal, and the neighbours who made up his small world knew no ill of him. His career was modest, but within its narrow limitations it was complete.

He had started in life as a soldier, a calling in which some of his ancestors had distinguished themselves; and he had spent the greater part of his years in the military camps. A military career was one for which he was particularly fitted. In a country of large men he was exceptionally tall, being but a few inches short of seven feet; strong of body and famed for his bravery. In those days when the long spear, the leather shield and bow with bronze headed arrows comprised the most modern military equipment, height, strength and bravery were the three essentials for military prowess. Though main reliance was placed on the bow and arrow, a favourite auxiliary weapon for close combat was a stout club five feet long and with a stone head weighing twelve to fifteen pounds. No physical weakling could handle a weapon like this and no moral weakling could stand the stress of combat. In battle, no quarter was given or asked. The game of war fascinated princes of the country as it always has done, and always will do, but it was still a crude game, lacking the modern and more fatal refinements, where many are killed and a few gain fame and glory. There was no elaborate machinery of war, no engineer-made artifices, those devices by which the cunning mechanic can defeat good honest brawn. The first book on military tactics was to be written a few years later by one of his own countrymen. Before its lessons were learned, stature, strength and bravery were what counted, and Kung the Tall was superbly equipped.

One of his feats was talked about by old soldiers in wine-shops many days' journey from his home, and was gossiped about by travellers until the story was heard in strange lands and, as often happens with narratives of unusual achievements, what he had done was falsely credited to others. His feat was badly recorded in the local histories and no one could embroider or magnify its simple gallantry. He and his fellow-soldiers, while engaged in the tedious and the long-drawn-out siege of a small walled city, noticed one dawn that the principal gate had been opened during the night. They hastily assumed that this was a token of surrender and entered the open gate in order to take possession of the place. No sooner were they inside than the heavy portcullis, or inner gate, was lowered and they realised that the open inner gate was a ruse to inveigle them to certain defeat and death. While the portcullis was still descending Kung the Tall seized it in both his powerful hands, lifted it and held it suspended whilst his companions escaped, and then followed them to safety. What made his feat of strength all the more extraordinary was the fact that he was at the time sixty years old. This display of strength and bravery inspired his younger companions to emulate him, and their subsequent valorous acts turned an unimportant siege into a famous feat of arms. One of them, who must have been the equal of Kung the Tall in stature and strength, seized a heavy wagon wheel, covered its circumference with leather, and using this as a shield succeeded without harm to himself in drawing the arrows of a hundred of his foes. On the same day the enemy, safe inside their ramparts, taunted the besiegers by hanging long pieces of fine cloth from the walls so that the lower ends dangled tantalisingly near. One of the besiegers, more agile than the rest, leaped and caught an end of the cloth and, though weighted down with his arms, was pulling himself to the top of the parapet when the enemy cut the cloth and he fell with it to the ground. The manœuvre was twice repeated and when he had secured his third prize in this way the enemy hastily drew the other pieces of cloth to safety inside the wall. Of the three feats of strength, that of Kung the Tall rightly gained the greatest fame, for it was a simple act of courage without bravado.

As Kung the Tall served under three successive dukes and was never more than a common soldier it might safely be assumed that he was a man of narrow mental limitations. But had he lived at another time his talents might have found greater scope for development. His career, like that of his fellow soldiers, was handicapped because although there was plenty of fighting and loss of life no great issues were involved in the outcome of the campaigns. There had been great battles of far-reaching importance before he was born and many others were fought after his death, but he lived in one of those periods of petty squabbling, which serve as interludes between great wars, and are so exasperatingly unsatisfactory to practical soldiers. These small conflicts between jealous feudal rulers were numerous and frequent, and the many lives lost created a surplus of females in the population, but in the main they consisted of conflicts between undisciplined warriors in which there was no opportunity for the development of military genius. There was also, for the first time in history, what appeared to be a successful movement to stop all wars. A visionary minister of one of the feudal states constituting what is now Northern China had cajoled all the princes into a peace conference where they signed a disarmament agreement which was designed to end warfare for all time. The minister was quite frank about stating that he did this in order to make a name for himself, and when his programme was adopted demanded excessive rewards. The treaty went a good deal further than a mere disarmament pact and by clauses covering economic and political questions sought to remove the causes of war. It contained the following:

'All we who covenant together agree not to hoard up the produce of good years, not to shut one another out from advantages that we possess, not to protect traitors, and not to shelter criminals. We agree to aid one another in disasters and calamities, to have compassion on one another in seasons of misfortune and disorder, to cherish the same likes and dislikes, and to support and encourage the royal house. Should any prince break these engagements may He who watches over men's sincerity and He who watches over covenants, the spirits of the famous hills and of the famous streams, the kings and dukes our predecessors, the whole host of spirits, the ancestors of our states – may all these intelligent spirits destroy him, so that he shall lose his people, his appointment pass from him, his family perish and his state be utterly overthrown.'

This was in the sixth century before the birth of Christ.

No one of the princes signing the agreement had any intention of honouring his undertaking if he found it to his interest to break it, and so the covenant did not last long, but it did succeed for a few years in applying a curb to the militaristic adventures of the warrior chieftains and instead served to store up enmities which had to be fought out by later generations. The little feudal state of Lu, to which Kung the Tall was subject, was too small and weak for ambitious military encroachments and had only to concern itself with the designs of stronger neighbouring states or with forays by neighbouring barbarous tribes who were quite easily defeated. The princes themselves had lost all semblance of the martial ardour and the honest bravery of their forefathers, and contended with each other through intrigues, stratagems and treachery. The affair of the besiegers at the city gate was occasioned by a conflict of such small importance that if the trapped soldiers had all been slaughtered, instead of saved, it could have made no difference to history; even to history which concerned itself with such minor events of the state of Lu, a little principality of which the reader will hear a great deal more.

After he became too old for active military employment Kung the Tall had spent the latter part of his life in peaceful civil employment in the service of the Duke of Lu. The service was so unimportant that there is no conclusive evidence as to exactly what it was, though he is said to have been the magistrate of a small town. No matter what his talents may have been it is certain that he was not heir to any of the easy political sinecures of the state since he was not a member of any of the local family clans, though he was destined, through his illustrious son, to be the founder of the

25

numerically strongest and longest lived clan of history. His ancestors for many generations lived in the neighbouring feudal state of Sung where they ranked very high in the feudal aristocracy. The family prospered here until the beautiful wife of Kung the Tall's great-grandfather innocently and tragically involved the entire family in serious political difficulties. A powerful minister, who had seen the beautiful wife, was infatuated, and in order to secure her brought about the execution of her husband on some trumped up charges. The wicked minister gained nothing through this iniquitous plot for, while she was being taken to his palace, the beautiful lady strangled herself with her girdle. A serious family feud was precipitated as a result of this, and apparently the years did not soften its bitterness for a few generations later the grandfather of Kung the Tall migrated to the state of Lu; which really means that he made the journey of a few days which was necessary in order to cross the boundary of one feudal state and enter another.

To return to Kung the Tall's balance sheet, there was one important item on the debit side which worried him much more than the absence of fortune and fame, and that was the lack of a son – a satisfactory son, a son who could perpetuate the family name and carry on the rites and ceremonies which are commonly known as 'ancestor worship'. After the fashion of his time, which has persisted now for twenty-five centuries, he had married early. His bride had been selected by the two families concerned, after due consideration of the relative social standing, the lucky stars as revealed by the necromancers and soothsayers and the evidence of such other signs and omens and portents as were available in those days. According to all the prognostications the union should have prospered.

After the marriage ceremony the wife repaired to a local shrine and prayed for the birth of a son, as Chinese wives had done before and have since continued to do. In due time a child was born, but this first baby was a daughter. This was a great disappointment for it was the universal desire that the first child be a son, but others had suffered the same disappointment and eventually had been more than content with a son younger than the first born daughter. When it was evident that another child was to arrive there were renewed prayers, and earnest supplications before the shrine. These proved to be of no avail. The second baby was a girl. The third baby was a girl. The fourth baby was a girl. The fifth baby was a girl.

It looked to Kung the Tall and his friends as if malignant fates had reversed the natural order of things. The relatives of the couple were embarrassed and were mutually recriminatory, for someone must be blamed for whatever happens in a family. Among vulgar people there would have been bickerings. These folk were too refined for such controversial satisfaction, but the necromancers and soothsayers who had assured a prosperous marital journey came in for their share of abusive remarks. Neighbours talked about it, and when Kung the Tall visited the village wine-shop the old codgers who were tippling and gossiping there frequently found it necessary to change the subject of conversation abruptly and begin talking about the weather or the latest political scandal. It probably appeared to his companions as exceptionally queer that a man of the huge size and manly vigour of their neighbour Kung should be cursed with this secret weakness which made it impossible for him to produce a son. It was a matter of neighbourhood gossip and speculation, but to the married couple it presented a problem of tragic importance to whose solution they devoted their undivided attention, consulting all the soothsayers available. It is more than probable that after the first few failures the disappointed husband went to the shrine himself and added his manly supplications to those of his wife.

In her way the wife was abundantly fruitful but she produced chaff, not wheat. The sixth baby was a girl! The seventh baby was a girl! Kung the Tall had been very patient and considerate with his wife. Most men having lost their tempers after the fourth or fifth female child, would have sought a divorce, a new wife and started over again. Kung the Tall must have loved the woman for he still forgave her and carried on.

The eighth baby was a girl. One more chance, madam! Give birth to a boy and you will be forgiven the eight daughters! The ninth baby was a girl. This was too much for human endurance! In all the history of husbands and wives, a long and not entirely uneventful history, no other husband had been treated so shabbily. Whatever love he may have felt for his wife was sorely tried; she had certainly failed in her first duty which was to provide a son for his family. He now did what any other sensible and

27

strong-minded husband in his time would have done years before. He got a divorce.

Before resorting to this final step, Kung the Tall had indulged in a marital diversion in the hope that he might break the bad luck of this incessant and unrelieved production of girl babies. He took to his bed a concubine, a procedure which then as now was looked upon as a liberty allowable under certain circumstances, but not entirely respectable. He probably asked his wife about it and under the circumstances she could do nothing but agree with the idea. In fact she may have suggested the concubine herself, as many barren Chinese wives have done.

At first this adventure appeared to have been crowned with success. The child born of the concubine was a boy and Kung the Tall, with thoughts of his ambition fulfilled, had visions of a lusty, big-boned lad who would grow up in his own tall image. He too might become famous for his bravery and feats of strength. Of course, critical neighbours and the family of the divorced wife would sneer at a son born of a concubine, but he could afford to be indifferent; any son could carry on the family sacrifice in which a daughter could not even participate. His joy and satisfaction lasted only a few days for the boy was sickly and a cripple. The mother hid the mis-shapen body under the quilts as long as she could, but when the father, anxious for a look at his man-child, brushed aside the bed-clothes and saw the twisted legs his pride and vanity was gone, his mouth tasted gall and in spirit he wore sackcloth and his body was covered with ashes. This puny and mis-shapen offspring of a concubine could never fill the proper place of son. Better, he thought, no son at all than one like this.

A well-known proverb of his country ran to the effect that a man past the age of sixty-four should not go courting, and this proverb was supposed to embody sound morals as well as correct social usage. The disappointed old man had passed this age five years before but felt and looked much younger than most men of sixty, and he could forget rules of propriety in the urgency of his desire for a son. Though old, he was healthy and spry and not a greybeard. He was by reason of his divorce a single man. After the manner of aged widowers who decide to re-marry he reviewed the situation carefully. This was no time for one of those family-arranged marriages which for him had turned out so disastrously. He was not, as on the occasion of his early marriage, a young man with no experience and needing the guidance of friends and relatives in the selection of a wife. With the nine daughters and the crippled son he had garnered plenty of experience in marital affairs and would take care of the present enterprise himself.

With this project in mind he approached an old friend and neighbour who had three marriageable daughters. The two eldest were considered as being a little past their prime, being more than twenty years old. Kung the Tall thought that in spite of his years his friend might consent to an alliance with one of the daughters, probably the eldest, and therefore the least desirable. In fact at her age it might be difficult to find a husband for her. This was the idea he suggested to his friend who with three marriageable but unbetrothed daughters on his hands was in a better position than others to appreciate the distress of a friend with nine daughters. The neighbour was genuinely sorry and sympathised with his friend's distress, but for obvious reasons the proposal did not arouse any particular enthusiasm. He discussed the matter, but cautiously refused to commit himself.

Usually a father took on himself the responsibility of selecting husbands for his daughters, but this situation was unprecedented, for the established marriage customs did not contemplate a suitor about seventy years old. The neighbour temporised and consulted the wishes of the three girls, which was a very unusual procedure for a father to follow and indicated that he must have been a man of unusual character. He put the case to them honestly and frankly. The aged suitor came of a family which was so old that it numbered among its forebears emperors of the legendary period. His name was one of the proudest in the country and would add dignity to any alliance. On the other hand he was poor and unattractive as a marital companion. He was an old man – an old man whose youthful austerity had not been mellowed by age. By no feat of the imagination could any hint of romance be injected into the situation. Of the many and diverse love songs of the period there was none which made even an indirect allusion to a betrothal between an old man and a young maiden. Most of the love songs dealt with the strong and lusty loves of rustic youth or of dainty young princesses who became the brides of dukes. Whoever married him might expect to become a young widow and though widows –

especially young widows – often married a second time this was not considered the correct thing to do. The best that his wife could hope for was a brief and problematical honeymoon with an old man followed by a respectable but impoverished and lonely widowhood.

The two older girls were not attracted and offered no encouragement and the prospects of the proposed match were far from hopeful. The youngest girl, who at the age of fifteen was barely of marriageable age, had not been seriously considered. But the father in his embarrassment turned to her, and she, like an obedient and dutiful daughter, replied that she would allow him to decide for her.

'Then,' said the father, 'you will marry him.'

This was also contrary to the ancient rule that a maiden under sixteen should not wed. The usual formalities of the marriage ceremony were either neglected or hastened through and a young girl was taken to the home where the nine daughters and the crippled son had been born.

Although the ceremony of praying at shrines and offering sacrifices to ensure the birth of sons had invariably been the affair of women, who were more directly responsible in the matter, Kung the Tall decided to leave nothing to chance on this occasion and attended to this important matter himself. Obviously the old shrine was unsatisfactory, so he searched the neighbourhood, travelled far afield and made careful inquiry about the efficacy of other places. He at length selected a shrine of sound reputation on a hill which was known as Mount Mu and went there to pray with the young wife, adding his supplications to hers. On a clear day the Great Mountain (Tai Shan) could be seen directly to the north of the shrine. This was then as it is now the most sacred mountain of China; whose very sight cast a beneficent influence, though none but the King of Chow could pray directly to the spirits of this greatest of shrines or offer sacrifice to it. A few months after a final series of visits to the shrine, the girl dreamed of a black god who appeared before her and told her that she would give birth to a son and that the birth would take place in a hollow mulberry tree. That possibility presented some physical difficulties but the dream appeared to be an omen, and omens and portents were serious matters and not to be brushed away in the sunlight as idle fancies of the night. She told Kung the Tall about the dream and he supplied

Before the birth of Master Kung his mother prayed for a son at a shrine on Mount Mu some distance from her home.

the logical explanation. A dry cave not far away was known as 'The Hollow Mulberry Tree' and this was doubtless the spot the dream referred to. When the pains of labour beset her the girl repaired to the cave. There on a summer day the child was born, a big lusty boy with a peculiar bump on his forehead. This was in the year 551 B.C., about the time that Nebuchadnezzar died, Cyrus became King of Persia, the Jews returned from their exile in Babylon, and Daniel came unscathed from the den of lions.

In gratitude to the spirit of the little hill on which the shrine where they had prayed was located the parents named the child after the name of the hill. In later years when his fame as a scholar transcended such trivialities as personal names the child born under such unusual circumstances became known as Kung Fu-tze or 'Master Kung', a name which in all its simplicity embodies the tribute of a great people to their greatest man. About twenty centuries after his birth, when the learning of European scholars became broad enough to give due recognition to the scholarship of strange lands, Portuguese Jesuits who learned of him, tried to express what was to them the awkward sound of his name by means of the Latin alphabet. They did this very carelessly for they dropped one consonant from the name and called him 'Confucius'. That is the name by which he is known in countries far from his birthplace, but to the countless millions of his fellow-countrymen who have for many centuries followed his teachings he has always been and will always be known as 'Master Kung'.

CHAPTER II

*The river country where the people who were later to
be known to the world as the Chinese first learned
how to feed and clothe themselves and then developed
their own civilisation without foreign aid.*

THE country in which the son of Kung the Tall had been so
opportunely born was a land without a distinguishing name
such as is now possessed by the least important of states. It was not
nameless because unimportant, but for the contrary reason that its
supreme importance made a distinguishing name superfluous. So
far as the old soldier and his countrymen were concerned there was
no other country. They knew nothing of the other civilised communities which lived around the Mediterranean, on the Euphrates
and the Nile, and these other communities were equally ignorant
of their existence. Theirs was not *a* country but *the* country; their
beloved spot of mud was the world. They occasionally referred to
themselves as 'we who live under Heaven', 'we of the Middle Kingdom' or 'we of the Flowery Kingdom' not as a means of geographical
identification but as a general term showing their collective unity.
They later adopted the name of the first strong dynasty which ruled
them and called themselves, with inordinate pride, 'the sons of
Han', a name which they still retain. They have never known
themselves as Chinese, a name which was ignorantly adapted by
Europeans from the short-lived rule of the Chins – a dynasty which
is held in universal contempt by the Chinese because its founder
sought to destroy all ancient knowledge by the burning of the books
and execution of the scholars. These people who were the founders
of the Chinese race, speaking and writing the same language, eating
the same food, wearing the same clothing and bound together by the
same common practical and cultural interests consisted at this time
of a collection of some ten to fifteen million souls who lived along
the banks of what is now called the Yellow River as their ancestors

34

had then been living for many centuries. The river, with its constantly shifting channels, like the country, was nameless, and for the same reason that it was not one river of many and thus requiring a definite name. It was *the* river, the *only* river that required consideration. It was not given a name until some years later when with the increase in population the people of the two great rivers overlapped each other and it was necessary to distinguish the Yellow from the Yangtsze. The people of the Yellow River were constantly increasing in numbers, continually extending their boundaries to satisfy that incessant hunger for more land, but they had at this time occupied only a fraction of the great expanse of territory they were in later centuries to populate so densely. With each generation they spread further afield, but many centuries were to elapse before they got very far from the banks of the shallow and unnavigable river occupied by them at this time. Their country comprised roughly the present Chinese provinces of Shantung, Honan and Shensi, though parts of these areas were uninhabited and others were still occupied by strange barbarian tribes. This was, so far as they knew, the only civilised land, theirs the only people of importance, themselves the only beings who were not to be classed with the barbarians who were but slightly removed from the wild beasts.

They were surrounded at all points of the compass by barbarians or the isolation of the great unknown sea. To the north, where the state of 'Manchoukuo' has recently been created and where Mongolia is still so designated on the map, there was a despised race no one had yet learned to fear — savage and barbarous tribes whose ancestors increased and migrated westward and later played a prominent part in populating what is now the Union of Socialist Soviet Republics. As these barbarous tribes grew in numbers and in warlike skill they later threatened the peace of the river people and so caused the building of the Great Wall, one of the greatest engineering accomplishments ever undertaken by man. But at the time of Kung the Tall the need for the completing of this great defensive work had not yet arisen.

A very large part of what is now the fertile and prosperous valley of the lower Yangtsze, the territory embracing Shanghai, Soochow and Nanking was then a reed-covered marsh, as the silt deposited by the annual overflow of the Yangtsze had not yet brought the low-lying land up to a level where it could be cultivated. The original inhabitants of these marshes were naked barbarians who cut their hair and tattooed their bodies. They cut their hair so that they could not be so easily captured by enemies. They were boatmen and the hideous designs with which they decorated their bodies were supposed to frighten the great fishes which lurked in the waters. Mixed with these barbarians was a slight overflow from the more cultured and comfortable Yellow River country, consisting principally of criminal or political refugees who brought with them a knowledge of writing and other civilised arts. Forgotten by their former neighbours, they inter-married with the barbarians, founded a ruling aristocracy and built towns which were to become proud and beautiful cities such as Soochow and Hangchow, but at this time were only sorry clusters of rude hovels. Ningpo, under the ancient name of Chin, had just come into existence as a village sheltering venturesome fishermen who went into the Chusan archipelago for fish which were larger and more delicately flavoured than the fish from the muddy river streams. These growing barbarian empires were regarded by their northern neighbours as of such small importance that their existence was ignored until their armies grew strong enough and their rulers daring enough to command attention. This period was just approaching when Master Kung was born. Beyond the Yangtsze, further south, and to the southwest were purely native tribes so uncultured and wholly barbarous that they were not given names. Some of them have persisted to this day and are no longer nameless, though they still constitute strange races uncultured and unimportant. The more advanced and energetic Chinese of the north drove these barbarous aboriginal tribes from the fertile river valleys to the hills and mountains where some of them still exist, speaking their own languages and maintaining their own strange traditions.

The west was a place of deserts and marshes through which the original Chinese stock may have migrated, though this is a much disputed point; in fact has occasioned controversies of amazing proportions considering the slender supply of facts and data available in support of any theory. If the ancestors of the Yellow River people ever had migrated from some other point the knowledge of the migration was long forgotten and archeologists searching for the ancient trail have failed to find the thread of history which would indicate the alien birthplace of the Chinese. The search has been rendered difficult by reason of the fact that the ancient Chinese in their lusty and vigorous growth had no time to concern themselves over such academic matters. If they had any nostalgia for places from which they migrated they had forgotten it, even in the ballads which mothers teach their children, the kind of songs which persist for generations. They had many legends of a long line of heavenly and earthly kings who had ruled the universe for tens of thousands of years but these were all black-haired people like themselves, and there was never any suggestion that they had come from strange lands.

On the east was the sea, a place of dark and terrible mystery. The river people were landsmen and had the landsmen's terror of the ocean. They were not even boatmen for very little of their shallow river was navigable. While the desire for a more plentiful supply of that supreme luxury – salt – drove them to the sea shores, the watery waste remained for a long time a place of mystery and terror – a symbol of oblivion. The fact that the brine-laden water, easily evaporated by the sun on the flat mud shores, gave them this wonderful salt, which river water could not provide, probably added to the mystery, if not to the terror. When they travelled to the sea they thought they had reached the end of things, beyond which no further progress could be made. It was the dwelling-place of strange and savage monsters. Not until several centuries had elapsed did rumours circulate that an island to the east was inhabited by a strange race of dwarfs who were later identified as the Japanese.

The map of eastern Asia at the time gave no hint of the later existence of the municipalities which dot the coastline to-day. What is now the great and wealthy metropolis of Shanghai was an expanse of soft black mud, nameless, unknown and uninhabited. It is doubtful if any of the country around Shanghai could then be seen even at low tide for the alluvial countryside has been created by the deposits of ages of silt from the overflowing Yangtsze and the process was not yet completed. The island of Hongkong was sparsely habited by tribes so abandoned to wickedness that they had become outlaws from the only slightly less barbarous tribes of the mainland. When Hongkong became a British Crown colony about one hundred years ago, it had been harbouring thieves for many centuries, bandits who were the descendants of thieves and roving vagabonds for countless generations. The neighbouring city of Canton did not come into existence until more than a dozen centuries after the birth of Master Kung. There was no hint of the future existence of such cities as Peiping, Hankow and Tientsin. The site of the former was a sparsely inhabited plain, and the sites of the latter two were reed-covered marshes. Even in the highly-civilised part of the country there were no large cities. Loyang, the capital and residence of the King of Chow, covered approximately one square mile and as large areas inside the walls were given over to palaces and temples the residents of the place could not have been very numerous.

Isolated as they were, not only by the ocean, deserts and marshes but by a wall of barbarism, the Chinese had, without aid from others, built their own civilisation along the banks of their own treacherous and fickle river. They had learned how to grow plentiful and useful crops and to build simple houses, though many of them lived as they live to-day in cave dwellings carved out of the banks of clay. They learned to give and take in marriage, instead of following the earlier custom of capturing wives from alien clans. Most of their practical accomplishments had to do with such matter-of-fact things as raising enough food to fill empty stomachs, and growing and spinning and weaving enough flax to clothe naked bodies. In more leisurely moments they had learned how to make silk from the wild cocoons which fed on oak leaves and later how to pamper the loathsome little grub, the silkworm, by feeding it on the more delicate leaves of the mulberry tree, and so produce a textile even more wonderful than that produced from the oak leaves. Considering the absence of other luxuries, this was a marvellous achievement which must have created as much of a sensation, aroused as many new ambitions, intrigued the imagination, as did the science of wireless telegraphy and the aeroplane in a much later period. It is no wonder that later Chinese attributed the discovery of the silk cocoon and the invention of the process of reeling and weaving to a semi-mythical deity for the product appeared to be too wonderful for mere human accomplishment. A few centuries later silk reached Europe for the first time and wise men who puzzled over it found nothing in their human experience which would explain the origin of this fine raiment. This was a secret guarded so carefully that it was not discovered in Europe until the time the Chinese learned the growth and uses of cotton about A.D. 1500. At this time seeds of cotton arrived by way of India and Persia, and the plant was extensively cultivated. The fact that from very ancient times they had spun and woven silk, and that the best that could be offered then by the foreign nations they came in contact with was the cheaper, but greatly inferior cotton, afforded to them only one additional bit of evidence to confirm their convictions of the superiority of their ancient civilisation over anything enjoyed by other people.

They mined and smelted iron for making tools and the metal was used in place of money as a commodity of universal usefulness, and therefore acceptable in exchange for all other commodities. The iron was of such superior quality that when it was later sold in Rome it became known as the best iron the world produced and brought prices high enough to justify the great expense of transportation. Copper coins of uniform size had recently been introduced but were a novelty and had not been generally accepted. Bronze was generally used for the making of arrow-heads, the fittings of harness and carriages and for bells, vases, urns, and other luxurious articles. Their bronzes, tripods and ceremonial vessels, even in the most critical judgment of to-day, were magnificent. They were excellent carpenters and made handlooms and carts which have remained practically unchanged right up to the present time. They had tables, couches and chairs and slept in beds. Those who, like their remote ancestors, squatted on their haunches, were looked upon as displaying extreme bad taste. Among the refinements of life were candles, vegetable oil-lamps, chop-sticks, sundials, umbrellas, flat-irons, bath-tubs and mirrors made of polished metal. Those who needed them because of their occupation or could afford a fashionable vogue, wore leather shoes. Hats were never either fashionable or thought to be useful, so they braved the sun with brimless caps which gave them no protection from its rays. They squinted to keep the sun out of their eyes and that possibly is the origin of the permanent squint which is a Chinese facial characteristic. The glories of Chinese porcelain were to come later and the rough pottery cups and jars which they produced were in comparison rather crude affairs. There were no teapots, for tea was a beverage enjoyed by the barbarians living much further south but almost if not entirely unknown on the

Yellow River. It is doubtful if the old soldier or his famous son even knew its taste. They did not know of the existence of grapes but made wine out of fermented grain which they flavoured with aromatic herbs and frequently drank a great deal too much of it. There were reformers who blamed almost all the evils of the times on the habit of heavy drinking, and preached a practical system of temperance which might stand as a model to-day. The reformers insisted that the first drink of the day should be taken after sundown, when the day's work was done and there was time for relaxation. The reformers were particularly severe about the clubs where men forgathered to drink.

They had discovered the uses of the indigo plant and were clad in blue hemp gowns. Though colour secured from the native indigo provided the cheapest and most popular dye, they developed many other sources of pigments and could match almost all the colours of the rainbow. The women embroidered and crocheted designs on their gowns and made them strangely attractive. Many wives, whose husbands could not afford it, wore silk though most of them grew their own cocoons and made their own garments. Women had no social standing except as wives and mothers and were compelled by common usage to remain unobtrusively in the background. Some of the more artful ones ignored the conventions, made themselves attractive by plucking their eyebrows, perfuming themselves and staining their cheeks and lips. A few succeeded so well in these vanities that they upset the usual traditions, created national scandals and so gained a questionable fame by providing the material for historical episodes. Later in life when the son of Kung the Tall began to give the weight of authority to maxims of conduct in politics and morals he sternly warned against the danger of permitting women to meddle in state affairs. His objection which was also voiced by many others was not based on any academic theory as to the inferiority of women, but emanated rather from sound and invariably sad experience. When sex was permitted to interfere in state affairs serious consequences had invariably followed.

The jealous wife had no reason to worry about curly-headed blondes. There were no curls and no blondes. The river people were all of straight black hair and light or dark brown eyes. The only people who were different were the strange albinos, unusual freaks of nature, few of whom grew to maturity for they were usually destroyed at birth. When they later came in contact with Europeans they proudly called themselves 'the black-haired people' as a symbol of the homogeneity of their race. They had in fact a great deal of difficulty in understanding that Englishmen, Dutch and others might be yellow headed and blue eyed and still be normal human beings. Probably doubts still lurk in the minds of some in remote parts of the country.

Most of the people were farmers, as food was the most important consideration and artisans were few in number as compared with to-day. The farmers were also weavers and in the idle winter months made their own cloth out of silk or hemp. First as a protection against barbarians, and later against the raids of partisans from rival clans, they lived in mud or stone-walled villages surrounded by their fields. The walls of similar villages seen along the Yellow River to-day are piled high with cobblestones which will crack a skull now as effectively as similar stones twenty-five centuries ago. The country was well wooded and there were many wild beasts still roaming about. Man-killing tigers terrified the country around the sacred mountain of Tai Shan. When soldiers were summoned to battle it was by means of signal flares made from wolf bones. Whether this was because of symbolism or convenience is not known but wolves were common enough to be a menace to the farmers. They grew little if any rice; for rice, like tea, was a southern product. They did grow barley, millet, wheat, beans and huge cabbages, the latter being one of their commonest foods. Among their favourite fruits were apricots which could be easily dried in the hot arid summers of the Yellow River country and kept to supplement their food during the winter months when fresh fruits were not available. They did not know and never learned of milk, butter and cheese as a food, being the only people who ignored the uses of dairy products. As wild game was plentiful they ate a greater proportion of meat than at present. Dried bear's paw was a highly esteemed delicacy. The Chinese anecdotal histories tell of a wicked old man who was sentenced to execution by his son. The condemned man seeing death was near made a final request; he wanted a bear's paw for his supper. The son was about to humour him but knowing his father's cunning he reflected that it would take a long time properly to cook this delicacy and he rightly decided that this was only a stratagem to gain time for escape. Instead he gave the old man a mess of cabbage and sent him on his way to the executioner.

Cooking had reached a very high state of development and there were famous chefs and among the nobility equally famous epicures. Scandal-mongers said of one powerful politician that he had acquired his power not by reason of his political ability but because he knew how to provide the prince with tasty dishes. His friends tried to explain that a man might be a good official as well as a good cook, but they could not hush up the gossip. The politician was famous for his skill as a cook and the prince was well known as an epicure so the conclusions were inevitable. A few recipes of this period have been preserved and the following will give some idea of the sophisticated tastes of the gourmets of that day:

'Take a suckling pig and having cut it open and removed entrails fill the belly with dates. Wrap it around with straw and reeds which are plastered with clay; and then bake it in a pit. When the clay becomes completely dry break it off. Having washed the hands, remove the crackling and macerate it with rice flour to the consistency of gruel, which is then added to the dressing of dates. Then fry the whole in a quantity of lard which will cover it. In a large pan of hot water place a small boiler on a tripod, which is filled with fragrant herbs and slices of the pig. Care must be taken that the hot water does not cover the inside boiler, and that the fire has no intermission for three days and nights. After this, the whole is served with the addition of pickled meat and vinegar.'

The fixed location of the North Star had been noted many centuries before, and with that as the logical starting-point had been built up a knowledge of astronomy which enabled them to make an accurate division of the calendar and to predict eclipses. The phases of the moon were used to mark the passage of time, though the system did not provide for an accurate calculation of the solar year and so the calendar required revision every few years. However, it was for the period an ideal practical method of marking the passage of time. The hunter in the mountains, the farmer in his fields could see the glory of the full moon as well as the king in his palace, and by that symbol know that a new month had begun. The system was officially abolished in 1931 but is still the method universally used by many millions of Chinese farmers and others, and it is difficult to imagine that such a simple method will ever be entirely superseded.

Physicians had evolved a school of medicine in which remedies were classified according to taste. Sours were used to nourish the bones, acid for the muscles, salt for the blood, sweet for the flesh and bitter to improve the general vitality. These medical men said, and it was generally believed, that it was not safe to entrust your health to a practitioner whose family had not been in the profession for at least three generations. This made it impossible for a new-comer to establish himself in the field except by birth or adoption. Physicians were wizards as well as healers and were expected to be skilled in magic. Quite a number of books on medicine as well as on agriculture had been written.

The art of writing except for the mechanics of inscribing the characters had been fully developed. It started with rude outlines of simple natural objects. These pictures, as for sun, moon, man, mountain, etc., remain in modified form in the Chinese characters of to-day. But the development of writing could not be confined to the narrow limitation of picture ideas and so the language grew to embrace all the abstractions required to express the ideas and thoughts of a highly cultivated people. The barbarous tribes which surrounded them could not write and the exclusive possession of this accomplishment which enabled the river people to send written messages and to make written contracts gave them a very important advantage over their less advanced neighbours; investing them no doubt with what must have appeared to be magical powers. The fact that they were later to become rulers of the continent was due, probably, as much to the cultural advantage given them by posses-sion of the art of writing as to their military ability. Neither paper nor ink had been invented though there were pigments for painting and for dyeing. The best substitute for ink was brick dust and water and this impermanent fluid was occasionally used to write characters on silk. Most of the writing done was laboriously in-scribed with a stylus on slips of bamboo, which has been aptly des-cribed as like writing on a shingle with a sharp nail. With these writing materials a book the size of the volume now in the reader's hands would fill a small truck. It was said of one industrious scholar that he read 'a hundredweight daily'. When, after the downfall of the Chow dynasty, the ambitious Chin emperor sought to destroy the old literature by his infamous burning of the books the bonfire made much more of a blaze than would have been possible with bound paper volumes, for what he burned consisted of huge heaps of well thumbed and thoroughly seasoned slips of bamboo.

Under these mechanical difficulties the art of writing had not reached that perfection which was later to make it the pride of every Chinese scholar. The written language consisted of characters of the same general form as are in use to-day but new ideas meant the coining of new words and this coinage was by no means uniform. It was many centuries later and probably as the result of the general acceptance of the Master Kung's teachings as set down by his disciples that the written language became, as it is to-day, uniform – perhaps the most uniform of any living language. At the time of Master Kung's birth each of the petty states had its own school of literature and the scratching of characters on hard bamboo did not lend itself to artistic development. It was not until several hundred years later when paper and ink, invented much earlier, had been improved, that Wang the Penman by the supreme skill of his brush perfected the writing of Chinese characters and elevated calligraphy to a permanent place among the most highly esteemed arts of the country. Thereafter the scholar was, in theory at least, an artist with his pen. In the days of Master Kung the artisan who could make things of beauty out of the incised characters was rare but held in high esteem.

Whatever the black-haired river people had in the way of culture or practical achievement was entirely their own, had been developed and brought to what perfection they had attained through laborious centuries of trial and error. No one had helped them and they were under no obligations to any other people for the borrowed finery of culture. They paid homage to gods and goddesses who had taught them husbandry, the cultivation of the silkworm and who had invented clothes and many other arts but they were all black-haired gods and of their own people. They acquired a confidence in their completeness and superiority which was not shaken until the age of steam, and, even as this is written, the advance of modernity has by no means destroyed it.

CHAPTER III

*Locally famous because of the circumstances of his
birth, the boy's fame grew and even as a youth he
attracted the attention of his elders by his knowledge
of the elaborate rites and ceremonies of the country.*

ACCORDING to one story which was first told more than 2,400 years
ago and has always been believed, the leaves of the shrubs and
trees on Mount Mu stood respectfully erect when the young wife
of Kung the Tall went there to the shrine to pray for the birth of a
son, and, when she left, the trees and shrubs prostrated themselves
in a gesture of adulation. According to another story, a fabulous
animal known as a *chi lin* appeared before the prospective mother,
bearing in its mouth a jade tablet inscribed with a message pro-
phesying future greatness for the son then about to be born. The
young girl tied a silken scarf around the single horn of the animal
and it disappeared the same night, only (according to the story) to
reappear more than seventy years later, just before the death of
Master Kung. According to a third story, at the time the child was
born two benevolent dragons patrolled the heavens to ward off evil
influences; five old men, representing the five planets, came down
from heaven and guarded the birthplace, and the mother heard
strange music from a mysterious source and a voice from the sky
announcing the birth of an illustrious son. When the son was born,
it is said that there was discovered written on his chest the phrase
'established the world by law'. These were the kind of stories the
people of that day liked to believe concerning the manifestations
attending the birth of great men, but the stories were not generally
accepted, often not recorded and usually not invented until the
fame of accomplishments had justified them. These stories did not
attain their full perfection until later but it appears probable that
the legends from which they sprung had gained a certain currency
during Master Kung's own lifetime. Legends of this description

45

about living men were not uncommon, for these people, like all who are superstitious, were highly imaginative and it was their habit of thought to associate the unusual with the supernatural. If, when the lad grew up, he heard and believed any of these flattering stories and prophecies as to his future greatness, we may be sure that he had many occasions to grow sceptical about their accuracy, for his life was such a continuous cycle of prosperity and adversity as would appear to deny the existence of ordinary good luck, let alone any pre-ordained greatness. During brief intervals he had full confidence in the greatness of his destiny. On other occasions he was doubtful and despondent, and he finally died full of the bitter disappointment which follows a consciousness of failure.

Whether or not the neighbours heard of and believed any stories of the strange circumstances attending his birth, we may be sure that for reasons much more plausible than these strange visitations, his birth was the talk of the village, and was the subject of some gossip covering a much wider area. The marriage of an old man of seventy to a young girl of fifteen and the prompt subsequent birth of a child would constitute a story of considerable human interest in any country and at any time. Similar events have been featured in the rotogravure sections of American newspapers of modern times and pictured in the illustrated European weeklies. The fact that the marriage was occasioned by the desire for a son and that the boy was born following the birth of nine half-sisters made the story all the more piquant and gave the sex-control faddists something to think about. It had in it all the elements of a success-story – success in old age – after the most disheartening sequence of failures as exemplified by the nine daughters. The event attracted even more attention here in the little feudal state of Lu, for the hungry imaginations of the people fed on the recital of strange events and the disparity in the ages of husband and wife did not constitute the only unusual circumstance. The boy was born with a prominent bump on his forehead. The place at the top of the baby's skull which is almost invariably concave was in his case convex – so decidedly convex as to form a very noticeable protuberance and to give the child a decidedly singular appearance which did not disappear as he grew older. As a part of the superstitious beliefs they had inherited from earlier and more primitive days the residents of Lu in common with all the other river people believed that any

On the night that the son of Kung the Tall was born, two dragons patrolled the sky for the purpose of warding off evil influences, while five old men, representing the spirits of the five planets, came down from heaven.

departure from the conventional and commonplace, especially as concerned births, was an omen whose significance was worth while inquiring into. Three-legged calves, big snakes, the discovery of rocks of strange appearance, birds which appeared when driven out of their natural course of migration – all these constituted events of such interest and importance that they were set down in the local official record, ranking in historical importance with eclipses, floods, droughts and visitations of locusts. Scholars specialised in interpreting what these strange things presaged and the boy was later to be called upon to show his skill in such interpretations though he never believed in such superstitious nonsense. The peculiar appearance of the boy's head, in conjunction with circumstances of his conception and birth, created a great deal of gossip and comment among a people who have always been frankly interested in everything connected with the propagation of the species. News of the event spread throughout the little principality of Lu and reached the ears of the Duke. He sent the father his congratulations. The honour of this recognition by the Duke of the good fortune which had come to the old soldier was no more than was due him, for he had spent a long lifetime in the service of the Duke and his predecessors.

There was no need to hide this baby under the bed-clothes, as the concubine had done with his crippled half-brother a few years earlier. He was a strong and lusty youngster, though probably an extremely ugly one for the bump on his forehead was not his only irregular feature. If in any way attractive as a baby, aside from his obvious good health, then there must have been great changes in his appearance as he grew up, for by any standard he was ugly, though he did possess great dignity. Though he was admittedly of striking appearance his most sedulously worshipful disciples never suggested that he was handsome. In later life his ears were huge and pendulous, his nose flat and terminating in a button-like protuberance. Two upper front teeth were always visible and his nostrils were cavernous and prominent. His eyes showed a great deal of white which was particularly noticeable and objectionable to his slant-eyed fellow-countrymen. A Chinese historian has pointed out that though almost all men are imperfect in one or two of their features, Master Kung even in this showed his superiority for he was imperfect in all. His ugliness was all the more conspicuous because of his great size. According to the Chinese chronicles he was ten feet tall, but as there is a good deal of uncertainty as to the length of the ancient Chinese standards of measurement no one knows just how tall he was. The generally accepted theory is that his height was more than seven feet, being slightly taller than his father. Men of great height are not uncommon in North China to-day and were probably not uncommon then, but he was tall enough to be noticeable. Wherever he went the people marvelled at him and called him a giant. Indeed, although it is a most ungallant thing to say regarding a lady who has been dead so many years, it appears probable that his mother was somewhat lacking in physical attractions. The ready acceptance by a girl of fifteen of a proposal of an alliance from an honourable but austere and impoverished old man of seventy, and the prompt clinching of the bargain by a father who had two older daughters to marry off, leaves an unexplained gap in the story which the Chinese historians have failed to clarify.

Kung the Tall, whose determination and virility had been the means of bringing the boy into the world, did not live long to enjoy his pride and satisfaction in his son, for he died when the boy was, according to the Chinese calculation, only three years old. Under the Chinese system of computing ages, a child is one year old throughout the year in which he is born. Thereafter at the beginning of each New Year, one year was added to the age of the child. As the Kung baby was born in the eighth moon, which we know as August, he became two years old on the incidence of the lunar new year four months later and was three with the commencement of the next lunar new year. So the boy had actually breathed for less than two years when he became fatherless and his mother a young widow. The old soldier died content. He had left an heir to his name – a son who could revere his memory, carry out the ancient devotional ceremonies connected with the cult of filial piety and continue the honoured family name of Kung. The old man's final days would have been supremely happy could he have known that his son was destined to make the Kung lineage continue unbroken through more generations than that of any other family known to the world. He left no estate. He had never been wealthy and the task of raising his numerous daughters and getting them married must have been more than a little difficult and expensive. It was customary then as now for the

When Master Kung was born, strange music came from a mysterious source, and a voice from the sky announced the birth of an illustrious son.

bridegroom's family, by a donation to the father of the bride, to liquidate the expenses of feeding and clothing her from infancy, but parents with marriageable sons often drove hard and profitless bargains, and a man with nine daughters was in a very disadvantageous trading position. Not only did he have an unusually large number of daughters to dispose of but the families of desirable bridegrooms naturally avoided alliance with a family which, apparently, could produce nothing but females.

Shortly after the death of Kung the Tall, the young mother moved to a village near the ducal capital of Zigzag Hill (Chufu). The family records contain no hint of the reason for this removal, but it was probably in order to make her home with a more prosperous relative who could help support her and the boy. The new abode was about eight miles distant from her former home. She was doubtless glad to get away from the neighbourhood of the nine daughters and the envious and jealous first wife. In spite of her extreme youth there was nothing vain or frivolous about the young widow. She was large, plain, solid and dependable. The only son of a young widowed mother is by her soft complaisance often turned into a spoiled and worthless youngster but she did not pamper the boy. He probably got a much stricter and better bringing up than would have been his fate if the father had lived to undertake the task. The latter's good nature under the indignity of the nine daughters shows him to have been weakly uxorious, and he might well have been equally easy-going with his son. The widow was what is generally known as a good house-wife – the kind who sees that everything is in apple-pie order no matter how uncomfortable it may make herself and others. There was a proper place for every humble belonging in the house and nothing was left lying carelessly about, as in less orderly households. Tasks were performed according to a routine as rigid and unalterable as the forms of a religious ritual. The clothing of her son, like her own, conformed to the conservative style of the day and was simple and comfortable. She did not dress him in any of the bright colours which children love, and taught him that gentlemen do not wear garments decorated with scarlet or violet, colours which some of the dandies of the town affected. Even in hot weather she did not allow him to run about in his undershirt but taught him always to wear a decent gown or jacket. He had separate clothing for sleep, which, while not an innovation, was so uncommon as to cause some comment. The nightshirt he wore in cold weather was comfortable and sensible for it was half again as long as his body.

The food was usually common and coarse but it was always clean and well cooked. According to the standards of her day she was a dietitian. Even though the supply of meat might be plentiful she would not allow it to overbalance the proportion of cereals and fresh vegetables. If the fish or the pork had that unmistakable odour which indicates a lack of freshness she would not serve it. She would not make rabbit stew in the hot weather when the flesh is not wholesome and she knew and used the proper sauces for each meat. As wild game was abundant they enjoyed a greater variety of meat than is available to-day. All meat was very finely minced which not only ensured a thorough cooking but provided morsels which could be easily handled with chop-sticks, those convenient table utensils which had now been in use for centuries. In only one minor detail did she relax and show a mother's weakness in gratifying the pleasures of her child. The boy acquired a taste for the pungent ginger root and she gave it to him frequently between meals, though it was not so much a food as a luxury, supposed to have a mild medicinal value as an aid to digestion. All his life he nibbled at ginger and all of his life he was careful of his diet, eating only wholesome and well-cooked food. Though he ate sparingly he would never permit his drinks to be counted and set no limits on his potations except that he would never according to his disciples allow his wits to become fuddled. His mother taught him to be as particular about his wine as about his meat and he would not drink wine bought in the market-place, where they often sold immature vintages of doubtful quality.

The young mother taught her son nothing of the prevalent beliefs in ghosts, omens and spirits – beliefs which were well-nigh universal at the time, especially among the women. She did not believe in them – or not all of them. Loud peals of thunder frightened her and filled her with forebodings, just as they frighten women to-day. Heavy winds were equally terrifying and she communicated these terrors to her son who never outlived them. Thanks to the remarkable and unusual common sense of his mother his mental growth was not handicapped by the belief in demons, ghosts and omens which coloured the thoughts of almost all the men of that day.

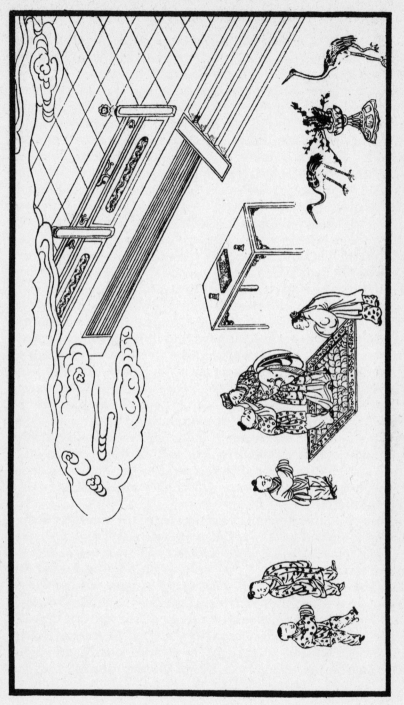

As a small boy Master Kung amused himself and his playmates by playing with the sacrificial vessels and imitating the ancient rites and ceremonies.

During his lifetime he consistently refused to discuss any of these spiritual manifestations which made up so much of the conversation of the peasants and were not entirely ignored by the scholars. There was one other rather strange inhibition which she impressed on his young mind and that was an aversion to feats of strength. It will be recalled that it was the Samson-like feat of the elder Kung in holding up the gates of the besieged city which gave him a brief line in history. From his huge size it would appear that the son might easily have emulated his father's prowess. In that period feats of physical strength and endurance were of much more importance than in later years when mechanical contrivances had robbed them of their utility, and a higher culture had discounted the nobility of their achievements. But the teachings of the mother created a fixed and unchanging aversion. Throughout his lifetime Master Kung not only refused to discuss feats of strength but appeared to have a contempt for anything connected with physical prowess which depended on strength rather than skill which comes from well-disciplined muscles. Even in these more skilful exploits he did not take the usual pride of the athlete. Archery and charioteering (or horsemanship) were two polite accomplishments which every gentleman and scholar was supposed to possess, and we know that he was an archer of no small ability. But when he was compelled to speak of his skill in these two accomplishments it was with apologetic deprecation. He carried this aversion to mere physical strength so far that he avoided all exercise except for mild countryside strolls. On his many and lengthy journeys in later life he habitually rode over the rough roads on the highly uncomfortable springless chariots or carts; where the average healthy individual would have preferred to walk. When he visited the great sacred mountain of Tai Shan he did not complete the pilgrimage by going to the top, but stopped half-way on the more comfortable lower levels. He was at that time a young man so did not have the excuse of old age for not completing the journey.

Under the watchful care of his mother the boy grew up serious-minded and studious, carefully observing and storing away everything in the capacious but orderly warehouse of his mind. There were no games, no laughter or gaiety in his mother's house and he had to look elsewhere for amusement. The austerity of his home was duplicated in the amusements he found. The comings and goings of officials connected with the ducal court at Zigzag Hill, the constantly recurring funerals and periodical sacrifices to spirits were all surrounded by forms and ceremonies, emblematic posturings and manipulation of ritualistic objects. These colourful ceremonies were so complicated and governed by such a fixed ritual that they could only be conducted properly by one who had studied them for years. They were more like an elaborate Masonic ceremony than anything else of the present time. Before he could have understood much, if anything, of the significance of these ceremonies young Kung was imitating them by conducting amateur performances, aided by the other small boys of the neighbourhood. With an improvised altar, sacrificial vessels of broken pottery, little jackets tucked up in peculiar fashion to represent ceremonial costumes the boys played at make-believe funerals and solemnly interred the coffins of imaginary dignitaries, or performed sacrifices to the spirits of equally imaginary ducal ancestors. On lighter but not gayer occasions they would ceremonially receive the visits of diplomatic envoys from neighbouring states. It was not unlike the play-acting games of boys and girls of to-day who mimic the ceremonial forms of their elders, but here the game was confined to boys. Little girls were not allowed to play with their brothers, for this privilege might give them absurd ideas of sex-equality. It was a man's world. At first the older people looked on these juvenile ceremonies with a condescending smile at the vain mimicries of youth, but soon their attention became serious and respectful. The childish pageants were not burlesqued and, considering the youth of the performers, they were professional in the finish of their technique. Their leader, six-year-old Kung, with his childish headdress, insisted on the most careful and scrupulous observance of the ritualistic forms and the older village people wondered how a boy so young could know so much about matters which were a mystery to most of them.

The mother sent the boy to school which he entered at the age of seven. There were no public or free schools as we now know them but the education of boys was looked upon as a public duty, a duty which was shifted to the shoulders of the schoolmasters. They set up schools in which no regular tuition fees were charged, the pedagogue depending for a living on the gifts of his pupils. The liberality of the gifts was regulated by the wealth and generosity of the

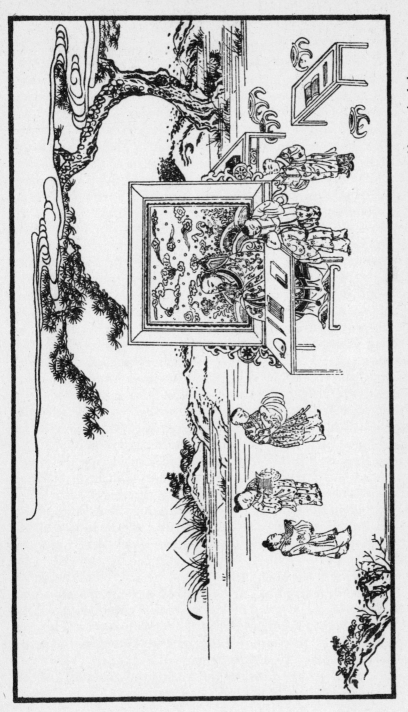

At the age of seven the future sage attended a school conducted by a local magistrate and presumably remained there for several years.

student's family. In a place like Zigzag Hill, with the wealth
which would naturally surround a ducal capital, there was no dearth
of well-to-do patrons whose contributions would be generous enough
to support a good school which young Kung and other poor boys
could attend at an expense within the means of their parents.
Although there is no definite record, it is presumed that he remained
in the school for the usual period, that is until he was about fifteen
years old. In view of the great fame the pupil later attained one
would presume that the teacher would come in for a certain amount
of well-deserved renown. He was the man who, according to the
belief which millions of Chinese have held for many centuries,
taught the greatest teacher of all time. But no credit has been
given to him by this race which has so meticulously given honour
to culture and to ancestry. Almost all those with whom the son of the
old soldier came in contact during his long life have been enshrined
in the memory of his fellow-countrymen, but his tutor is forgotten.
There are no memorial temples, no tributes to him in a rather
verbose biographical literature. All that we know about him is
that he was a Mr. Yen and that he had been, or was, a local magistrate. The probabilities are that with his active, inquisitive mind,
Young Kung taught the teacher instead of the teacher teaching him.
Whatever may have been the reason or the inspiration, the boy after
his years in this little village school found his principal if not his
only enjoyment in study, and at the age of fifteen had made up his
mind that he would devote his life to scholarship.

CHAPTER IV

*Even when employed as a collector of tithes the young
scholar continued his studies and collected disciples
around him. His marriage the birth of a son and
the death of his mother three events which followed
closely on each other.*

THE necessity of making a living had faced Master Kung from
the time of his birth and grew more urgent as he emerged from
childhood and completed the education afforded by the modest
village school. The problem was complicated by the limited class
of employment he could with propriety undertake. He was an
exceptionally large boy and could at a very early age have been
apprenticed as an artisan or have become a soldier like his father.
But he was the descendant of dukes and kings, was of noble blood
and the family traditions had to be upheld. Also by his own scholarly inclinations as well as his mother's pride was he limited to
more intellectual employment. His difficulties were increased by
the fact that, although the members of his family had lived in the
little state of Lu for several generations, they had originally come
from the neighbouring state of Sung and so the Kung family were
looked upon as *émigrés* and therefore not entitled to official employment, which was presumed to be restricted to men of ancient Lu
descent. A matter of three or four generations' residence in the
place did not remove the stigma of alien origin. If his father did
serve as a magistrate in his later years, which is by no means certain,
it was because of his long and faithful career as a soldier and in spite
of his Sung descent. Whatever position young Kung secured would
have to be through his own abilities and without the aid of any
family prestige.

At the age of seventeen he secured his first employment, the
task of keeping the granary accounts for the Chi family, one of the
three great baronial houses in the ducal state of Lu. It was a rather
responsible position for one of his age and, for the reasons mentioned

above, he must have secured it according to the poor-boy formula –
by having first acquired a reputation for intelligence, industry and
honesty. The occupation was only on the border-line of gentility
and did not involve the kind of work any young scholar would
willingly undertake. The details of the work were, from to-day's
viewpoint, unusual and require some explanation. Under the
ancient system of land tenure which had been in operation for
many centuries each family, consisting perhaps of seventy to a hundred individuals, was given a form of freehold title to a tract of land
of, say, a hundred acres, though the exact area is uncertain and
probably varied in different places. The freeholders consisting of
nine branches of the family were each allotted a tract of equal size
where they would raise grain for their own individual use as well as
pigs, chickens, hemp, and mulberry trees for feeding the silkworms.
With nine tracts in the possession of the freeholders, the tenth tract
consisting entirely of grain land was set apart and known as 'public
land', the produce of this area going to the duke in whose domain
it was situated. The freeholders were supposed to cultivate this
land with the same or even more care than they bestowed on their
own fields. In the state of Lu the collection of this grain from the
public lands was in the hands of the barons or heads of the three
great families, of whom more will be heard later. They were, in
effect, tax farmers and grew to power through having control of the
revenues. Grain, principally millet, was grown on the public lands
and that part of it which reached the duke's storehouses was used to
feed his own numerous household retainers and soldiers and to pay
his officials. The theory on which this system of tithes had been
established and carried on by previous dynasties was that this would
be a single tax, the only source of revenue for the state. At that
time all wealth was agricultural, and could be measured in terms
of grain and it was assumed that one-tenth of the produce should
be ample to meet all governmental expenses. Young Kung's position was the humble, rather difficult and certainly unpopular one of
estate supervisor and tithe-collector. He was required to keep a
watchful eye on that portion of the public lands for which he was
responsible, seeing to it that the peasants did not neglect its cultivation and, at harvest time, that the baron was not cheated and that
the proper amount of grain went to the baronial granaries for even-
tual transfer to its rightful owner, the duke.

A responsibility like this would never be an easy one, but his position was made all the more difficult by reason of the fact that some years previously one of the dukes of Lu, hard pressed as a result of his own extravagances, and the avaricious demands of the powerful barons, had doubled the tithes by increasing the proportion from one-tenth to one-fifth. In practical administration this meant that the tithe-collector had not only to see to the cultivation and harvest on the public lands but also to collect, in addition, a tenth of the crops produced on the private fields which the farmers were wont to consider as belonging exclusively to themselves. The original provision for the collection of one-tenth of the produce had been established by one of the early kings of the golden age of the country and was generally accepted as a perfectly just and equitable system of taxation; any departure from it was resented as an injustice. Though they had a reasonable ground for complaint it must be said that the farmers of Lu were not nearly so badly off as others, for in the neighbouring state of Tsi the exactions of the ruler were so onerous that the tillers of the soil had to be content with the retention of only one-third of their produce for themselves. In spite of the many difficulties encountered young Kung carried out his duties to the satisfaction of his superiors and as a result was soon given the more onerous and presumably more remunerative position of keeper of the herds. This work was like the other except that it had to do with oxen and goats raised on the public pasture lands. Obviously it required a great deal more care and attention to check up on the increase and secure an honest return of live-stock than to do the same thing with grain.

It is impossible to conceive of any task which would have given him a keener appreciation of the sorrows of his fellow-countrymen. In both of these positions he was the representative of the powerful officials against whose oppressions the people cried out most bitterly. The extra ten per cent which was collected was an especially sore point, for this was generally regarded as an illegal and unjust tax and this feeling was probably shared by the young official whose duty it was to collect it. The work was naturally distasteful to him but at any rate it provided him with honest labour which enabled him to support his small family. Employment of this nature by a man so young could not fail to have an effect on the formation of his character. No one has to listen to more lies, evasions, subterfuges,

Young Kung's first employment was as collector of the tithes of grain for the duke, the tithes amounting at that time to about one-fifth of the entire produce of the farmers.

petty dishonesties, and stories of genuine cases of distress than are poured into the ears of a collector of crop rents, and these experiences crowded into his young formative years gave him more of an insight into practical affairs and human character than would have been afforded by a century of scholarship. Such an experience would either blunt his sensibilities to human distress or make his sympathies richer and more generous. Happily it developed the latter trend. His experience brought him into personal and intimate contact with the common people, gave him sympathy and understanding and strengthened his half-formed resolution to achieve their happiness and bring about a return to the 'golden age' through a reform of the government and a restoration of the ancient virtues of the people.

He naturally had no pride in this employment and even his disciples, when speaking about it in later years, were a little apologetic. As for young Kung, aside from the natural distaste he had for the work, he disliked it because it did not provide him with the mental stimulus and recreation his active young mind demanded. He had the indifference, bordering on contempt, for mere mathematical gymnastics that is shared by most philosophers and artists. To him the calculation of figures, addition, subtraction, multiplication, division was mere mental drudgery; mathematicians, like clerks, the slaves of the foot rule. Referring to his duties as keeper of the granary he told a friend:

'My calculations must be correct; that is all I have to care about.'

Later when he was put in charge of the public lands and herds he found the duties a little less easy but still requiring no special mental effort for he observed:

'The oxen must be fat and strong and of superior quality, that is all I have to care about.'

No doubt these remarks not only reflected his indifference to the mental strain of clerkly duties but also his disclaimer of any responsibility for the collection on behalf of the duke of what he and others generally considered to be an unjustly large proportion of the produce of the land. Other remarks which he made show that he appears to have taken rather lightly one of his theoretical duties which was to exercise a kind of supervision over the methods of cultivation. With their paternalistic form of government and highly centralised authority, the feudal rulers had elaborate and

very definite rules for the conduct of agriculture and animal husbandry, and these the young tithe-collector was supposed to enforce.
Standard text-books had been written on agricultural as well as on
many other subjects. He never became a text-book farmer and
wisely allowed the peasants to solve their problems from their own
practical experience. Later in life when he was asked to give some
advice on farming he laughingly declined and said:

'Better get advice from some old farmer.'

With duties too trivial and too easily disposed of to occupy his
mind, he spent his spare time in studying and giving instruction
to the boys who loafed and played around the grass lands where the
cattle were pastured. Some of them were doubtless the same boys
with whom he had played at ceremonial observances years before.
In this casual way there grew up the band of disciples who were to
follow him devotedly throughout his lifetime, gain renown for
themselves and by their records of his teachings make his fame
immortal.

As soon as he was certain of regular employment his mother
selected a wife for him. A marriage was arranged with a girl from
the state of Sung, his ancestors' native state, and they were married
after all the simple formalities had been complied with. This early
marriage, he was but nineteen, was in accordance with the strict
ritual demands of the family and what any other Chinese boy would
have done under similar circumstances. The necessity of providing
an heir was encumbent on him as on all others of his race. A son
was born the first year, but aside from this accomplishment, and the
relatively unimportant birth of two daughters, the marriage was not
a success. According to some accounts there was an early divorce
and, whether there was or not, there can be no doubt that the wife
after the first few years played little or no part in his life. He was a
dutiful and affectionate son, whose scholarship was the pride of his
mother's heart, but only sons of young widows do not usually make
successful husbands. In the case of Master Kung the temperament
and talents which made him an ideal son would make him an impossible husband for a wife possessing any gaiety or spirit. The obedience which he gave as a matter of duty to his mother he demanded
in the same or more generous measure from his wife. She was the
first person over whom he had any social authority and doubtless
he practised on her his theories of a sternly formal deportment and

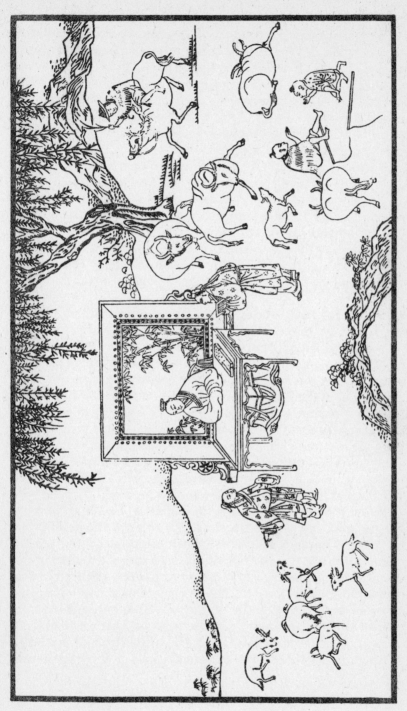

Having established a reputation for industry and honesty in the collection of tithes of grain for the duke, the young man was given the more important and difficult task of collecting the tithes of live-stock.

discipline which embraced the most minute details of everyday existence, ranging from such diverse items as the colour of a person's clothing to the point of the compass faced when sitting down to meals. A man who was so formal, as he was, that he would not sit on a mat that was the least bit awry, who would not speak when at meals, who was fussy about the length of his nightgown, must have been a somewhat difficult person to live with. His rather peculiar, not to say unattractive personal appearance, may have had something to do with the family differences. He was not amorous, as his father had been, and was never a woman's man. Later in life when he became an authority on all the niceties of human relationship he ruefully admitted that he had never learned how to behave toward girls. When he was at all intimate with them they presumed on him and became unmanageable; when he kept them at a proper distance their feelings were hurt and they pouted.

When the son of Master Kung was born the Duke of Lu sent a ceremonial present of a carp. The Kungs were apparently getting on in ducal esteem, for when Master Kung was born the duke merely bestowed his congratulations on Kung the Tall. The carp is a symbol of courage and achievement; courage because when the flesh of a live carp is cut there are no tremors, as with other fish; achievement because a carp in the breeding season will, like a salmon, ascend the most violent rapids. The Japanese, who in modern life cling to many customs and symbols borrowed from ancient China, which the Chinese have themselves forgotten, use the carp as a symbol of manliness in all boys' games and festivals. It had some similar significance in China at this time. Flattered by the notice he had received from the duke, Master Kung named his son Carp Primus, anticipating other sons who would, after the Chinese fashion, be named Carp Secundus, Carp Tertius, and so on. But in this he was disappointed for Carp Primus was the first and only son.

Likewise, whatever hopes the young father may have held for a son of his own tastes and abilities they were not realised. Carp Primus must have inherited a certain light mindedness from his mother, or the austere scholarship of his father may have soured him concerning all similar pursuits. As soon as he was old enough to fend for himself he avoided trouble by keeping out of his father's way. He promised to study the classics and probably fully intended to do so, but the fact remains that he never achieved even mediocre fame as a scholar. He and his mother, who was his one affection, probably had more interesting if less important matters to occupy their minds. He flits through history a light and trivial figure unmentioned except for the good but unheeded advice, the curt rebukes of his father and the fact that his only son became a worthy descendant of the sage and perpetuated the family name. It will not be necessary to mention him directly again except on the occasion of the death of his mother and then of himself.

In spite of his distaste for the work of tithe collecting, Master Kung, might have carried on with it, been promoted to more responsible positions and so become one of the thousands of bright young scholars whose services were used by the dukes and whose youthful ideals grew cold through the disillusionment and sophistication which petty official employment usually brings. With a mother, a wife, and a child to support and no prospects of other employment it was not an easy matter to escape from the environment into which he had been placed. Under any circumstances the conditions of life under which he was born did not make a change of occupation easy of accomplishment, for life ran in formalised grooves from which once a man was placed he seldom departed. The consideration of first importance to him lay in the fact that his duty to his family, especially to his mother, far outweighed any duty he might owe to himself, including that to his own conscience regarding the collection of unjust tithes. A son might be excused the most dishonest and most discreditable conduct if his actions were necessary to prevent the discomfort or distress of his parents, but would be considered guilty of the most atrocious misconduct if he allowed his own personal scruples to interfere with his filial duties. That a son should steal rather than see his parents go hungry was taken for granted as a procedure about which there could be no question.

Master Kung was torn between his dislike for his work and the necessity of providing for his family when his problem was solved for him in a rather tragic manner by the death of his mother which occurred soon after the birth of Carp Primus. This meant a definite break in his employment, for according to the strict ceremonial usage of the time, which is still observed, all official employment must be given up during the period of mourning. Aside from the

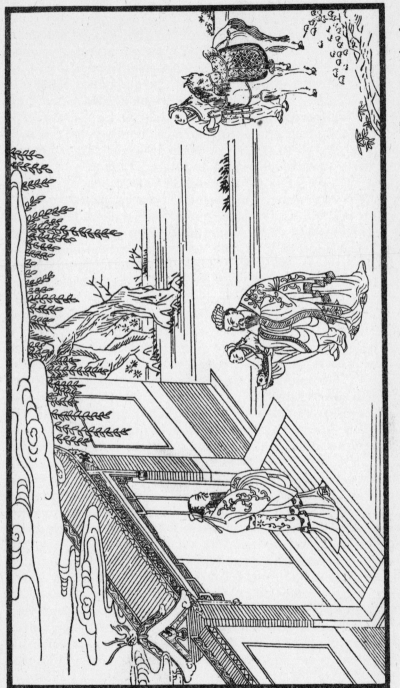

On the birth of Master Kung's only son the duke sent him a carp as a congratulatory present. The son was therefore named Carp Primus.

observation of certain simple ceremonies, this period was given over entirely to study and reflection. With the decay of the old civilisation and the general laxity of morals which prevailed in the state, the observance of the old funeral rites and ceremonies had been neglected. Children cut short the period of mourning for their parents and did not observe the proper decorum, eating rich foods, visiting the barber, wearing good clothing and enjoying festivals and other amusements when they should have been living in seclusion and exhibiting manifestations of grief. Observance of the proper ceremonies for the death of a parent was one of the most sacred of human obligations and Master Kung did not in the slightest degree abate its observance, but mourned his mother for the entire prescribed period of twenty-seven months. During this time the active duties of official employment were out of the question. He surrendered the care of the sheep and the oxen to others and never went back to them.

Having conducted the funeral services and arranged for the burial of his mother, Kung set about the care of his father's grave which he had of necessity neglected for a very extraordinary reason. He had not only never visited the grave but did not even know where it was. He was an infant when his father died, his mother had moved to a village about eight miles distant and through some strange idiosyncrasy had kept her son in ignorance of his father's burial-place. Since she would not tell him of its location he could not ask others. After her death he was able to institute inquiries he had been debarred from making during her lifetime and learned for the first time that the coffin had been deposited on the 'Road of the Five Fathers' near his birthplace. An old woman of the neighbourhood, the mother of one of his friends, told him of its location and also added the rather distressing information that the body had never been properly buried. It was the custom then as now to effect a temporary interment immediately after death which would be followed later by the formal funeral and permanent entombment. Sometimes this permanent burial was delayed for a few months because of lack of funds, or while waiting for an auspicious day, but to leave this important ceremony neglected and unperformed for a period of twenty years was most unusual.

It must have been particularly distressing to Master Kung with his exacting ideas as to the observance of all the ceremonial forms and especially all of the forms connected with funerals. The conduct of the widow in this connection is inexpressibly shocking to all Chinese, but no Chinese historian has ever made more than half-hearted attempts to explain it. By some it is pointed out that she was very young at the time and that maidenly modesty prevented her carrying out the ceremonies in which she would have to appear as the chief mourner. Others consider that lack of funds to provide a proper entombment caused her to postpone it. Again, a family quarrel may have been at the bottom of the neglect. With the children of a first wife, a concubine and a second wife living there was plenty of opportunity for differences of opinion as to whose privilege or responsibility it might be to take care of the funeral.

In this connection it would be a deliberate and inexcusable concealment of history to omit to mention the fact that there is room for doubt as to the legitimacy of the birth of Master Kung. The first of China's great historians who lived a few centuries later referred to the marital companionship of Kung the Tall and the young girl as a 'wild union'. This was generally understood at the time to mean that the usual simple marriage rites had not been observed. It would not have been extraordinary if this were true for the marriage ceremony had not at that time acquired the importance and sanctity given to it in later centuries and at this particular period the standards of the past had been lowered. The constant petty warfare, together with the barbarous punishments which were inflicted on the men, had reduced the number of marriageable males to a figure much less than that of the marriageable females with the consequent laxity in the marriage relationship. Some centuries later the wedding formalities were of much greater importance and scholars who followed the teachings of Master Kung, known as Confucianism, were shocked at the implication which naturally followed the suggestion that his father and mother had not been married. In order to rectify matters in their own minds they placed a new interpretation on the phrase regarding the 'wild union' and said that it referred to the disparity between the ages of the couple. Orthodox historians who followed them have either strengthened this interpretation or kept a discreet silence on the matter while many modern scholars say quite frankly the birth of Master Kung was illegitimate even according to the lax standards of the day. At the time this was not a matter of any vital importance and there was no particular stigma attached to illegitimacy. The inner-courts or harems of the nobility, the chief officers, and wealthy families were crowded, and, as will be seen later, some of the prominent men who rose high in the councils of the state were born as the result of chance roadside encounters. If the young girl was not actually married to Kung the Tall, there was no reason why she should be responsible for his burial.

However indifferently his mother may have observed the usual and decent funeral formalities, the son left nothing undone. He recovered the sadly decayed coffin of his father, removed it to the grave he had prepared for his mother, and buried the two of them side by side with appropriate ceremonies. The burial-place was neither at his birthplace nor the village to which his mother had removed, but at a small village called Fang, where the Kung clan had established themselves when they migrated from Sung to Lu. This place could be considered as the ancestral home of the family. The construction of the grave gave him a great deal of anxious thought. It was not then the custom to erect mounds over graves and he in the burial of his parents originated this practice, or at any rate has been given credit for it by all Chinese historians. After placing the coffins in the proper position, they were covered with a mound of earth about four feet high. The marking of the graves with a mound was not a mere whim of fancy or vanity. It appears that even then he was dreaming of larger fields of activity, did not expect to spend a lifetime in the restricted vicinity of his birthplace, and was making his plans accordingly.

'In olden times,' he said to his disciples and friends, 'they raised no mounds over their graves. But I am a man who belongs equally to the north and the south, the east and the west. I must have something by which I can remember this place.'

After the two coffins had been properly placed side by side and the earth had been partly heaped up, he left the disciples to complete the work of erecting the mound while he returned to his home. The disciples were late in rejoining him and explained that after the mound over the grave had been completed a heavy rainstorm had suddenly broken and washed it away, so it had been necessary to remain and rebuild it. If Master Kung had shared the common superstitions of his countrymen he would have looked on this as an omen significant perhaps of the bitter disappointments which were to follow him through life. In any event the mishap caused him great distress and he wept bitterly. Although he went to all this trouble to mark the graves of his parents there is no record nor hint that he ever visited them again and the care of the graves must have been attended to by proxy. Nor, indeed, did he ever again so far as known mention either his father or mother and they are never referred to in the voluminous writings of his disciples.

CHAPTER V

The glorious past but troubled present and doubtful
future of the country which impressed themselves
on the boy's mind as he grew to understanding.

As young Kung in his collection of tithes came into close contact with the farmers and began to give heed to the conversations and arguments around the wine-shops and taverns where the men of the village congregated, he found himself surrounded by political discussions open and heated, or cautious and sly and, to one with a political bent, of the most absorbing interest. The discussions were not trammelled by the comparatively simple politics in which people of to-day find interest and amusement but were based on a political machine which was vastly more complicated, interesting and exhilarating. In comparison, it might be said that the Chinese politicians of those days played chess while to-day they are content with checkers. The stakes and hazards were large. A loser in the game might be castrated, boiled alive or suffer the extermination of his entire family including that of several preceding generations who were still alive. The rewards were equally great; real castles were taken and real kings put in check while the pawns played their traditional unimportant part. However, by clever intrigue, bold manœuvres and an element of luck a pawn might assume royal powers, as indeed many of them had done. The fact that under these promising opportunities and with the rich rewards the career offered, Master Kung never became a professional politician, showed him to be a man of such high principles and rugged strength of character as, by that circumstance alone, to set him apart from the majority of his fellow-countrymen. In order to understand the turbid state of politics of the times in which he lived, it is necessary to go back and briefly review the early history, especially the history of the thoughts and dreams of his countrymen.

The river people had always believed in fairies and the belief persisted throughout the centuries of disillusionment and sophistication which changed them from a nomad people of the hills and wooded valleys to dwellers in cities with massive walls which they erected for protection against fellow-men of their own race. The fairyland in which they lived was a very real one to them and there were many kinds of fairies, good and bad but mostly good. So sincere was this belief that many people would, with perfect honesty in their hearts, tell of fairies they had seen and talked to, fairies, who in one way or another had brought them good or evil. There was one fairy-story they all believed and their faith in the story had a most profound effect on their philosophy, their politics and the development of their history. This story detailed the existence of the birthplace of their race which in many respects was not unlike the Garden of Eden. In that period there was no evil and all was good, chiefly owing to the beneficent rule of three ancient kings, known to posterity as Yao, Shun and Yu. Neither of the three rulers was of princely descent for there had been no princes before them. Each had been a commoner and was elevated to the throne by common consent, universal recognition of the fact that he was best fitted to rule as a benevolent despot. These three ancient rulers, who lived more than 4,000 years ago, embodied all wisdom and virtue and served as models for all the generations of rulers who followed them. Because of the good example which they set, the people of their time were distinguished by sobriety, industry, honesty, obedience and all the other personal and political virtues.

Under their benevolent rule no law enforcement officers were necessary because no one violated any of the few laws which existed. There was no dishonesty and doors and windows were not locked; indeed a man might leave his treasures piled up in the courtyard, or out in the street for that matter, with no fear of theft. There were no tax-collectors because the grateful people took their light contributions to the royal store-houses cheerfully and without compulsion, many of them giving more than their due so that the taxes were always overpaid. The rulers, like their subjects, lived comfortably but austerely. There were no soldiers, because no wars; no policemen, because no crime; no poverty, because no wealth. Not only were there no crimes but no evil thoughts. The most conservative Chinese writers of ancient days show no rhetorical restraint when describing the lives and deeds of these three men and indeed seem to find the richest words too poor and mean to do them justice.

All nature showed its approval of this ideal state of human conduct and worked in harmony with sinless man. Wild beasts came out of the forests to the fields, harnessed themselves to the plough and helped the farmers turn the soil. The skies provided rain and sun in just the correct proportion and in the proper season to ensure bountiful harvests. When locusts or other insects threatened the growing crops, birds of the air miraculously appeared and devoured them. The rulers themselves contributed to this ideal state of affairs. The last of the three ancient kings subdued disastrous floods by dint of superhuman effort extending over a long period of years, instead of safely and comfortably riding floods out like Noah did. The fact that he did this about the time that Noah was building his ark adds interest to the comparison. He straightened the courses of such important waterways as the Yangtsze and the Yellow Rivers and drained marsh lands which had covered a great part of the country. So great was his devotion to duty, so concentrated was he on the important task in hand that twice after long absences he passed his own door and returned to his labours without crossing the threshold or greeting either of the two sisters to whom he was married. People lived then to a great age. Yao and Shun each lived well beyond the century mark and Yu was more than ninety years old before he ascended the throne. This idyllic condition had existed because of the wisdom and virtues of the rulers and the obedience of the people, everything forming a natural harmony with nature. This in very brief outline constitutes the fairy-story which had such a profound influence over the lives and characters of the people who were fellow-countrymen of Master Kung.

The perfect virtues of the three great rulers of this golden age were not always duplicated by their successors. For a thousand years there were successive dynasties, some patterned in a weak and imperfect way after the golden age, some tyrannical and oppressive, some ruled by emperors of such excessive and revolting wickedness that the story of their lives makes one shudder even at this remote time. One of them was so completely and thoroughly and outrageously bad that the traditionally wicked Nero, by comparison, was a fairly respectable and mild-mannered citizen. An example of his less revolting acts was the butchering in cold blood of distinguished scholars in order to determine whether or not their hearts were constructed like those of ordinary people. To add to this picture of depravity, it should be mentioned that his consort aided him in these and even more gruesome scientific investigations.

The history of the dozen centuries succeeding the death of Yu, the last of the three virtuous rulers, was a long and dreary one with a few bright pages. The people were overtaxed, impressed as soldiers, and their women ravished. That many of them drank too much is not to be wondered at. The beneficent influences of nature were withdrawn, drought and floods wreaked devastation, there were no heaven-sent birds to grow fat at the expense of the locusts which destroyed the crops. Wild beasts attacked the farmers instead of aiding them in the cultivation of their fields. The people in their misery still sang old ballads of happy days. The old men over their wine-cups told old stories of the golden age and the young dreamed of the time when the fairies would again rule the country, when all would be happy, peaceful and prosperous.

About a thousand years before another and quite different people saw their similar hopes and dreams come true through the birth of Jesus of Nazareth, the river people's hopes were aroused in somewhat similar fashion. A new and virtuous ruler conquered the last of the wicked dynasties to found the great Chow dynasty which was to rule the country for more than eight centuries. The founder of the dynasty was said to have been of miraculous conception. A girl, who was a virgin, was walking in the country and there saw the huge footprints of a god. Something, perhaps vanity, moved her to walk with her own tiny feet in the tracks of the monster footprints. She did so and at once felt a thrill by which she knew that she was pregnant. The birth of a son which followed was painless. Sceptical people refused to believe the story and for some reason a good many attempts were made to get rid of the boy, though none succeeded. In the most dangerous situations his life was always saved under circumstances which can only be accounted for as miraculous. He had been thrown into out-of-the-way places so many times that he finally was given the nickname of 'The Castaway' which he retained even when he sat on a throne, and, so far as he and his subjects knew, ruled the world. In him and in his immediate successors were found the virtues of the old rulers.

Having established his capital at a place near the present ancient city of Sianfu, he set about consolidating and extending his kingdom. He did this by the eminently practical and economical method of creating many orders of nobility and distributing these orders where they would best fit into the widespread political machine. Each order was accompanied by a grant of territory and certain prerogatives. The most important posts, the key positions, as they might be called, were given to his own relatives with the title of duke. To one of the greatest of these dukes was allotted the little principality of Lu where Master Kung and his immediate ancestors were born. The descendants of the old vanquished dynasties were weak and vacillating and a more ruthless monarch might have settled them for good and all by slaughtering the survivors, but he observed the amenities of seigniority by making them barons, earls and viscounts. They accepted the largess and with their descendants soon disappeared from the pages of history. There were also a great many powerful families which sprang from common stock, and whose rapid increase in numbers had built up clans of the same family name so large that they had to be reckoned with; for the family clan in China has always, in theory at least, acted as a unit. The clan heads were grateful for the title of baron which was bestowed on them, but with their titles and new dignities and powers they grew ambitious and later gave those of higher rank a great deal to worry about.

By a nicely balanced gradation of power the common people were subject to the direct overlordship of the barons, earls and viscounts; these dignitaries were subject to the direct overlordship of the dukes and the dukes were subject only to their royal master. Grateful for the honours, the powers and the riches these titles and appointments brought them, the dukes and those of lesser rank gave the king the most loyal fealty and he, like other founders of dynasties, thought in his pride and vanity that he had established a royal line which would last for ever. There appeared to be no faulty rivet in the machine. He suffered from no disillusioning knowledge of history, for history had barely begun. But his successors were later to learn the bitter lesson many other princes in other lands have learned, that the gratitude of their subjects is a virtue which is not always bequeathed from father to son, and so grows weak as the generations pass.

For an encouragingly long time the system was a success; it worked perfectly and the river people were nearer a return to the golden age than they had ever been before. There were several centuries of uninterrupted peace during which the country was happy and prosperous and the arts flourished. The new ruler and his immediate successors took the three old rulers of the golden age as models and enjoined their examples on the grateful dukes who in turn admonished the lesser nobility thus giving the people good examples to follow. Tax burdens were lightened, officials were honest, the few laws were mild and were administered justly. There were optimists who believed, or pretended to believe, that nature was beginning to show her appreciation of this state of affairs, and in proof advanced the ancient fallacy that the climate was changing, becoming more beneficent.

A century or two after the first dukes were set up in their growing little principalities, their successors began to put on airs. The king in his capital had a court and so each duke inaugurated a little court of his own, modelled as nearly on the king's establishment as his income and his abilities would permit. The king had a premier and an elaborate staff of civil and military officials and so each duke had one, though most of them ruled places so small that they needed very simple administrative machinery. Soon each one had his own court historian, ritualist, musicians and that height of royal vain-glory, a court fool. All these vanities cost money and the taxes, which had started out being very small, gradually grew larger and as is usually the case with taxes, were never reduced.

The dukes were formed into a league and the king had set up a system of paternalistic discipline over them. They willingly pledged themselves to band together in defence of their ruler against attack and to take joint action in disciplining any duke who might encroach on the territory of a neighbour. When as a result of death, or for other reasons, a new duke succeeded to power, he renewed the vows and pledges of his predecessor. In order to cement and make permanent the machinery which had been set up, the king's court officials built up an elaborate ritual and ceremony which every member of the nobility was required to observe. An important part of the ritual provided that each duke appear at the court at regular intervals and renew his vows of fealty.

In spite of these vows, which were given in a most impressive manner, and which included clauses pledging the council to membership in a brotherhood working for common good, their vanity and ambitions soon outweighed the obligation of pledges. Most of them were ambitious for more territory or larger revenues and, those who could, set out to attain their desires at the expense of their weaker or less fortunate fellow-rulers. One of them, whose territories commanded the salt marsh delta around the mouth of the river, established a salt monopoly which proved so profitable that the duke soon became richer than the king. It was said in illustration of the unexampled prosperity of his principality that every woman owned two needles, a long one and a short one. But subjects of the other feudal rulers had to pay more for their salt. One ruler set up trading stations in which he established his own salaried courtesans. Thus traders were attracted to his market and the duke made money by levying a duty on trade. The visiting traders, as a matter of course, left a part of their money behind which also helped to swell the ducal coffers. A tax on the iron hoes which every farmer required was another revenue-producing measure which again enriched one duke at the expense of others, for he had a virtual monopoly on iron.

These rivalries bred jealousies and ambitions and dukes who were strong enough to do so began stealing territory from their neighbours. They were supposed to maintain troops which could be called out only for defence of the king against barbarian invaders but instead they used these troops for raids on each other. The conflicts were invariably inconclusive though much territory changed hands and a great many soldiers lost their lives. No state was ever completely obliterated for such an event would have needed a great deal of explaining at the capital; but they ravished each other's territories, levied tribute, set up baronies of their own and carried on enough plots and intrigues to keep historians busy concealing them. Rivalries and petty warfare between the dukes had reached the point where rulers of weak states had their fields ploughed on lines parallel to the boundaries of strong neighbouring states so that the progress of invading war chariots would be impeded. Rulers of strong states adopted the opposite course and had their fields

ploughed at right angles to weak neighbours as visual evidence of
the rapidity and effectiveness with which their war chariots could
accomplish an invasion of the country if occasion arose. Assassina-
tions were frequent and troublesome people were poisoned cheerfully and efficiently.

Some of the dukes had grown so proud and ambitious that while
they swore fealty to the king they were casting envious eyes on the
throne itself, were intriguing and bribing eunuchs and court officials in the very shadow of the throne. Long before Master Kung
was born these intrigues and stratagems had so far destroyed the
power of the throne that it was a mere shadow. The dukes no longer
carried out the pretence of paying fealty to the king, first postponed,
then neglected and finally abandoned the ceremonial visits to the
court. They ceased to consult the king on political matters and
finally reached a point where they did not bother to secure his
perfunctory approval of policies, or appointments.

While the scheming dukes had carefully undermined the power
of the king they had, either through design, superstition or mutual
jealousies left him a shadow throne with no power except over minor
court servants, but had maintained the prestige of the court regarding ritual and ceremony. They may have calculated that by keeping the king occupied with these shadowy emblems of power they
were given more opportunity to carry on their own interesting and
sometimes profitable intrigues. The decline of the royal house was
hastened by the birth of weak and dissolute heirs, a contingency
which many other royal houses have found it difficult to avoid.
King Yu Wang, who came to the throne in the eighth century before
Christ was hopelessly weak and sacrificed the state to please a whimsical court beauty. At her instigation he deposed his legitimate
queen and dispossessed the legitimate heir. The beauty had strange
and expensive tastes. She enjoyed the brittle sound of torn silk and
for her pleasure the store-houses of silk sent as gifts to the king were
torn to shreds. In a fit of boredom she did not smile for a week and
in order to amuse her the king ordered to be lighted on the hilltops
the flares of wolf bones which served as a signal to the vassal princes
to rally in force to repel an attack by the barbarians. As a practical
joke which brought a smile to the lips of the queen this ruse was
eminently successful but it was followed by the inevitable sequel.
A few months later there was an actual attack by barbarians, aided

by the father of the deposed queen. The signal beacons were lit again but the princes feared another practical joke and did not respond. The king was killed and the whimsical mistress taken captive.

This political corruption which had been started by the dukes and spread upward to officials of the court had also spread downward as political cancers are wont to do. Powerful families, barons and others with hereditary prestige and power, jockeyed for ascendancy over others and, when they could do so with safety, usurped the powers if not the places of the dukes. The internal relations of these usurping families were not serene, for in each great family there were many collateral branches which struggled with each other. Ambitious and crafty ministers got the barons in their power and ministers of lesser degree usurped the authority of the greater ministers, so that the whole theory of gradation of power on which the dynasty had been founded was reversed. The result was anarchy in which any successful adventurer might find great profit for himself. Under these conditions almost everyone was a participant in this great political game, which was entrancing in its interest but was bringing about the downfall of the nation and was destroying everything that had been so good and so wonderful during the period of the golden age. Barons who had been created in order to add to the prestige of individual dukes, when grown powerful, ousted the dukes or feloniously usurped their powers. As the whole civilisation of the country was based on the idea of loyalty and obedience of each to his immediate superior, the result was anarchy and confusion. In order to understand the completeness of their despair over the conditions of their country, it is necessary to visualise the complete isolation in which they lived. They could not escape their ills and look forward to better days by migrating to other countries for there were no other countries. They were as isolated as though they had been on a foundering ship.

The State of Lu in which young Kung was born, had, like the others, fallen on evil days. It was one of the smallest of the states, in a roughly rectangular shape about 200 miles long from northwest to southeast and covering an area of less than 20,000 square miles. The present city of Tsinanfu, the capital of Shantung province, is located within its ancient borders, and according to a couplet in an old song the whole expanse of the state could be seen from the top of the sacred mountain of Tai Shan. At the time of Master Kung's birth it probably had a population of less than one million. Although a small state it was renowned as being one of the most enlightened and had a reputation for scholarship which embraced what was the then known world. The founder of the ducal line of Lu had been a brother of the king and shared the latter's benevolence and scholarship. His successors had been of lesser moral and mental calibre, and the semblances of a benevolent rule disappeared though the traditions of scholarship remained.

CHAPTER VI

*The death of a wealthy minister of the state of Lu
and his dying request which gave the promising provincial scholar an opportunity to visit the capital at
Loyang and add to his knowledge.*

ALTHOUGH in his arrangements for marking and identifying the
burial-place of his parents, Master Kung appeared to anticipate
a lifetime of travel to distant points, his ambitions in this direction
were disappointingly slow of realisation. After giving up his position as a tithe-collector and devoting his entire time to study and
teaching he followed this avocation for more than ten years without
incident and, so far as is known, without ever leaving the town of
Zigzag Hill where he was living. During this period his fame as
an accomplished scholar and as a teacher of young men became well
established in his neighbourhood, but it was purely a local reputation and did not extend beyond the boundaries of the state of Lu.
Other scholars of less ability had travelled far, found employment,
and gained knowledge and experience under the patronage of feudal
rulers of other states, but he remained where he was, his opportunities for learning as well as for teaching limited to the narrow con-
fines of his own neighbourhood. The death of his mother had
broken the routine of his employment as a tithe-collector and
definitely committed him to a career as a scholar and teacher. It
remained for the death of another to make a break in the humdrum
routine of the schoolroom, provide him with an opportunity to
enlarge his horizons and so become a scholar with a national rather
than a provincial reputation. Though he was by no means an
opportunist it will be seen that every move in his life was occasioned
by some fortuitous circumstance, and the fates played with him as
with lesser men.

When Master Kung was only seventeen years old and was still
looking after the collection of grain from the farmers, a well-known

member of the Meng family, one of the three great families of Lu, accompanied the duke on a ceremonial visit to the semi-barbarian King of Chu, acting as the duke's master of ceremonies. On the way to Chu the ducal party was entertained by a local feudal ruler, and there was an even more elaborate entertainment when they visited the Chu capital. On both of these occasions it was the duty of Minister Meng to conduct and guide his duke through the ceremonies and to make the proper responses to the official speeches. On both occasions he made a lamentable mess of it, for he was unfamiliar with the ritual to be observed and had had no previous experience with formalities of this nature. As a result he had been compelled to surrender his place of honour to an officer of less ability but more knowledge of the ritual and diplomatic formalities. Under any circumstances his failure would have been very embarrassing, but it was especially humiliating here for Chu was a semibarbarian state with rude customs, while Lu was one of the most cultured of all the states and in matters of social usage was accustomed to set an example to all the others. He was deeply mortified and on his return home he set about a study of the ceremonies with such determination and success that a few years later he was able to represent the duke at more important and difficult conferences with entire credit to himself and to his master. He was determined that his twin sons, who would succeed him in official life, should never be called upon to feel the humiliation he had suffered.

Schoolmaster Kung's knowledge of forms and ceremonies first attracted Minister Meng's attention and approval. When he learned later that the schoolmaster was the direct descendant of a famous scholar of a former generation whom he greatly admired he became thoroughly convinced of the schoolmaster's genius and destiny and selected him as tutor for the twins. Minister Meng was still a young man and was not to die until nearly twenty years later, but in order to make his commands to his sons all the more mandatory he put them in the well-known death-bed form: 'When I am dead and gone.' As a preface to his commands he told his sons of the famous philosopher ancestor of Master Kung who had lived in the neighbouring state of Sung. This philosopher, who had a great reputation as a literary critic and an adviser to a succession of dukes, was so excessively modest that every time new honour was given him he became more unpretentious, so humble indeed that he took pride in his own humbleness and boasted about it.

'On the occasion of my first honour,' wrote the philosopher for the benefit of posterity, 'I bowed my head; at the second honour, I bent my shoulders; and at the third I walked stooped over. Now I slink along the wall and no one ventures to cast blame on me. I have but one pot and in it I cook my porridge and my grits and so appease my hunger.'

For some reason which the brief comments of history do not make clear, the philosopher, in spite of his great humility aroused the envy or resentment of the prince, and he was killed while in the prime of life. The family tragedy did not end there for it was his son who had a beautiful wife with whom a powerful minister of the state became infatuated, leading to the execution of the husband, the suicide of the wife and later to the migration of the Kung family to Lu, as told in an earlier chapter.

In his final advice to his sons the minister referred to a belief held by some mystics that a man whose destiny had been unfulfilled and ambitions unrealised, during his own lifetime, might finally attain his goal through the inherited talents of a descendant. They believed that this law of inherited destiny operated with particular potency in the case of one whose career had been cut short by a tragedy as had been the case with the excessively humble scholar. It appeared to the minister that the schoolmaster was so destined, that the mantle of his illustrious but unsuccessful ancestor had fallen on him.

'When I am no more,' he admonished his twin sons, 'you must take him for your teacher.'

The minister died when Master Kung was about thirty-three years old and the twin sons joined the band of disciples. This was distinctly a step upward for the teacher, for these new disciples came from one of the three leading families of Lu, families which stood high in the councils of the duke and had a good deal to say about the administration of state affairs. The membership gave the band of disciples a social and political prestige it could not otherwise have acquired and as we shall soon see opened up new opportunities of learning.

The birth of the two sons had come about in a rather interesting manner. Minister Meng was travelling in a near-by state when a

girl of the neighbourhood dreamed that with her skirt she had made
a tent for a son of the Meng family. As the minister had no sons
the girl thought this dream was an omen which she should tell the
visitor about. On her visit to him for this purpose she took a companion with her and the two made an agreement that if either of
them should gain any advantage as the result of this unusual adventure the other should share it. When Minister Meng heard the
dream he agreed that it was an omen of unmistakable significance.
Both girls joined his inner-court without any particular formalities
and the following day he went on his way leaving them under the
charge of a concubine. He seems to have been detained for some
time on his mission for when he returned the girl who had had the
prophetic dream presented him with a pair of twin boys. Her companion had been given an equal opportunity but there was no
offspring. However the lucky girl with the twins kept her promise
and the care of one of the boys was turned over to the other. For
the girl with the dream to take her friend with her on an enterprise
of this kind may appear at this late day to be a rather extraordinary
procedure, but according to the customs prevailing at that time there
was nothing unusual about it. Monogamous marriages were confined to poor men who could not afford anything more luxurious.
When a duke, a baron, or a wealthy official married, it was more or
less taken for granted that his bride would be accompanied by her
unmarried sisters, cousins or other dependent female relatives or
friends, who automatically became secondary wives and shared the
privilege and responsibilities of marriage. This arrangement was
so well-established and customary that it excited no comment and
is only mentioned in the historical records on the occasions when
jealous sisters quarrelled over the succession of their sons.

When it is said that twin sons were born, the statement requires
some amplification for in China there could not be, in the strict
sense of the word, any such thing as twin sons though there were
twin daughters. In the case of important people the succession to
titles or to official prerogatives as well as to the duties of family
sacrifices demanded that one son must be definitely established as
the elder, even though his entry into the world may have preceded
by less than an hour the birth of his younger brother. Common
people had no concern with titles and prerogatives but the obligations of filial piety were equally compelling, and one son was always

The old statesman of Lu, ashamed of his own lack of knowledge, left instructions that his son was to be placed under the tutelage and guidance of the rising young scholar.

given seniority over the other. Minister Meng had settled this problem at once by giving the first-born of the twins his own family name and bestowing a different name on the other.

The two new disciples, probably inspired by the suggestions of their master, conceived a bold and ambitious scheme; accompanied by their teacher they proposed to go to the imperial capital at Loyang and there study the archeology, the music, the rites and ceremonies, at the fountain-head of information and authority. The political power of the capital had at this time reached a very low ebb but it was still the cultural centre of the country, the residence of the most famous scholars, historians, astrologers and musicians. The usurping dukes had seriously encroached on the political powers of the king, but they were scrupulous to respect his spiritual prerogatives. So long as they were allowed to rule the country and collect its revenues they were quite content to leave the king in undisturbed possession of his imperial library, museum of archeology, college of historians, bands of musicians and other religious and scholastic appurtenances. In former days, before the rule of the kings of Chow had become so weak that the feudal rulers no longer feared them, the Duke of Lu, accompanied by his re-tainers, had made periodical visits to the capital to renew his vows of fealty and furbish his ritualistic retainers' knowledge of the ceremonies. This troublesome pilgrimage had finally become a mere pretence and as the rulers in Loyang became weaker even the pretence was abandoned. The dukes were too busy with their own local intrigues to bother with long and uncomfortable journeys to call on a ruler who can probably best be described as a pope with no temporal power and whose spiritual following was fast disap-pearing. No official visit from Lu to Loyang had been made for many years and it was necessary to secure the duke's permission even for the unofficial visit of a band of scholars. If it had been undertaken without his sanction those who took part in it might have been suspected of treacherous or treasonable designs. As matters turned out, the duke not only gave his permission but also his support by providing the travellers with a chariot, a team of horses and a servant. A small band of disciples joined School-master Kung on the trip, but one of the two whose connection with the schoolmaster had made the journey possible remained at home. The elder son of Minister Meng could not go on what proved to be an historic journey, as he was prevented by the duty of mourning the death of his father whom he succeeded in office.

The trip from Zigzag Hill in the feudal state of Lu to the capital, Loyang, covered a distance of only a few hundred miles but it was at that time a journey of rather ambitious proportions and not to be lightly undertaken. The little band of scholars took at least a week, probably nearer two weeks, to cover the distance. As they had but one conveyance it is to be presumed that most of them walked. The vehicle which the Chinese historians with their polite choice of phraseology term a 'chariot' was the springless two-wheeled cart which can be seen throughout North China to-day and is known to thousands of tourists as the 'Peking cart'. It would not be considered by them either an elegant or a comfortable vehicle though in remote parts of the country there are some old gentlemen who still look upon it as the mode of conveyance most suitable to the dignity of age and gentility. The clumsy vehicle has always supplied the dividing line which separated the common man from his superiors. This was the first time Master Kung had enjoyed the distinction of riding in a chariot but thereafter he seldom moved about in any other way for it was a dignity which he never gave up except when compelled to do so by direct necessity. Wherever he went his heavy body was transported by horses or more frequently the slowly plodding ox, while most of his disciples travelled with less dignity but more comfortably on foot.

Naturally his wife did not accompany him on this visit to the capital. Even if they had been companionable, which they were not, such a proceeding would have been unthinkable. Wives always remained at home and never accompanied their husbands even when the latter went to live for years in distant parts of the country. In the case of Master Kung and his wife separation brought no pangs or even mild regrets on either side. They may have been living apart at the time of the Loyang visit and whether they were or not it is extremely doubtful if they ever saw each other again.

His visit to the capital was filled with the eager researches of the ambitious student whose appetite for knowledge fed on what he already possessed. He inspected and carefully examined the imperial treasures, mostly bronze tripods, urns and sacrificial vessels, including some of such excellence that they have never been

Pictures of the ancient kings were seen in the 'Hall of Light' at the capital in Loyang.

excelled. All the books of the empire were to be found here, a collection which was huge in cubic as well as literary contents, for each volume comprised a good cart-load of bamboo tablets. Aside from historical records, the books included works on poetry, ceremonials, medicine, astrology and agriculture. Each ducal court had its library and that at Lu was one of the best but it was a small affair compared to the treasure-house of learning in Loyang. There were architectural wonders also, for though the architects of the Chow kings never created any buildings worthy of being remembered, their structures were magnificent as compared with the best buildings in the feudal states. One of the most imposing was the 'Hall of Light', a huge structure set apart for the ceremonial reception of visiting feudal rulers who had formerly come to renew their vows of fealty. These colourful receptions of feudal princes were no longer common, had in fact practically ceased, but the useless paraphernalia remained. The hall was kept in good repair and the scholar from Lu was pleased to find that the place of honour in the hall was given to pictures of the three ancient kings, Yao, Shun and Yu. These were the three who had ruled China during its golden age, whose example the founders of the Chow dynasty had set out to emulate, at first with marked success and later with such conspicuous failure. The presence of these three pictures in the 'Hall of Light' gave him renewed faith in his belief that the ruin of the country might be averted through a return to the principles exemplified by the conduct of these men.

Schoolmaster Kung was not content with purely academic researches in the library and museum but pushed the rules of propriety to the limit in searching out and interviewing anyone who could add to his store of knowledge. He sought for and obtained introductions to historians, astronomers, musicians, poets and philosophers. He listened to the palace music, observed the differences between the musical instruments of the various states as exhibited here, took music lessons from the best teachers and learned to play some of the instruments himself. The ancestral temple which ministered to the spirits of the deceased kings of Chow was much larger and architecturally superior to the ducal and baronial ancestral temples at Zigzag Hill and the ceremonies more complete and elaborate. He studied the architecture of the temples carefully and made thorough inquiries regarding the ceremonies. At Lu, as in the other feudal states, even the ancestral rites had been neglected and corrupted, but at the capital they were maintained in their original completeness and purity. Here he was not a teacher but a disciple, more ardent in his search for knowledge than any disciple of the hundreds who were to follow him later.

Of the many scholars and philosophers he met and talked with the most notable was the one who is known to the world by the Latinised name of Lao-tsze, a mystic whose teachings were after his death to form the basis of Taoism, the only native religion of China whose followers have always been at odds with those who follow the philosophy of Master Kung. He was one of the official employees of the court, having a scholastic position as keeper of the archives, a sinecure which gave him ample time to study and develop his philosophy. At the time of the Loyang visit Lao-tsze was eighty-three years old, more than twice the age of Master Kung, and there was as much disparity in the ideas and beliefs of the two men as there was difference in their ages. There was no disagreement in their minds as to the conditions under which they were living and the serious problems which the country faced. Both thoroughly appreciated the distress of the country and the threatened collapse of civilisation which appeared to be approaching. Master Kung was a reformer who wanted to regenerate the world through a return to the ancient doctrines; Lao-tsze had no faith in practical reforms by individual effort and believed that peace and happiness for the individual were only to be found in abandoning the world and living the life of a recluse until such time as the fates might bring about the existence of a happier state of affairs.

Even at this time his followers, who were in despair over conditions, had begun to find remote caves, secluded vales or mountain retreats for themselves and to retire from the haunts of their fellow-men. In the course of his later travels Master Kung was to encounter quite a number of these ascetics who urged on him the vanity and impracticability of his ideals and urged him to join them. The two men had many scholastic tastes in common, but that which brought them closer together than anything else was an absorbing interest in the ceremony and ritual of funeral observances. In fact the exact date of Master Kung's visit to Loyang is definitely fixed by the incident that a funeral they were attending together was interrupted

On his visit to the Chow capital at Loyang, the scholar from Lu asked the sage, Lao-tsze, about ancient ritual and music.

by an eclipse of the sun which was of course recorded by the court astrologers.

Although there is no record of the fact, there can be no doubt but that Master Kung tried to convert Lao-tsze to his ideas of reform, as, in truth, he tried to convert every important person with whom he came in contact who would listen to him. The attempt was not successful and the octogenarian mystic on the other hand was very sincere and earnest in his attempts to demonstrate to the young philosopher the futility of his ideas. Taking advantage of his great age he lectured the visitor in the following kindly vein:

'Those old emperors and others whom you talk about are dead, and their bones are mouldered to dust; only their words remain. When the superior man lives in propitious times he mounts aloft; but when the period is against him he moves as if his feet were entangled. I have heard that in times like these a good merchant, though he has rich treasures carefully stored away, appears as if he were poor, and that the superior man whose knowledge is complete is yet to outward appearances stupid. Follow their example and put away your proud air and many vain desires, your insinuating habit of thought and wild will which cannot prevail. These are of no advantage to you. This is all which I have to tell you.'

As a matter of fact that was not all the old philosopher had to say to the young one. During the stay of the latter in Loyang they had frequent meetings and it is a matter of great regret that there is no record of the conversations of these two men whose teachings were to have such a profound influence on the lives and thoughts of their countrymen. The only other recorded conversation was on the occasion of the younger man's departure for his home when the old philosopher gave him further kindly advice which he evidently thought might help to keep the younger man out of trouble.

'I have heard,' said Lao-tsze, 'that rich and noble persons make parting gifts; but people who are neither rich nor noble, but are good, give sincere words in farewell. I am neither rich nor noble but I am held to be a good man, so I will give you these words to take with you on your way:

'Shrewd and clever people are always near to death, for they love to criticise and pass judgment on others. Those who know a great deal about practical affairs, and do things on a large scale, endanger their persons, for by their actions and their knowledge they reveal the mistakes of mankind. He who is only the son of another has nothing for himself, for he owes all to his father; he who is only the official of another has nothing for himself, for he owes all to his superior.'

Master Kung who had great admiration for the scholarship and respect for the sincerity of the older man listened but was unconvinced. Lao-tsze's doctrine of non-resistance was exactly counter to his while the other's thinly veiled contempt for established authority came dangerously near being revolutionary. His own political ideas were bent along quite different lines. According to his manner of thinking, the distress in the country was not due to the structure of the political machine as it had been set up by the ancients, but to its faulty functioning brought about largely by the usurpation of powers on the part of the dukes, barons and officials. In Loyang he had visual evidence and first-hand information as to the depths of impotency to which the royal court had sunk. No powerful feudal envoys came to visit it. No one sought rights or favours from a king who was powerless to grant them. The nobles and officials around the court engrossed themselves in petty palace intrigues in which concubines and eunuchs played conspicuous parts. Even this distressing condition of affairs with the first-hand evidence of degeneracy and weakness did not shake his faith.

Aside from Lao-tsze's admonition against the folly and danger of being too frankly outspoken, Master Kung had another lesson on the same subject from an entirely different source. One of the interesting sights of the capital was a bronze statue of a man whose lips were sealed with three locks. The figure represented a cautious Minister of Agriculture who had served under one of the three great rulers of antiquity. On the back of the statue was an inscription reading:

'Be careful of your speech. Don't talk too much for much talk leads to calamity.'

He called the attention of his disciples to the statue and the inscription and admonished them against laxity in speech. Lao-tsze's counsel, the message conveyed by the statue, or both, must

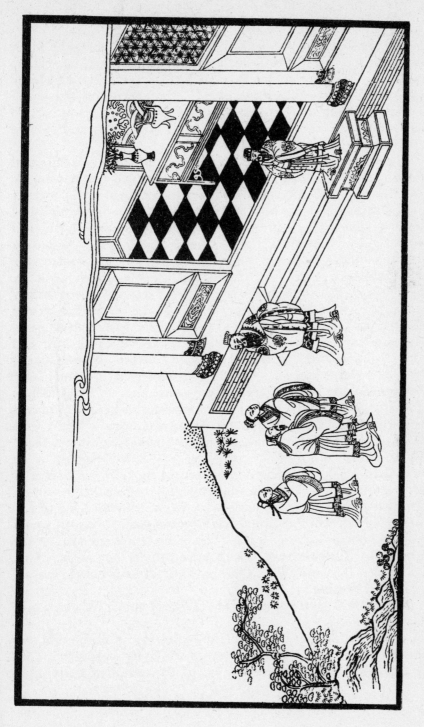

He called the attention of his disciples to a statue with its lips sealed, and cautioned them to be careful in their speech.

have made a lasting impression on him for this was advice which he frequently repeated.

'What is the good of being ready with the tongue,' he told his disciples many years later. 'They who encounter other men with smartness of speech for the most part merely cause themselves to be hated.'

The music of the capital was of entrancing interest to Master Kung. He had studied music in Lu and had practically exhausted the musical accomplishments of his native state but here at the imperial capital he found different airs and a more versatile equipment of musical instruments, for the ballads and music of all the feudal states were collected at the court. It was the duty of one class of officials to travel through the states, learn the new ballads which were being sung by the people and repeat them to the king who in this way kept himself in touch with the thoughts of the people. Master Kung discussed music with Lao-tsze and also with a famous music master of Loyang, and sought to learn from the latter something about the fundamental principles and the psychology of music. Later the music master said to a friend:

'This scholar from Lu has all the marks of a sage. He has the eyes, the forehead, the back and the stature of a sage. His profound knowledge and good memory all fit him for such an office.'

'Presuming he is a sage, what would he do?' said the friend.

'The ancient doctrines laid down by the monarchs of old have declined and are forgotten,' replied the music master. 'The rules of music and propriety are incomplete and those which are known are unheeded by this careless generation. A sage is needed to complete and establish them.'

Master Kung heard of this conversation and modestly said:

'How can I qualify for such a task? I have no knowledge, only a mere liking for propriety and music.' But the remarks of the music master confirmed the resolution he had arrived at some years before and gave him encouragement and confidence. He knew from that time on what his life work was to be, and to its accomplishment he devoted all of his talents.

Two years before the visit of the Lu scholars to Loyang, the king had died and the selection of his successor brought about such a violent conflict between opposing parties and rival factions of the royal family as to make it appear that the Chow dynasty had finally come to the inglorious end which many had so long predicted. The troubles had their origin in the inner-court of the palace, for father and son, elder brother and younger brother contended against each other because the distinction between the sons of the legitimate queen and the sons of the other ladies of the court had not been kept clear, nor was the identity of the paternal parent always a matter beyond doubt. In the midst of the minor fighting and general confusion the situation was further complicated by the death of the presumably rightful heir to the throne, which occurred in the same year as the death of the former king, his father. The elimination of this important contender from the scene of action created fresh opportunities for others and added new and more troublesome complications. At the time the visitors from Lu were at the capital one of the pretenders had, after many delays, been seated on the throne, but his position was by no means secure for there were several contenders in the neighbourhood each backed by a body of armed supporters of respectable size. These intrigues in the royal family naturally had their repercussions in the feudal states, for even if they were not directly concerned with the practical politics of the royal succession the manœuvres of the plotters at the royal capital at Loyang inspired the schemers around the ducal courts to similar exertions, so there was a renewed political and military activity.

In the quarrels over the succession to the throne in Loyang, the last wishes of the deceased ruler, as well as the rights of the legitimate heir, had been ignored by the plotters, each of whom dragged still lower the power and prestige of the ruling family in his efforts to gratify his own personal ambitions. The three powerful families in Lu were playing the same game for similar stakes on their own restricted stage. Duke Chao was then in the twenty-fifth year of his occupation of the ducal palace which he had entered with circumstantial pomp and ceremony at the age of nineteen. At that time one of the candid historians of the day commented on the fact that he had 'the heart of a boy' which was his euphonious and polite manner of saying that the mind of the young ruler was immature and that he was more interested in youthful sports and amusements than in the serious duties which his noble office obligated him to assume. The passing years did not add to his mental maturity and though he was now forty-four years

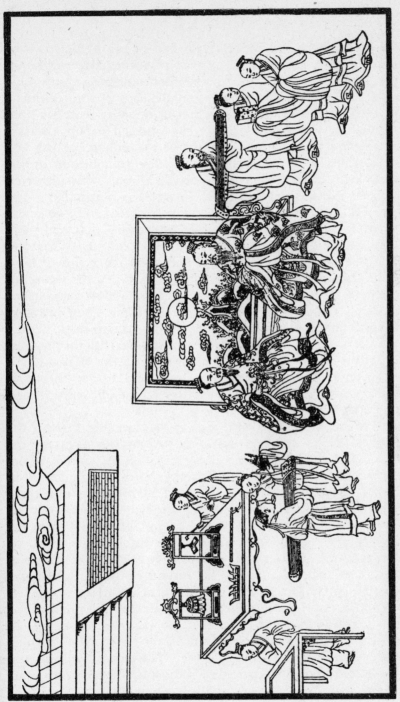

Master Kung discussed music with Lao-tsze and also with a famous music master of Loyang, and sought to learn from the latter something about the fundamental principles and the psychology of music.

old he was still more interested in the concubines of his inner-court, in rabbit catching, archery, and cock-fighting than in the affairs of state. His lack of interest in serious matters had made things easy for the usurping barons of Lu and the ambitious officials with the result that the duke now had much less power than he had possessed when he assumed the title a quarter of a century before.

The process of decay of the ducal authority in the state of Lu was typical of the similar processes which were going on throughout all the other states. Duke Huan, who had enjoyed an inglorious reign two centuries before this time, had in his inner-court a favourite concubine to whom three sons were born. As the existence of a legitimate son and heir provided for the ducal succession, the only way in which the duke could gratify the ambitions of the concubine and his own affection for these secondary sons was to create three baronies for them and turn over to them and their successors the collection of tithes in three divisions of his duchy. It was in the service of the most powerful of these baronial families that Master Kung had found his first employment. In passing it may be remarked that a great deal of the blame for the decay of the Chow dynasty could be traced directly to the inner-court system. Almost without exception the legitimate marriages of the dukes and other members of the nobility were arranged for them with some political object in view, and quite naturally resulted in a goodly proportion of mismated couples, and it followed that the favourite concubine would have more power and prestige with the duke than the legitimate spouse. With sons of numerous concubines contending for place over sons of the legitimate consort, with jealous wives and concubines and intriguing eunuchs taking active part in the controversy the household of every feudal ruler was a small hotbed of political strife and the family feuds which were created continued through generations.

The successors of the three first barons acquired more and more authority for themselves at the expense of the successive dukes, each of whom became more powerless than his predecessor. Though cautious at first in their exercise of illegal authority, the barons became more brazen and open in their encroachments. Formerly the army was under the direct control of the duke but some years before this the single small military unit had been split into three divisions, each being stationed in the territory of one of the barons, so that, in effect, the three separate bodies of troops became baronial rather than ducal armies. The ducal castle was supposed to be the only military stronghold in the state but, as the power of the barons grew, they built their own personal castles which rivalled the strongholds of the duke in importance. A trivial incident which occurred during the childhood of Master Kung illustrates the extent to which the prestige of the duke had been lowered and that of the barons augmented. A diplomatic emissary from a neighbouring state was on a visit to Zigzag Hill and was being given the usual official entertainment. This included an archery contest, but, when arrangements were being made for it, it was discovered that there were not enough archers in the duke's employ to stage the affair and he was put to the humiliation of having to borrow some from one of the barons.

Powerful ministers of the barons had not, in the meantime, been idle, and had lost no opportunity to increase their own powers so that during the few months that the scholars were in Loyang the state of Lu had made much more than the usual progress toward what appeared to be inevitable anarchy. To be enmeshed in political troubles was not a new experience at Zigzag Hill, but those which had come to a head while the students were in Loyang were much more serious than usual. As a result they cut their visit short. They could have remained much longer with both profit and satisfaction for they had only nibbled at the feasts of learning which were spread before them and were hungrier now than when they arrived.

CHAPTER VII

The scholar from Lu and his disciples return from a visit to the capital to find their native state disrupted by feuds which resulted in the exile of the duke who died seven years later without returning to his home.

HOWEVER much they may have desired to remain longer in Loyang, Master Kung and his disciples could not have been very greatly dissatisfied with the progress they had made in their studies and the scholastic prestige they had gained because of their pilgrimage. Naturally their visit to the capital had been the subject of a great deal of envious or congratulatory comment among the other scholars of Lu and their return to their native state was an event of some importance in scholarly circles. Master Kung, as the leader of the expedition, came in for a certain amount of fame and he resumed his teaching with a more firmly established reputation and with an increase in the number of his followers. He could now speak with the certainty of first-hand knowledge about the rites and ceremonies of the imperial capital and was an authority to whom the older but less travelled scholars were compelled to defer. He had the stamp of academic approval which goes with the doctor's degree and there could be no longer any doubt about his position in learned circles. He was the leading scholar of Lu, the state which stood highest in scholarship, and disciples came to him from other states. He was now no longer a purely provincial scholar whose learning had been restricted by the limitations of the feudal capital, but one of the favoured few who had enjoyed access to all the learning of the country and who had conversed with its greatest musicians, historians, astrologers, ritualists and philosophers. Under these circumstances his disciples not only increased in number but also in family rank, for other men of importance followed the example of Minister Meng in sending their sons to him.

He did not enjoy this patronage very long without disturbance for he had been back from Loyang less than a year when the political troubles which had been brewing at Zigzag Hill during his absence came to a climax. The difficulties which faced the duke here were not essentially different from those under which most of the other feudal rulers suffered for all were saddled with the dead weight of the great baronial families or of dictatorial ministers. The occasion for the creation of the three baronial estates of Lu has been described in the preceding chapter. No doubt for some time after the titles were created the successors to the three estates, with their prestige and power as barons, strengthened the position of their ducal superior and helped him in the administration of the state. As one generation after another succeeded to the baronial title the blood relationship of the barons with each other and with the successive dukes grew thin and watery and counted for nothing as against their mutual jealousies and conflicting ambitions. Their loyalty wavered, they secretly intrigued against their ruler and finally grew more or less openly contemptuous of the power of the duke.

Their control of the collection of tithes and taxes gave them a great and almost entirely uncontrolled and unregulated power which they did not hesitate to use to their own political advantage. In their collections of the hated tithes and taxes they were careful to use the name and authority of the duke so that the grumblings and resentments of the people might be turned in his direction. But in their distribution of the wealth collected they conveniently forgot the authority of the duke, defrauded him of his rightful portion and kept his household on short rations while the baronial families grew rich. They built war chariots for themselves and maintained standing armies of their own, and at the same time kept the duke so impoverished that he could not maintain the remnant of his own ducal army at its proper strength. With control of the revenues and the army the three great families had the duke entirely in their power and he did not dare attempt to exert any authority of his own. With the duke placed in this political isolation the three families were free to intrigue against each other. They developed intense rivalries and jealousies, each trying to gain more power and revenue at the expense of the other. A political situation which was complicated enough by this three-cornered rivalry was made still more complex by the fact that in each family there were jealous rival branches. The three-cornered feud with its many ramifications had been smouldering secretly for some time and broke out into open flame very shortly after the return of the scholars from Loyang.

The immediate occasion which brought the secret rivalries and animosities into the open was a hotly contested cock-fight in which the backers of each bird had cheated. In narrating this incident the Chinese historians naïvely say: 'The cocks of the Chi family and of the How family were in the habit of fighting,' a cautious phrase which shifts to the courageous birds the responsibility for the sport enjoyed by their masters. The head of the Chi family, the most important baron in the state, owned one of the birds while the head of the How family, only one of the bourgeois local families of some wealth but small political importance was the owner of the other. On the occasion of the historic contest Baron Ping of Chi concealed freshly ground mustard in the feathers of his bird disposing the irritant so as partially to blind the other bird when he buried his beak in the neck of his adversary preparatory to delivering the fatal thrust with his spurs. Those who have attended a cock-fight will readily understand how effective a trick of this sort might be even over a bird of greatly superior fighting powers. In some way the head of the How family heard about this unsportsmanlike stratagem and in retaliation he sheathed the spurs of his bird with razor-sharp metal spurs such as are used in all orthodox cock-fights to-day, but were not provided for in rules of that period. They may, with a fair degree of certainty, be set down as a Chinese invention and it is possible that this is the first time they were ever used. Whether mustard prevailed over metal spurs, or metal spurs over mustard has not been recorded, and it is probable that the contest between the two birds was never fought to a conclusion but was forgotten in the unsportsmanlike brawl which followed the discovery of the mutual deceptions. On technical grounds neither side had a leg to stand on and any referee would have disqualified both contestants. The decision of a referee availed nothing in the settlement of the matter. Blood was up among spectators as well as contestants and soon the feud was too violent and widespread to be confined within the limits of the cockpit. The Baron of Chi, who had really been the first to display poor sportsmanship by the use of the ground mustard now completed his record as an unfair sport by playing the part of a bully and using his political power to publicly rebuke his adversary. He followed this up by confiscating for his own uses a residence belonging to the How family. It was a dangerous thing to harbour animosity against a powerful baron especially if you were wealthy and possessed property which the baron could confiscate but the injured How family were so angry that they forgot all caution and joined the forces of the baron's secret enemies.

About this time another trivial incident added to the political troubles and aligned new enemies against the powerful baron. When the time came to celebrate one of the ceremonial sacrifices in honour of the memory of the deceased father of Duke Chao it was found that only sixteen dancers were available for the ceremony as the others had been, illegitimately and without authority, attached to the ancestral temple of the baron of Chi. This was a brazen piece of effrontery on the part of the baron. The number of dancers, archers, ritualists and others attached to each ancestral temple was very carefully regulated and graded according to rank. For the baron to maintain a more elaborate sacerdotal establishment than the duke, was bad enough but, for him to despoil the establishment of the duke in order to do so, was a much more serious matter involving as it did a grave insult to the memory of the ducal ancestors. The temple officers in charge of the sacrifices were greatly humiliated and incensed by their inability to carry out the proper religious ceremonies, and so they also harboured grudges against the powerful and arrogant baron. The shortage of ducal archers because of a similar reason had occurred several years before but was still fresh in their memory.

With the personal animosity which these two incidents had created, an uncle of the baron's considered this might be an opportune time to pay off an old score. His grudge against the baron which was of long standing, had originated in rivalry over the favours of a dissolute woman and been fed by the overbearing demeanour of his nephew toward him. In carrying out the assassination he had in mind he was certain of the support of the How family, and of the ceremonial officials whose dancers the baron had stolen and thought he might be fairly certain to secure the acquiescence if not the active support of the duke. The latter had no reason to love this powerful satrap who had not only deprived him of his

political powers and curtailed his legitimate revenue but had
humiliated him by filching his archers and his ceremonial dancers.
The uncle's plot though complicated in the ramifications of the
machinery necessary for its execution was quite simple in its objective, which was nothing more nor less than to kill the baron in the
simplest and easiest possible way. No doubt he would have poisoned him or accomplished his murder in some other secret way if
there had been any opportunity to do so but the baron was aware
that there were a great many men who would be happy to see him
dead and so he took the necessary precautions. Under the circumstances it appeared improbable that the assassination could be
carried out except in a more or less public way and in order to be
certain of the eventualities which might follow, it was necessary to
learn the attitude of the duke. With this idea in mind the uncle
presented one of the sons of the duke with a very fine bow and took
him outside the city to try out the new weapon, and in the secrecy
of the forest disclosed his plot to assassinate the baron. The duke's
son, in turn, discussed the matter with his two younger brothers
and the three rather timorously agreed to help at least to the extent
of sounding out their father. They were afraid to ask him directly,
and as an approach to the subject which might arouse his interest
but at the same time protect their own skins, they compelled an
attendant to inform the duke of the general idea behind the plot and
report to them what the ducal reactions were. The attendant was
excited over the sensational news he had to deliver and broke into
the apartment of the duke when the latter was asleep. Angered at
being disturbed the duke threatened the attendant with a spear
and shouted that he would seize the plotters and punish them. The
attendant ran away but the duke did not carry out his threat and
gave no orders regarding the punishment of the plotters.

The would-be assassins were frightened and kept out of the way
of the duke for several months but when he showed no anger toward
them and made no move to punish them they became encouraged
and made the attendant speak to him again. As on the previous
occasion, the duke threatened with his spear but he listened to the
message first, did not come so near with his spear and the attendant
did not have to run away so quickly. A few days later the attendant
spoke to the duke a third time. On this occasion there was no
threatening spear and the duke only reprimanded him, saying: 'This

is a matter beyond a small man like you.' With this encouragement
the plotters ceased their roundabout negotiations and disclosed the
entire details of the project to the duke who heartily endorsed it
and hesitated only because of fear that the assassination could not
be successfully carried out. With this idea in mind he consulted
with his various advisers from whom he received divided counsel.
The head of the How family who had been the baron's adversary in
the cock-fight and was one of the principals in the plot was quite
enthusiastic about it and considered that the project of killing the
baron could be accomplished very easily. Some agreed with him
while others held opposing views but in the end the duke endorsed
the project and put himself at the head of the plotters.

In all their calculations the schemers had felt sure that once the
issue was raised they could count on the support of the other two
baronial families who had long ago grown tired of the domineering
attitude of Baron Ping of Chi. The plotters were logically correct
in their theory for it would appear that any reduction in the power
of the strongest of the three baronial families would leave more
power to be shared by the other two. Secure in this conviction and
with everything in readiness for action they mustered their forces
consisting principally of the small ducal army and ordered the
capture and execution of the baron. When matters reached this
crisis one of the other powerful families, the Shuh-sun clan, recon-
sidered the matter and with a new orientation of thought. Glad as
they would have been to get this troublesome rival out of the way
they suddenly realised that when dukes started executing barons
and reducing illegitimate baronial estates, a dangerous precedent
was being established and there was no telling to what lengths it
might lead. There was a conference of the Shuh-sun family where
one of the officials presented his opinion quite succinctly by saying:

'If there is no Chi family, there will be no Shuh-sun family.'

The other family officials agreed with him and with their armed
forces they went to the rescue of the beleaguered baron. The plot
appears to have taken him by surprise for he put up no resistance
and until the arrival of this help, he was in considerable danger.
The troops at the command of the plotters had him surrounded in a
house and the soldiers with their bows unslung were squatting about
on their haunches waiting for the duke to get up courage enough
to give the order for the execution. He was as timorous in this hour

of easy victory as he had been when the project was first broached
to him and while he was still worrying and hesitating the Shuh-sun
soldiers arrived and went into action. In a short time the rescuers
were victorious and the baron's enemies driven from the field. The
first and most important casualty in the fighting which followed
was the death of the unfortunate Mr. How who had put metal spurs
on his fighting-cock. There was really very little bloodshed, and
the fight was not actually a decisive one and the duke was never
in any personal danger. There was no reason why he could not by
the exercise of any courage and political sagacity have remained
in Lu and taken advantage of the situation and put himself in a
better position than he had previously enjoyed even though the
assassination which he sponsored had failed in its purpose. The
partial success of the plot had taught the baron a very salutary
lesson which if followed up might restore him to something like the
subordinate position he was legally entitled to occupy. There was
nothing decisive or heroic about the duke and he was very thoroughly frightened by the unexpected turn events had taken and
could think of nothing but flight for he did not have courage enough
to face the vengeance of the baron. One of his faithful ministers
who had advised him against the plot, had anticipated failure and
had prepared in advance a policy by which the duke could extricate
himself from his difficulties and emerge in better position than
before. He was to disassociate himself entirely from the plot, blame
his ministers for it, exile some of them and execute a few of the
plotters who were of the least importance. To show his sincerity
in the matter, the minister proposed to be included among those
who were exiled. He argued that the baron had been thoroughly
frightened himself and this had been a chastening experience for
him. It was a perfectly sound programme involving no difficulties
but the duke was as cowardly as he was stupid. He was afraid to
remain and discuss this sensible proposal of his minister and fled
hastily to the neighbouring state of Tsi, accompanied by his younger
brother, his three sons, and a band of followers including his
ministers and most of his small ducal army.

CHAPTER VIII

The scholar and his disciples escaped from the political turmoil in Lu by following the duke into exile but he failed in his attempts to secure an official appointment in the state of Tsi.

MASTER KUNG was engrossed with his Loyang experiences and his newly augmented band of disciples and had kept distinctly aloof from the political turmoil which followed the cock-fight though he must have known at all times what was going on, for many of his disciples belonged to the important families who were mixed up in the affair in one way or another. The young official of the Meng family who had arranged the trip to Loyang had at first sided with the duke but, with the other Meng forces, went to the aid of the baron when he saw that the Shuh-sun family was taking that action. Master Kung did not accompany the refugee on his inglorious flight into exile but followed him a little later accompanied by a party of his band of disciples. With the duke driven from his throne (though driven by his own cowardice) divested of even a pretence of power and affairs governed by the usurping and secretly rebellious families, he felt that continued residence in his native state was impossible for him. Although his ideas may have been slightly modified later in life, at this time the keystone of his political creed rested on loyalty to constituted authority. He might tolerate loyalty to a semblance of power which was apparent rather than actual, just as his countrymen have never made a very strict distinction between theory and fact or between appearance and reality. But with the duke in exile and the rebellious families refusing to allow him any semblance of authority the situation could not be concealed or ignored. According to his political and social theories the only way in which the government of the state of Lu could be restored was by the return of the duke. He hoped to form some connection

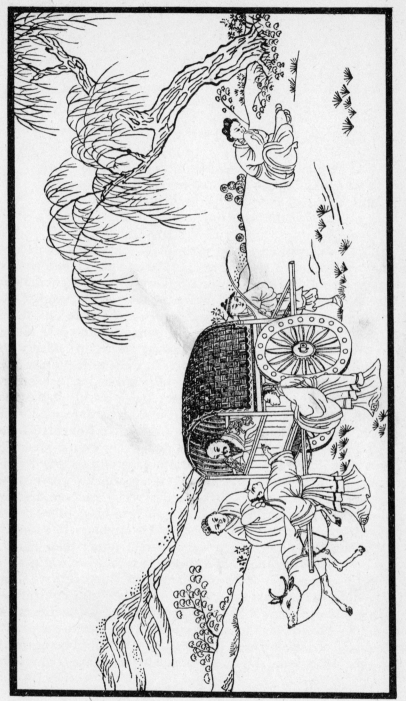

On his way to voluntary exile in the state of Tsi, Master Kung stopped to hear the story of the woman whose male relatives had all been killed by a tiger.

with the exile and possibly be of some help in bringing about the return.

As the scholars were leaving the border of Lu for the state of Tsi, the Master and his followers passed near the edge of the great sacred mountain of Tai Shan which on a clear day could be seen from any point in Lu. Master Kung was attracted by the heartbroken wails of a woman who was crying by the roadside and sent one of his disciples to inquire the reason.

'My mother's brother, and my husband were killed here by a ferocious tiger,' she said, 'and now my son has met the same fate.'

'Why do you not move away from such a dangerous neighbourhood?' inquired the disciple.

'But the officials here are not oppressive,' the woman explained.

Master Kung was told of the incident and said to his disciples:

'You hear that, my children! An oppressive official is more to be feared than a dangerous tiger!'

If Master Kung had been compelled to leave his native Lu for another state he could not have chosen one that fitted in better with his future plans than the state of Tsi. He was travelling to a strange and new country but with the knowledge that he was not unknown to the rulers of the state and with the confident hope that he might here secure the official appointment which would enable him to make practical use of his talents, help the exiled duke and advance the reforms on which his heart was set. Though a desire to aid the exiled duke may have been uppermost in his thoughts at first, the futility of attempting to do anything for this cowardly refugee soon became apparent. He then turned his attention towards development of the contact he had previously established with the head of the state. Several years before this Marquis Ching of Tsi, accompanied by his favourite and most gifted minister, Yen Ying, the hunchback, paid an official visit to the Duke of Lu at Zigzag Hill. While there he had met Master Kung, and asked his opinion concerning an academic question of government. The visiting marquis did not put into practice the advice given but expressed himself as very much pleased by the aptness of the reply he had received and the knowledge of ancient political history displayed. The state of Lu was full of scholars but Tsi formerly had been one of the semi-barbarian states where learning was not so common. Though hunchbacked Yen Ying, of whom we will hear

later, was a match for any of them in the accomplishment of scholarship and in the adroitness of oblique diplomacy, he was unique.
With few competent scholars to fill the official positions and particularly with the encouragement the visiting marquis had given him,
the philosopher set out with the high hope of every young man when
leaving his home town in search of fame and fortune in a strange
new country. He was not only counting on the support of the
marquis, but also on the friendship of his fellow-scholar Yen Ying
for on the latter's visit to Lu they had enjoyed many talks together
on pedantic subjects in which scholars find so much spice and relish.
Some important months were to be added to his life before he
learned that the Marquis Ching liked to talk showily about reform
but with no idea of putting reforms into practice, and that Yen
Ying's was a bloodless scholarly friendship which involved no human
obligations.

The visitor had not been long in Tsi before he was received by
Marquis Ching. Even if he had been unknown to the ruler, a
stranger who travelled about the country accompanied by a band of
devoted disciples who were constantly increasing in number was
sure to attract the attention of the officials of a little state like this.
The marquis asked his advice as to the government of the state and
Master Kung who never overlooked an opportunity to put in a word
for a needed reform replied that the art of government lay in the
economic use of the revenues. This bit of advice like the advice
Master Kung was to give later to many rulers and officials had a
distinctly personal application. The marquis, like all his fellow
feudal rulers, was collecting exorbitant taxes from his subjects and
squandering the public revenue on an expensive military establishment and other princely vanities. His exactions from the farmers
were so heavy that two-thirds of their crops went to him and they
had to clothe and feed themselves on the scanty third that was left.
His predecessors had established highly profitable monopolies of
salt, and his wealth exceeded that of any other ruler including the
King at Loyang. However he pretended to be very much pleased
by this thrifty advice. As a result he proposed granting the philosopher freehold possession of a considerable estate which would
ensure his permanent residence in the state. Though the motives
for this generous gesture were mixed, doubtless he intended in this
way to give an appearance of reform and secure public approval,

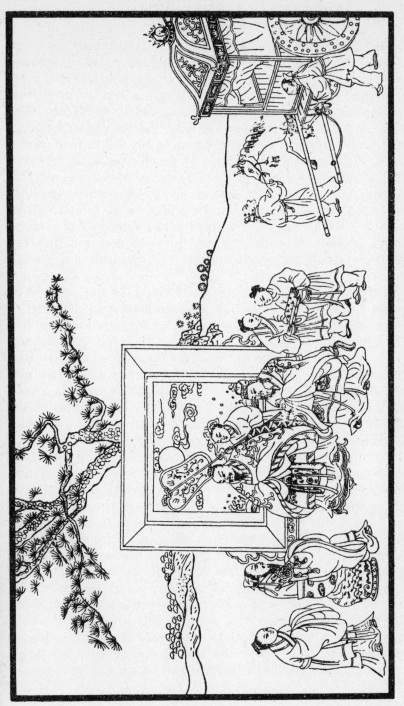

Marquis Ching, of the state of Tsi, with his minister Yen Ÿing, visited the state of Lu and asked the advice of the scholar about methods of government.

on the pretence of having adopted policies he had no intention of carrying out. It was an old political trick then and has not yet lost its usefulness. The visiting scholar saw through the subterfuge at once. The grant of an estate would not be a means of promoting his ideas for it was not accompanied by any powers, but on the other hand it would be a method of silencing him and neutralising his influence. Full of high ideals and refusing to compromise with political expediency, he refused the offer. His disciples were not so punctilious, and many of them while listening with eager approval to the idealistic political theories of their master had both eyes wide open for the easy and well-paid political appointments which might fall their way. One of them remonstrated with him over his refusal of the freehold and was promptly rebuked.

'A gentleman,' said the Master, 'does not take something for nothing. The marquis did not accept my advice but offers me a reward. He does not understand me.'

While he made no progress politically, and had no opportunity to improve the position of the exiled Duke of Lu, Master Kung's stay in Tsi was in other ways quite satisfactory to him. When in Loyang, he had been absorbed in the study of music and here in Tsi he found the music even more entrancing. He had gained a hint of its marvels while still *en route* to the Tsi capital, for his attention was attracted by the gait of a boy who was swinging a wine-jug as he moved along a country path. The movements of the boy were not those of the awkward country yokel, but were full of the unstudied grace of one to whom rhythm has become second nature. No boys in Lu walked like that or swung wine jars like that. He saw at once that he was approaching a country where rhythm had reached a much higher development than either in Lu or Loyang. Eagerly he told his driver to hurry on to the capital that he might hear and enjoy the superior melodies. He was not disappointed and the study of the music of Tsi so engrossed him that he forgot everything else for three months. During that period he neglected his food so completely that he did not know what he ate; he even forgot to nibble at ginger and drink his usual jugs of wine. He was as fascinated and as absorbed as an intelligent and appreciative lover of music might be at his first opportunity to enjoy a season of grand opera.

'I did not know,' he cried, 'that any music could be so excellent as this!'

It was said that this music could not be credited to the creative talents of the musicians of Tsi, but was the genuine music of the ancient King Shun, which had somehow been forgotten in the other states but was preserved in this. Each of the little principalities had its own court musicians, some of whom developed themes of their own, while others perpetuated the ancient compositions and by constant and careful repetition of the ancient tunes kept them free from change. Master Kung had learned all he could about the music at Zigzag Hill and at Loyang, and now he mastered the music of the Tsi capital. Chinese music was not merely an arrangement of harmonious sounds – even to-day harmony as the westerner understands it is not a necessary component of Chinese compositions. The ancient music expressed ideas and emotions in a manner whose artistry has been half if not wholly forgotten. As in the case of many other peoples, Chinese stories and legends were perpetuated in songs and ballads long before they were put into the more permanent form made possible by a common written language. As the more highly technical culture of writing replaced oral ballad traditions, the art of the latter was lost and Chinese as well as foreign scholars are at a loss as to how they should appraise it though all agree that the music of that day was of much greater significance than the music of to-day. Considering the messages which the illiterate African negroes of to-day can send by the use of their drums, it should occasion no surprise that the very highly cultivated residents of China should by means of their music have been able to record more complicated narratives, even to go into forms of literary expression which we assume to-day to be confined to the drama or the written word. Owing to the difficulties of writing, the written word was rare and the drama did not exist.

The Chinese historians in their comments concerning this period make no explanation of this profound significance of music which appears to have been to them a commonplace which would be generally understood. One incident they record tells of Master Kung's ability to interpret themes. He was attempting to learn to play the zither and after ten days had made no progress.

'We will try something else,' said the teacher, but Master Kung replied:

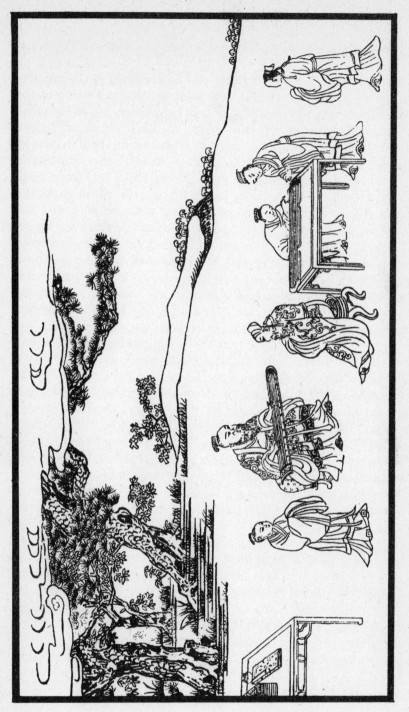

Master Kung's unusual understanding of music was shown by his ability to identify the character of the composer of a selection though he was hearing it for the first time.

'I have practised the melody, but have not yet acquired the rhythm.'

They continued studying and practising the same tune and again the teacher tried to urge his pupil to greater progress by saying:

'Now that you have practised the rhythm, we will proceed.' The pupil was still not satisfied and said:

'I have not caught the mood.' After a while the teacher spoke again:

'Now that you have practised the mood, we will proceed.'

'I have not yet ascertained the kind of men who composed the music,' said the pupil and the teacher observing him said:

'You must think deeply and seriously. You must look into the subject with a cheerful mood, high hopes and an open mind.'

'Now I know who he was,' cried Master Kung. 'His complexion was so dark as to be almost black. He was tall and stout and his eyes when they looked into the distance had the calm gaze of a sheep. His mind was that of a king who could rule the four quarters of the earth. No one but King Wen could have composed this song! If it was not King Wen, who else could have composed anything like this?'

The music master rose from the mat on which he was seated bowed twice and said:

'You are my master. According to the traditions of the ancient musicians it is actually reputed to be a melody composed by King Wen.'

The marquis continued to ask his scholarly visitor for advice which he never followed and continued to consider the idea of adding to his collection of potential political talent by making the scholar a permanent resident of the place. A few months after his first offer he again approached him, proposing to confer on him an estate with the accompanying political powers. The marquis had not made this offer because of any sudden conversion to new ideas, for he had been steeped in wickedness too long for any change to be possible now. In fact when he died some years later it was said of him:

'He had a thousand chariots but on the day of his death the people could not find a single virtue to praise.'

With his advancing age he became more conscious of the fact that his ministers were imposing their will on him and that some were plotting to upset the succession and depose his family in favour of another, a scheme which found great encouragement and impetus from the flight and exile of the neighbouring duke. He was anxious now to use the scholar from Lu as a counterpoise to neutralise the influence of the others and as one on whom he could depend for help against any treasonable plots. Of all the neutral scholars in Lu, Master Kung had been the only one even to consider giving aid to the exiled duke and this unselfish loyalty profoundly impressed the old marquis. Master Kung's ideas in the meantime had changed, and he was willing now to take half a loaf instead of insisting on the whole though he never compromised with his ideals. His plans to reform the world by means of high ethical teaching had not accomplished very much; indeed had accomplished nothing in the way of practical results. He had been teaching for more than ten years and a return of the country to the golden age was no nearer than it had been when he was checking up on the oxen and sheep. The lowest least scholarly official had more power than he and greater opportunities for accomplishment. He would gladly have accepted this opportunity to practise in a small way the theories he hoped all the rulers of the country could be induced to adopt.

During the months he had been in the state, with his growing band of disciples the professional politicians who made up the official household of the marquis had kept a watchful and suspicious eye on him. They represented the entrenched power which is always against the newcomer, especially against the newcomer with revolutionary ideas, and as soon as they heard of this new project of the marquis the ministers in the service of the state banded themselves against it. This philosopher from Lu, if given any power, might upset the established and profitable order of things, and would certainly interfere with the political plots in which each of them had a hand.

Their spokesman was the scholarly hunchback, Yen Ying, whose acquaintance Master Kung had made in Lu and on whose friendship he had at first relied. This Tsi minister, whose reputation for sound statesmanship, wit and diplomacy had survived throughout the centuries and is now looked on as one of the sages of China, is deserving of more than a passing reference, not only because of his unique character, but because of the rather questionable part he was to play later in this story. He was noted as being the most parsimonious man in the country, and in truth his reputation for sordid stinginess has seldom if ever been excelled. Although a powerful minister, and therefore a man of great wealth, he would not allow his women-folk to wear silk and denied both them and himself the clothing a well-to-do peasant would wear. He possessed one robe of fox fur which he wore for thirty years until it was so bare that from its appearance no one could tell what animal had produced the original fur. He was notorious for the poor table he set and everyone dreaded his official dinner invitations. At the annual sacrificial ceremonies it was customary for men of his rank and wealth to place whole animals on the sacrificial altar, but he contented himself with an offering of a single shoulder of pork. This was carrying parsimony to a rather absurd degree, because the sacrificial meats, after being exhibited on the altars during the ceremony were later taken away by the donors and provided the substance for the feasts which always followed the observance of the sacrifices.

He was not only parsimonious but intensely jealous of his official position and intolerant of any rivalry. In his youth there had been three older ministers who stood in the way of his advancement and he concocted a clever scheme to get rid of one of them. He persuaded the marquis to propose a prize of two peaches to the two ministers who offered him the best advice on certain problems of state. With only two prizes, and three contestants, it was a foregone conclusion that one would fail to win and might reasonably be expected to feel so humiliated that he would resign, thus leaving only two rivals to contend with. The scheme was far more successful than he could possibly have anticipated, skilful as he was in all kinds of political artifices. Two contestants appeared, and, as there were no other contenders, they were awarded the peaches. After they had eaten the prizes with considerable relish and satisfaction, the third contestant arrived. When he presented his plan the marquis was compelled to admit that it was so far the best, that he really deserved both the peaches but could not be awarded either of them as they had been consumed by his competitors. In their chagrin and humiliation over this development the two who had eaten the peaches committed suicide. The third contestant was so grieved at having been the indirect cause of the death of two men whom he held in the highest esteem that he also committed suicide. The scheming hunchback had by one sly trick eliminated all three of his rivals and after that he was careful to see that no other rival got a foothold. He did not forget his jealousy when he discussed with the marquis the latter's plan to give official employment to Master Kung.

'These learned fellows like Mr. Kung are an impractical lot who can be taught nothing,' he said. 'They are haughty and conceited of their own opinions, so they will never be contented with any inferior position, but will always be striving for more power. These fellows live by travelling from state to state, trying to impress rulers with their wild schemes and when they fail to get any official support they have recourse to begging and to borrowing, contracting debts which they never repay. How can such people be allowed to participate in state affairs? They set an absurdly high value on such showy observances as funeral ceremonies, give way to their grief and waste their own and the money of others on great and elaborate burials. Their example is injurious to the manners of the common people who should not be tempted into such extravagances. Mr. Kung has a thousand fads and peculiar ideas. It would take generations to exhaust all that he knows about the ceremonies of such a simple thing as going up and down stairs. Admittedly the royal house of Chow has been weak and the rules of decorum are out of order. But in a troubled period like this, when we have so many other important matters to consider, it is not the time to examine his complicated rules of propriety. If you, prince, decide to employ him to make changes in the good old customs of our state, you will not be making the welfare of the people your primary consideration.'

There was more than a little sophistry as well as downright deceit in the scholarly hunchback's statement of facts, in which he was, of course, speaking for the other ministers as well as for himself. Either convinced by this presentation of the case or intimidated by the determined front of his ministers, the marquis dropped the project for the moment. He did not, however, entirely abandon his plans to attach Master Kung to his official family and came forward a few weeks later with still another proposal which would have given the master a sinecure with a revenue in Tsi comparable to that of the great families of Lu. Yen Ying and the other dignitaries of the state became really alarmed at this proposal and plotted to

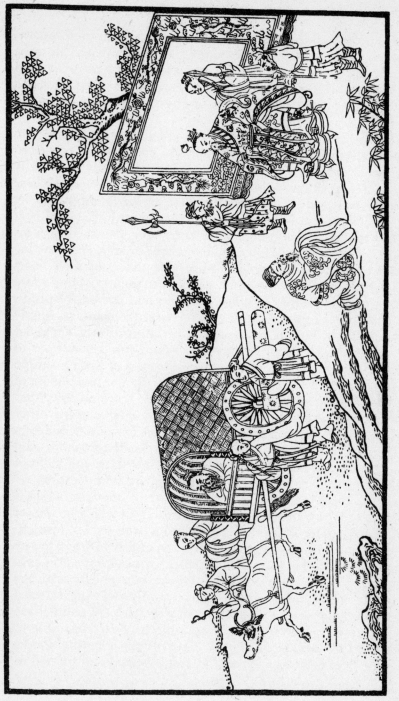

Minister Yen Ying persuades the Marquis of Tsi that Master Kung would not make a suitable public servant, whereupon the latter returned to his native state of Lu.

settle the matter definitely and finally by killing the unwelcome visitor. At the same time, they brought renewed pressure to bear on the ageing marquis. The scholar stayed on in Tsi, but was no longer patronised by the marquis. In fact the latter appears to have weakened under the determined opposition of his ministers or become bored at Master Kung's persistent preaching of reforms he had no intention of adopting for he tried to put a stop to his visits and gave him some well directed snubs. At last the marquis said:

'I am too old! I can no longer use Mr. Kung's services.'

Under these circumstances, even the superior music of Tsi could not keep Master Kung and he returned to his native state, accompanied by those of his disciples who had not in the meantime secured official employment in minor capacities. He had been gone less than two years and except as he had increased his own knowledge and influenced his disciples, the years were devoid of accomplishment. Whatever plans he may have had to aid the exiled duke had come to naught and it is doubtful if the two ever came in direct contact with each other.

CHAPTER IX

The death of Duke Chao followed by the deaths of the heads of two of the principal families of Lu threw the government into the hands of Yang Hoo who failed in his attempt to replace the heads of ruling families and make his dictatorship permanent.

Eight years after the historic cock-fight which had led to his exile, the death of the refugee Duke Chao created a new crisis in the affairs of Lu. The years he had spent away from the state of which he was the ruler had been unhappy ones, and he had plumbed the depths of humiliation. At first he had been hospitably received by the Marquis of Tsi who exerted himself on behalf of the deposed ruler and attempted to ameliorate somewhat the humiliating position in which he was placed. With his own troops he took possession of the unimportant city of Yun which, though on the border between the two states, was actually located in Lu. The refugee duke and his retainers set up their residence there and so were able to maintain the pretence that he had not fled from the state of which he was sovereign but was temporarily maintaining his residence in a suburb of the capital. A pretence like this was very comforting to the duke, though of course no one was deceived. The fact that he had made a cowardly flight from his own state and that he was a refugee on its borders where he existed by the sufferance of a rival ruler was of course well known to everyone. It was the subject of lively though discreet discussions in all the wine-shops and inner-courts, but it was unthinkable that anyone should put the actual facts of the case into blunt and frank phraseology. The ducal authority still existed in the small city of Yun so the duke in this safe though remote location carried on the usual ceremonies, offered sacrifices at the appointed seasons, held audience with his ministers and maintained a powerless refugee court. Baron Ping, anxious to observe the outward proprieties, sent him periodical presents of food, horses and clothing

138

until the duke's retainers seized and held the messengers, after which the gifts were discontinued. At the same time the resourceful baron bribed officials of Tsi and of other neighbouring states to keep an eye on the movements of the refugee and to thwart any attempt that might be made to restore him.

The flight of the duke of course created a tremendous stir in the capitals of the various feudal states. Under the general terms of sovereignty, as delegated to the dukes by the Chow kings as well as under the many specific covenants and alliances which the various petty rulers had made with each other, it was their solemn duty to place their armed forces at his disposal and to restore him to power. There were quite a number of pretentious conferences held to discuss the matter, but at these conferences the feudal jealousies came into full play and so offset and counterbalanced each other that the conferences ended in tedious discussions and nothing was done. Each feudal ruler was afraid that if any action were taken it might result in some other gaining an advantage. The powerful Duke of Tsin did go further than any of the rest of them and summoned Baron Ping to him for investigation and possible punishment, but the baron had, by bribery, secured the support of the Tsin ministers and, acting under their advice, obeyed the summons and emerged from the conference with a distinct diplomatic victory. The Duke of Tsin had expected him to refuse to come, which action would have made it possible to charge him with treason and so attack him on that basis. Instead the baron, ably coached by the bribed officials, came barefoot and in the sack-cloth of mourning costume, and made an impassioned plea for the return of the duke whom he promised to follow and support. Baron Ping was quite safe in making these protestations and promises, for during the duke's long absence his supporters had grown weaker, the opposition to him had grown stronger and the refugee preferred to remain under the humiliating protection of a neighbouring ruler rather than return and face the animosities in his own state. Baron Ping's diplomatic coup was so successful that it put a stop to any further efforts on the part of the feudal rulers to interfere with the affairs of Lu.

The duke had to content himself with the empty honours shown him by his followers at the refugee court of Yun, but the followers themselves were divided into factions and doubtless Baron Ping's genius for successful bribery prevented any effective action they might have taken to improve his position. At first the people of Yun were flattered by the presence of the ducal exile and gave him their loyal support. Soon after the duke established himself there Baron Ping made a half-hearted attempt to take the place, but the people of Yun put up such a determined fight that he abandoned the attack. But as time went by the attitude of the people of Yun changed. The followers of an impoverished duke do not make the best of neighbours and as the months passed they became more and more overbearing, their exactions more onerous and their payments more uncertain. At length the people could bear no more. In the concise manner of the Chinese historians it is set down: 'The people of Yun dispersed.' The duke and his principal followers were then absent on one of their perennial visits to the Marquis of Tsi and when they returned it was to a deserted city. When their crops were harvested the inhabitants had moved out, scattering in all directions, leaving the duke and his followers to the sole occupancy of the deserted and destitute city. This removal to new homes did not present any new or serious problems. There was plenty of vacant fertile land and it was customary to move to new fields as old ones became exhausted, though it was unusual for an entire city to be abandoned at one time except on the occasion of a flood, pestilence or other major calamity. The presence of the impoverished followers of the duke had in fact provided a calamity equal to those of nature.

The abandonment of Yun by its inhabitants was the climax to Duke Chao's misery and humiliation, for it left him without a foothold in his own state and without the shadow of a pretence that he was not a refugee. The Marquis of Tsi would have no more to do with him, would not even receive his visits and the officials of Tsi, disgusted by his cowardice and his grovelling pleas for help, openly mocked at him. He then went to the state of Tsin where he was grudgingly welcomed by the duke who a few years previously had planned to rally the armed forces of the feudal states and restore him to his capital. Here he died a few years later at the age of fifty-one. The three sons of the duke who had encouraged the plot against Baron Ping's life had followed him into exile and the eldest of these was, of course, the rightful heir to the throne. Baron Ping who had usurped the ducal functions during the long absence of Duke Chao, took upon himself the responsibility of selecting a successor to the duke and would not consider the legitimate claims of the heir who by his participation in the murderous plot had shown himself to be a personal enemy. Instead he selected the dead ruler's younger brother, who had prudently followed the refugee into exile and had with equal prudence refrained from any aid to his brother or other political activity which might prejudice his chances to succeed to the ducal throne.

The coffin containing the body of the duke was brought to Lu for burial, escorted by his sons and other relatives and retainers. At the feudal boundaries the escort discreetly retired after handing the coffin over to the escort from Lu, consisting of partisans of Baron Ping. The younger brother who had been promised the succession, did not halt at the feudal boundaries or slacken his progress to fit that of the slowly moving funeral cortège. For eight years he had been living on the short rations that might be expected by the dependant of an impoverished refugee nobleman and he was anxious to enjoy the luxuries of full ducal estate. He forgot the duties which as chief mourner he owed to the dead elder-brother and hurried on to Zigzag Hill arriving there some time ahead of the coffin. Baron Ping ignored the brother and took charge of the funeral ceremonies. Even in the performance of this duty he could not forget his hatred for his master who had unsuccessfully plotted to take his life and went out of his way to perpetuate in death the humiliations the dead man had suffered when alive. He buried the duke on a road to the south of the plot given over to the ducal tombs, thereby separating it from the other tombs of his ancestors, a procedure which could only be compared to that of burial in unsanctified ground. This action was stupid as well as spiteful and he was strongly advised against it by his ministers.

'You could not serve him when alive,' said one of them, 'and now that he is dead you would separate him from his fathers and think that this action will be a monument to yourself. You may do so now but the strong probabilities are that hereafter you will be ashamed of yourself.'

The death of the refugee duke and the irregular ducal succession, which had been dictated by Baron Ping, revived old frictions and created new ones, and Master Kung's presence in the state introduced a potential new factor in the extremely complex political situation. He was not a member of any of the local parties, and was not even a member of one of the family clans as his family had migrated from Sung several centuries before under circumstances which have been described in a previous chapter. He was, of course, a member of the Kung clan but it was then numerically too small to be of any political importance, and, considering the distinguished talents of the Kung ancestors in the state of Sung, had played a very unimportant part in the affairs of Lu. On the other hand, his support as an individual would be an asset of great importance to any family or faction and in the attempts to gain his support he had to listen to the claims put forth by many partisans. With his band of talented and personally loyal disciples, he could bring to the aid of any party in Lu an organisation of scholarship far superior to anything else in the state. In his detached and neutral position Master Kung could with perfect propriety have given his endorsement to any party and that support would probably have enabled the faction which held it to obtain an ascendancy over the others. His aid was sought by every faction but he found none which met with his approval and so held aloof from all, devoting himself to study and to teaching his disciples, but at the same time keeping a watchful eye on the political intrigues going on around him.

One of the most persistent in his attempts to gain the favour of the Master was Yang Hoo, the principal minister of the Chi family, one of those who had risen to power from the lower ranks by his own abilities. Though without the scholarship which was supposed to be the first requisite of an official, he was a clever and ambitious politician and a bold and resourceful soldier. Chinese historians have dismissed him with the brief and contemptuous reference which official chronicles reserve for unsuccessful rebels, but the facts as admitted by the historians themselves award him a much larger and more honourable place in history. An appraisal of the sketchy and inadequate historical data available shows that he might be classed as a political adventurer, soldier of fortune or an unsuccessful national hero. Some might consider him an Oliver Cromwell or a George Washington of his day, who might, under more fortunate circumstances, have accomplished the regeneration of his country but along drastic and revolutionary lines. He was what in common parlance is called 'a rebel against constituted authority' but in this instance the phrase did not fit because there was no actual constituted authority. All authority had been usurped and the fiction of legal authority was so fragile that it was not taken seriously by anyone except academic old scholars, and was put to no practical use except by adroit and unscrupulous politicians. Unhampered by scholarly inhibitions, and with no false ideas concerning the powers and abilities of dukes and barons and other dignitaries, Yang Hoo started to scrap the worn-out machinery of state and build a new structure according to an improved pattern of his own devising. That he did not succeed was due partly to the corrupt and dissolute period in which he lived, and probably in a larger measure to the centuries old tradition regarding the sanctity of the dissolute kings, dukes, barons, viscounts and others of lesser degree.

During Duke Chao's absence, Baron Ping had not only usurped the ducal power but had even worn the ancient jewelled badge which was his ruler's emblem of authority. On the face of things it would appear that Baron Ping, who obviously had ambitions in that direction, might easily have seized the ducal title for himself. That he did not do so was due to Yang Hoo's restraining influence, for this ambitious man had other plans. He was, in fact, trying to accomplish by means of political guile and armed strength changes as far-reaching as the reforms which gripped the heart and dominated the unselfish aspirations of Master Kung. At the time of the latter's return to Lu, Yang Hoo was playing a very large part in public affairs and had established a practical dictatorship over the greater part of the state. There was a rising tide of rebellion in the country, and Yang Hoo was the principal exponent of the movement; the boldest, most successful and most ambitious, for he had courage and abilities far superior to those of his colleagues and his schemes and activities were not confined by feudal boundaries. He was most anxious to secure the support, the advice and the help of the famous scholar, and soon after Master Kung's return the dictator asked him to call, but the invitation was ignored. The men had met before and under circumstances that were unpleasant and mortifying to Master Kung. During the period when he was looking after the ducal tithes he had by mistake presented himself as a guest at an official banquet to which he had not been invited. Yang Hoo, who was noted for his rudeness, had gone out of his way to tell the young scholar that he was an intruder and furthermore had delivered the message publicly. This had happened about twenty years before, but the scholar had not forgotten it. To be publicly reprimanded for this social error was particularly humiliating to one who prided himself on his observance of the proprieties. Although he was too great a man to harbour petty resentments, he was at the same time too proud to lightly forget this injury to his dignity.

Having failed in his more direct attempts to reach the scholar, the resourceful politician decided to attempt to get to him by taking advantage of the rules of decorum and propriety which he was so careful to observe. He sent a present of a roast pig, being careful to see that it arrived at a time when Master Kung was out, and therefore unable to personally receive the gift and return his thanks by the messenger. Etiquette demanded that under such circumstances the recipient of the gift should pay a personal call on the donor in order to express his thanks, and this, of course, had been a subterfuge of Yang Hoo in order to compel the scholar to call on him. Master Kung knew he had been tricked and decided to pay the trickster back in his own coin. When he set out to pay his duty call he selected a time when he knew that Yang Hoo would not be at home. But the host returned unexpectedly and the scholar could not escape the interview he had tried so hard to avoid.

'Come let me speak with you,' said Yang Hoo. 'Can a man be called benevolent when he keeps his jewel of knowledge in his bosom and leaves his country in confusion?'

'No,' replied Master Kung, for Yang Hoo, in his question had quoted one of the well-known adages of the country.

'Can he be called wise,' pursued Yang Hoo, 'who is anxious to be engaged in public employment by which he can be of benefit to the state and yet is constantly losing the opportunity of being so?'

Again the Master agreed by answering in the negative.

'The days and the months are passing away, and the years do not wait for us,' concluded the politician.

'Right! I will go into office,' agreed Master Kung.

No doubt Yang Hoo thought he had gained his point and that the popular and highly esteemed scholar would join and strengthen the autocratic government he had set up but it will be noted that there was no time definitely stated in his promise, and Master Kung did not in fact go into office until several years later, and then under other patronage than that of Yang Hoo. He remained in political

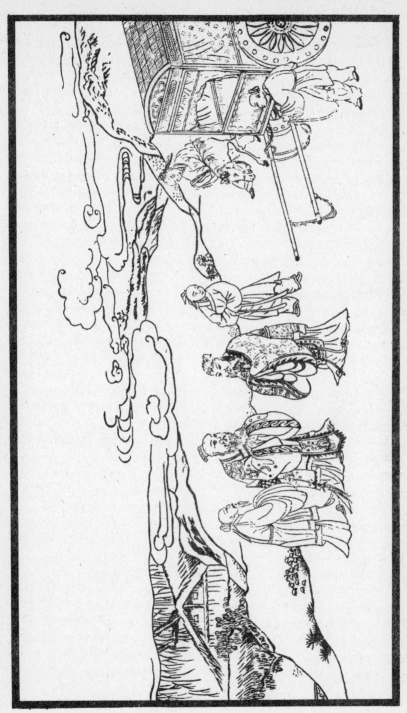

Trapped into meeting Dictator Yang Hoo, of whom he disapproved, Master Kung listened to the arguments of the other, and promised to take office.

isolation in Lu, continued teaching his disciples, carefully observing all political movements but taking no part in them. The incident of his encounter with Yang Hoo is one of the most famous in the life of Master Kung and while others might criticise him for what appears to them to be obvious deception, or at any rate, for lack of frankness, Chinese scholars have nothing but admiration for what they consider as a fine example of a combination of firmness and complaisance. Yang Hoo was not unaccustomed to rebuffs and discouragements and Master Kung's failure to carry out his implied promise to join his forces did not in the least deter him in going forward with his plans.

In Master Kung's forty-seventh year, five years after the death of the refugee Duke Chao, and the accession of his younger brother, Baron Ping went on a journey, fell ill on the way and died before he could return to his home. Only a few months later the head of the Shuh-sun family, the second in importance of the three great families of Lu, also died quite suddenly. In each case the family succession went to a young son of feeble character and mediocre talents. The third of the powerful families of Lu, the Meng clan, had several generations before this decayed to such an extent that it no longer counted for much in state affairs and the heads of the family were interested in little beside the revenue their ministers could secure for them. Under these circumstances the government of the entire state fell quite easily into the hands of Yang Hoo for there was no one strong enough to even consider offering any opposition to him.

This ambitious man now was exercising supreme power and his authority was not threatened from any quarter, but he sought to make it even more secure, to regularise it and to remove all factors which might prove disturbing in the future. That there was jealousy and dissatisfaction among collateral branches of the Chi family was shown by the energy with which the uncle of Baron Ping had promoted the plot to assassinate his nephew. There was an equal amount of family rivalry and jealousy in the Shuh-sun family and his plan was to dispose of the heads of both of these families and put in their places the heads of the collateral branches, who were naturally ardent supporters of the plot. As for the weak and unimportant Meng family, he intended to dispossess the entire line and make himself head of the clan. With his power and great abilities the Meng clan would at once become the strongest of the three, would dominate the other two families and all the affairs of the state. Having accomplished this there would be no difficulty in getting the weak duke to legitimatise his position and thus he would be prepared to travel much further on the road to fame and power which was then so opportunely open. The breakdown of authority in Lu was being duplicated in one fashion or another in all the other states and the old outworn government of the Chow kings could not much longer hold in check the ambitions of a man of Yang Hoo's ability and courage.

He lost no time in putting his plans into effect. Within a few months he had imprisoned two prominent men, including a cousin of young Baron Huan, the new head of the Chi family, and drove into exile all the minor officials of that family who stood in his way. He treated the young baron in a very cavalier fashion, imprisoned him, and released him only after he had made a covenant regarding governmental affairs which further solidified the dictator's position. In order to make his power manifest, and thus humble the young baron he intended to depose, he published the covenant in the market place so that all might see who was the real ruler of the state. He followed this by a still more humiliating proceeding. He turned his attention to ceremonial affairs and corrected the position of the ancestral tablets of the dukes of Lu as they appeared in the ducal temple. In their vanity and arrogance, Baron Ping and his predecessors had rearranged these tablets to suit their own ideas, undeservedly deposing some and honouring others beyond their due. Since these tablets represented the spirits of the dead noblemen, it was an act of sacrilege to interfere with them as the barons had done. Yang Hoo not only restored the tablets to the proper and orthodox order but publicised the fact by holding a ceremonial sacrifice in the temple. It was a bold and generous gesture to indicate that spiritual as well as temporal matters in the state of Lu would be set right through the revolution he had under way.

With his preparations all complete Yang Hoo moved rapidly. The first task was the execution of Baron Huan. In order to accomplish this with as little trouble and bloodshed as possible he invited the baron to a feast in the garden of Poo in the suburbs of Zigzag Hill which was to be the scene of the execution. He was so certain of success that he ordered an assembly of all the war chariots at the capital so timed that they would arrive when the execution had been completed and he would announce, and by armed strength, enforce the new order of things. Plotters in the Chi and Shuh-sun families were playing their part in the complicated strategy, but he had purposely ignored the weak Meng family, whose powers he planned to usurp for himself. It was at this point that his plans went wrong. It is more than probable that in the gossipy little state the members of the Meng family had learned of the dictator's ambitions concerning themselves and prepared for action. Whatever suspicions they may have had were confirmed when the Baron of Meng learned that without his knowledge his war chariots had been ordered to assemble a few hours later at Zigzag Hill. Instead of waiting for the appointed time he sent his small force of war chariots off at once, accompanied by his chief military officer. The Meng warriors, being the first to arrive on the field, had command of the situation for no other armed forces were assembled. As soon as the Meng commander learned of the murderous preparations in the garden of Poo, he ordered his soldiers to attack the followers of Yang Hoo who being mostly unarmed were easily defeated and the frightened baron rescued. Yang Hoo had at his command a much superior armed force, but he had not anticipated any resistance and was attempting to make the execution of the baron as quiet and unostentatious as possible. The intended victim had not been brought to the garden with any show of military strength, but had been escorted by three hundred unarmed foresters who were easily routed by the Meng soldiers.

Yang Hoo's defeat came so suddenly and unexpectedly that he had no opportunity to reorganise his forces. News of the failure of his plot and of the success of the Meng warriors spread quickly, and many who had been the most ardent of the plotters hastened to deny any knowledge of it and to ally themselves with the winning side. It appeared obvious that if his plans could be upset and his forces defeated by opposition which the weak Meng family could put up he had no hope of success. Yang Hoo in profound disgust at the failure of his plans and the craven desertion of his colleagues acknowledged defeat by a dramatic gesture of contempt and defiance. He threw off his armour and went to the ducal palace where he seized the great bow and symbol of jade which had been given the first duke of Lu by the Chow king as the most sacred emblems of authority. In such veneration were these ancient symbols held that their loss might, in the minds of the people of Lu, presage the direst of calamities and the downfall of the state itself.

With these emblems in his possession, and accompanied by his followers Yang Hoo departed towards Tsi. He had travelled but a few miles when he halted, ordered a meal and lay down for a sleep. His timorous followers urged him to flee, for they expected at any moment the arrival of the pursuers. Yang Hoo laughed at their fears and said:

'The cowardly Baron Huan is so glad to be rid of me that he will not bother about trying to get me back.'

When he was thoroughly rested they went on, seized a pass which they held for some time and then proceeded to Tsi where Duke Chao had fled to exile a dozen years before. As Tsi's easiest opportunity of territorial expansion was by encroachments on Lu, it was a fixed policy of the state to offer haven to any political refugees from the other state, and they gladly offered their hospitality to the deposed dictator. While on his way to Tsi he had concocted an entirely new plot which he had ready for presentation. He tried to interest the Marquis of Tsi in a project to conquer Lu and seize the whole state instead of nibbling at it piecemeal as Tsi had been doing for years. He had half convinced the aged marquis when a minister who had selfish plans of his own put up such an argument against the scheme that it was abandoned. Although the name of the minister is not recorded, it is more than probable that it was the envious hunchback Yen Ying who had prevented the employment of Master Kung about ten years before and was still jealously guarding his position.

The same minister was, with equal probability, the one who was the means of cutting short Yang Hoo's stay in Tsi, and for very sound reasons. It was obvious on second thought that a man with such bold ideas would find followers and become a menace to the state, so it was decided to send him to exile in the barbarous country in the neighbourhood, the present port and summer resort of Tsingtao. Yang Hoo expressed himself as being very well pleased with this arrangement and when the marquis reflected on the success this redoubtable warrior and clever politician might have by organising these savage tribes he hastily changed his mind and sent him to exile and confinement in the opposite direction. This, of course, was the direction Yang Hoo wished to travel.

He was being transported to this place of exile as a prisoner when he by some means secured all the war chariots of the place, sawed their axles in two, wrapped up the wheels in the hemp that was used to bind prisoners and sent the useless vehicles back to the commandant of the garrison. He then hid himself in a baggage wagon and so escaped to engage in many other plots and battles.

CHAPTER X

Master Kung considered taking service with a rebellious officer but did not do so. Appointed to the governorship of a town he accomplished some very notable reforms leading to his appointment to the ministry of Public Works and later to the more responsible position of Minister of Crime.

ALTHOUGH Yang Hoo, the erstwhile dictator of Lu, had been defeated and compelled to flee from the state with some of his followers, their flight did not by any means completely clarify the political situation or rid the state of all the malcontents. One of his colleagues and fellow-plotters, Commander Pieu New, was among those who remained behind to be a thorn in the side of Baron Huan and other members of the Chi family. He was in command of the garrison of the city of Pi, which though nominally the castled stronghold of the Chi family of which Baron Huan was the head, was actually held as his own property by this rebellious commander who ran things to suit himself without reference to the wishes of the baron and in poorly concealed defiance of the latter's authority. The only reason the defiance did not become open was because the timorous baron did not dare push matters to a conclusion. Yang Hoo had not been successful but some other resolute man might have better luck. Pi was some distance from Zigzag Hill, and though Commander Pieu New had shared the plot with Yang Hoo and had been one of his most active collaborators, the brief fight had come to a conclusion before he had time to take any part in it. When Yang Hoo fled the Commander of Pi fell heir to his political fortune and rebellious elements rallied around him as their leader. Though the ambitious stratagem had not been a success, it had gone so far that the heads of the powerful families were very much frightened and the way was open for another intrepid man to complete the programme which had been carried so near to success. The Commander of Pi undoubtedly had some such ambition in mind. Safely surrounded by his own loyal supporters, and confident of his ability to widen his own sphere of influence, he sent a messenger with an invitation to Master Kung to join him. As on the occasion of a similar proposal from Yang Hoo, Master Kung did not indignantly reject this offer, though he knew that it came from a well-known rebel. On the contrary he gave it his careful and serious consideration. His beloved state was seriously in need of his services but gave him no opportunities and indeed the state was in such a desperate condition that it appeared as if complete anarchy would soon engulf it unless some strong man should step in and take charge of affairs. If this eventuality should develop would it not be better for him to aid this leader rather than to leave him to pursue his own erratic course? There were few left who, even if they desired to do so could give him much assistance. Some of the ablest ministers of the state had fled with Duke Chao while others had gone into exile following the defeat of Yang Hoo, leaving none but inexperienced and incompetent men to guide the affairs of the state. When they heard that he had received this invitation and was giving it serious consideration his disciples were horrified at the possibility of their master giving his support to a rebel.

'Indeed, you cannot go,' said Tze Loo who acted as spokesman for the others. 'You must not think even of going to see him.'

Master Kung pointed out to them that the great Chow dynasty itself had been founded by a rebellion against the preceding weak and corrupt Shang dynasty, that its beginnings had been modest and obscure but had grown in power and worthy accomplishments. From similar small beginnings, he said, he might aid in the establishment of another dynasty of equal power. He was anticipating history for under conditions slightly less aggravated than those which brought about the downfall of the Shang, the Chow dynasty was overthrown a few centuries later and the powerful though short-lived Tsin dynasty set up in its place.

'It can surely not be by mere chance that the commander has summoned me,' he said. 'If he understands how to make use of me, perhaps there can be established here an eastern Chow!'

Interpretation of this incident has created a great deal of controversy among Chinese scholars, and orthodox Confucianists have written volumes in their attempts to explain it away. Most of them, starting on the premise that an alliance with the rebels in Pi would be an act of treason, Master Kung could not have seriously considered it. On the other hand, to what legally constituted authority in Lu could he offer his allegiance? The new duke held the ducal symbols of authority by reason of an illegal appointment for he was not the rightful heir. His power, which in theory was supreme in the state, was actually very much circumscribed by the baronial families who in their turn were dominated by their own officers. As to the legal aspects of the case, it must be obvious that when the dukes ignored the authority of the king, the barons ignored the authority of the dukes and officials ignored the authority of the barons, all legal authority had, in fact, ceased to exist and the rebels in Pi stood on as sound a legal footing as any of them. That Master Kung actually did consider joining the rebels in Pi does not appear to have been questioned by his faithful disciples who about twenty years later set down his conversations on the subject nor by the Chinese historians who wrote about it before the beginning of the Christian Era. Later historians who were attempting to uphold the then established monarchial system placed their own interpretation on the event, as they did on many other events in the life of Master Kung and interpreted his sayings to suit their own political purposes.

While the invitation from the Commander of Pi was still under consideration, Duke Ting unexpectedly appointed Master Kung as governor of a township. The place was so unimportant that there is some doubt as to which town it was, and several small places have for twenty centuries disputed for the honour. It appears more than probable that news of the offer made by the Commander of Pi had reached the ducal ears, and his action was precipitated by the fear that the scholar and his numerous disciples would join forces with the rebellious element rather than because of any approval of Master Kung's well-known ideas of reform in the administration of the state. The heads of the great families were still frightened over their narrow escape from Yang Hoo's plot and fearful of what might follow for the former dictator had not yet arrived in Tsi and was still in the neighbourhood holding possession of a mountain pass in Lu. Why he and his former colleague, the Commander of Pi, did not join forces when there was ample opportunity to do so

can only be accounted for by the general impermanence and insta-
bility of all political partnerships. Apparently this one did not
survive the first disaster. The frightened rulers, fearing further
developments, hastily decided to neutralise the influence of Master
Kung by giving him an unimportant official post which would keep
him employed and remove any temptation he might have to join
the opposition. No doubt the growing number of disciples also
had something to do with this appointment. They constituted a
numerous and very active lobby, and as most of them had been
born in Lu and had many relatives and important family connections in the state they were able to bring a great deal of political
pressure to bear. Whether the master was appointed to this
obscure post because of ducal approval of his ideas of reform, fear
of his joining the revolutionary forces or in order to silence his
disciples is a point on which there might be a great many honest
differences of opinion, but after all, it is a matter of academic
interest only. The importance of the incident lay in the fact that
Master Kung was approaching the half-century mark and after
studying and teaching theories of government for thirty years he
was now, for the first time, given an opportunity to see how his
theories would operate in practice. His enemies, composed of
envious scholars and corrupt politicians, were both hopeful and
confident of failure and his faithful disciples were equally confident
of his success.

The governor of a township like this was in his own small realm
a dictator who ruled with little or no interference by his superiors.
The ancient custom, which has been followed even to the present
generation, and is just now in process of being broken down, was
that so long as a local magistrate collected (and, more important,
remitted) the requisite taxes, and no revolts or serious troubles
broke out in his territory, his superiors permitted him to work out
his own problems, to try his own experiments and take the consequences of his own mistakes. The district of which Master Kung
became governor consisted, like all other townships in the country
of a small walled town in which the officials, gentry, artisans and
tradesmen lived, and the countryside dotted with farms whose produce supported the town. It was not one of the largest districts in
the state and probably had a population of less than thirty thousand.

As soon as he was installed in office Governor Kung plunged into the work of administration with all the energy and zeal of the reformer but with much more than the reformer's usual success. Irregularities in the levying and collecting of taxes and tithes were straightened out, and put on an honest footing so that while the state revenues were increased the burdens of the people were made lighter. When only a humble tithe-collector he had been powerless to correct abuses which came to his attention but now he was able to make good use of the practical experience he had gained. For the first time in his life he had authority and he used it to the utmost in carrying his ideas into practice. The introduction of an honest system in the collection of taxes and other simple administrative changes were logical and were to be expected from any honest man, but additional reforms which he put into effect were of a much more radical and idealistic character. Different foods were prescribed for old and young, different tasks for the strong and the weak. It may interest food faddists to learn that the young were restricted in the amount of meat they were allowed to eat, so that there would be no lack of meat for the old. Heavy meals of pork and mutton were presumed to be conducive to health and to prolong the life of the aged. The sexes were rigidly separated. Men walked on one side of the road and women on the other. Lu was one of the most puritanical of the states and carried restriction of the sexes to the point where it must have interfered with the normal increase in population. Other and more warlike states, with a view to the production of replacements for the army adhered to a less rigid code. The separation of the sexes in Lu was carried to such an extreme point that a question once arose, and was seriously discussed, as to whether or not a man should rescue his sister-in-law from drowning if this humane act involved laying his hands on her person. Fortunately the problem was solved by the application of the laws of humanity rather than by the strict puritanical rules of propriety though it was felt that the situation presented some elements of scandal.

Under the régime of Governor Kung so great was the improvement in the morals of the people that all became honest and objects dropped on the road were not picked up by the first passer-by, but left there for recovery by the rightful owner. There was no necessity to lock doors and windows for there were no thieves. The counterfeiting of curios by giving them a false appearance of age

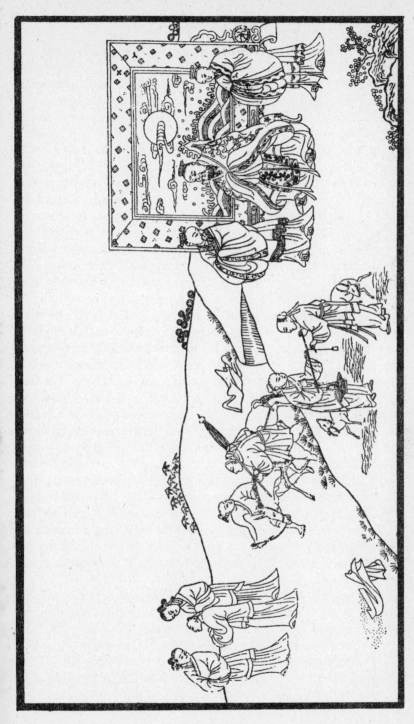

Under Master Kung's rule as governor the people became so honest that objects dropped on the street were left there for the rightful owner to recover.

was prohibited, for even in that remote period there were enthusiastic collectors of antiques whom the skilful artisan found it easy to deceive. To the collector of to-day the idea of misrepresenting the age of a curio of the Chow dynasty appears somewhat ludicrous, since the most humble object of that period would now be prized in any museum. Standards of commercial probity went even farther than this. The herders driving their live-stock to market were not allowed to water the animals on the way so as to give the oxen and goats an artificial weight. He introduced a uniform system of weights and measures, abolishing the use of scales of varying standards which were in use by the crafty tradesmen. The trade of the place was facilitated by doing away with a troublesome regulation which required travellers to report to officials who kept them under a kind of surveillance during their visit. Instead strangers 'were received as if they were returning to their own homes'. Finally, as a part of his programme of trade reform all goods were sold at fixed prices, which must have been the most revolutionary change of all to a people with such love of the joys of barter.

He paid a great deal of attention to the observance of funeral ceremonies and regulated the thickness of the wood in the inner and outer coffin so as to set some reasonable limitation on their cost. Wealthy families, by their showy and ostentatious funerals, had established extravagant standards which the poorer people found it difficult to maintain, and the undertakers grew rich through the sad misfortunes of their neighbours. He initiated the custom of burial on hillsides where nature had provided a mound instead of in level fields where an artificial mound would be necessary, and productive land taken from cultivation. It will be recalled that in the burial of his parents about thirty years previously, he had raised a mound over the graves. Others followed his example and his new regulation was designed to correct an abuse which his precedent had created. Neighbouring magistrates were so impressed with the wisdom of this method of burial on hillsides that most of them adopted it. With the growing population they were just beginning to realise that there was a limit to the land that could be put under cultivation. There was still plenty of unused land in the country but the graves were beginning to encroach on the more valuable fields located near towns. The custom has become universal in China, thus saving for cultivation millions of fertile farm plots, which would otherwise be given over to graves. The only places where graves are found on level land is in the flat country such as is found around Shanghai where there are no hills.

Governor Kung was responsible for these changes in connection with burials and one of his disciples inspired by his example was instrumental in furthering a still more important reform. The custom of human sacrifices was an ancient one, and, although many condemned its inhumanities, it was still observed in some places. In the case of a wealthy man, his horses and chariots were also buried with him. The wealthy elder brother of one of Governor Kung's disciples died and the disciple took charge of the funeral arrangements. The widow, as well as the steward, of the dead man approached the brother with the suggestion that a few lives be sacrificed in order to provide attendants for the spirit of the deceased in that mysterious land beyond the grave. The unfortunate persons used to provide these sacrifices were usually servants, eunuchs and concubines who were forcibly immolated and had nothing to say about the matter. The disciple heartily agreed with their suggestion but pointed out that if they were sincere in their desire to serve the spirit of the deceased no one could do so better than the widow and the steward who were so well acquainted with his wants while on earth and could give him in the land of the spirits the same faithful service to which he had been accustomed on earth. This suggestion put a rather different complexion on the matter, the widow and the steward said nothing further about it and the brother was buried without human sacrifices. Thereafter widows and faithful old servants became more reluctant to suggest a ceremony fraught with such dangerous possibilities, human sacrifices steadily decreased in number, and a few centuries later died out entirely though the sacrifice of horses continued for some time.

Duke Ting was so impressed by the progress made in this one small township that he asked Governor Kung if he thought the same theories of government could be carried out successfully over a larger territory, and the latter confidently replied that the same principles could be used successfully not only in the state of Lu but in the government of the entire country. The salvation of his country and through that, the relief of his suffering countrymen, was the accomplishment on which his heart was set, and he was hopefully confident that with the successful demonstration of his policies in this small area the rulers of other states would fall in line and the moral bankruptcy which was threatening the country be averted. The duke was evidently impressed, though the increase in ducal revenue through honest remittances may not have been without its influence in ducal decisions. Whatever may have been the cause, Governor Kung certainly had no reason to complain about his own progress for he was advanced in power with really remarkable rapidity. After a brief but highly successful career as governor he was brought to the capital at Zigzag Hill and promoted to a position corresponding with that of Minister of Public Works, where among other things he corrected the measurement of land, and transferred peasants from wornout farms to more fertile tracts. He did not hold this position long for he was soon promoted to be Minister of Crime, a position which does not find its exact counterpart in modern officialdom. His duty was to attend to the suppression of all crime and he functioned as investigator, prosecutor, judge and executioner. The position was a very important and difficult one. The disturbed condition of the state following the collapse of authority and the rebellious movement fostered by Yang Hoo had brought about a general moral breakdown and there had consequently been an abnormal increase in crime. With the lawless elements numerous and powerful, and with a growing lack of respect for authority as represented by the weak duke and barons, the suppression of crime was by no means an easy problem to solve, but he attacked it with initiative, enterprise and considerable courage.

One of his very first acts threw terror into the hearts of the evildoers. The state was full of petty criminals and Judge Kung realised that the prosecution and conviction of these would accomplish nothing but add to the already large prison population. Some bold step was necessary in order to put a stop to the wave of crime and he decided to take it though certain it would lead to severe criticism and possibly dismissal from office. He seized the most notorious criminal and trouble-maker, a man who was of considerable importance in his own circle, and ordered the execution after the barest formality of a trial. In order to show that he accepted full personal responsibility for his action, the execution was carried out in his presence. This rather precipitate exercise of authority surprised and annoyed a great many people and one of his disciples remonstrated with him about it. In justification of his act Judge Kung enumerated six vices any one of which, he said, justified the death penalty, these vices being:

1. Robbery and stealing.
2. Possession of a wicked and treacherous disposition.
3. Obstinacy and possession of a fiery temper.
4. Lying and using arguments which are plausible but false.
5. Using foolish words and treasuring them in mind.
6. Propagating evil while assuming virtues one does not possess.

He concluded that as it was well known that the rascal had been guilty of all these offences there was no question about the justification of the death sentence and its execution. In modern parlance the man was a well-known public enemy whose crimes were known to all and he had been condemned and executed on these plausible though not strictly legal grounds. Those who are interested in such comparisons will note that there is very little in common between the six vices enumerated by Judge Kung and the ten commandments of Moses. From the twentieth-century point of view this execution appears barbarous but in general the punishments for crime were, by present-day standard, exceptionally harsh. As will be seen by Judge Kung's list enumerated above there were many minor offences which were considered as meriting the death penalty and he did not bother to enumerate the major offences. Yet the punishments of Lu were much less rigorous than in some of the other states. Castration and the cutting off of feet, hands or kneecap, branding and flogging were common in most of them, while some occasionally descended to punishments of almost unbelievable barbarity. In the year of Judge Kung's birth the premier of the state of Tsi was cut into quarters and one part sent to each corner of the state as a warning to other officials. A few centuries earlier the king at Loyang as a punishment for insurrection, boiled alive one of the feudal rulers.

Judge Kung was confronted by some practical problems which probably had not been contemplated in his theories, but he solved them to his own satisfaction, and generally to the satisfaction of the millions of his followers who have lived after him and modelled their lives and their thoughts on the precedents which he established.

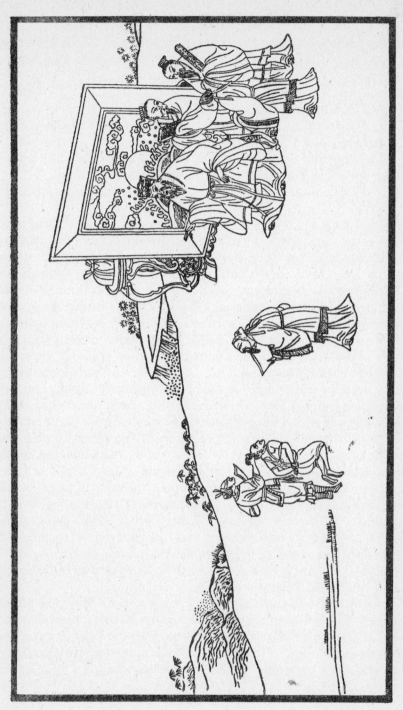

While acting as Minister of Crime, Master Kung ordered the execution without thorough trial of a notorious trouble-maker.

A father brought before the judge a wicked and unruly son, guilty of a crime for which the usual punishment was death. This was a situation so unprecedented, so contrary to the established usages of filial piety, of duty of son to father, father to son, that he had no rule to go by: so threw them both into prison while he thought things over. He kept them imprisoned for three months, treating them with equal severity and when the father withdrew the charge he released them with a stern lecture. Baron Huan who was growing a little apprehensive over the increasing power of this rising official accused him of inconsistency, reminding him of his saying that filial piety was the most important thing to be insisted upon if the state was to rest on a secure foundation.

'What hinders you now,' he said, 'from putting his unfilial son to death as an example to all the people?'

'When superiors fail in their duty,' replied Judge Kung, 'and yet propose to have their inferiors put to death, it is not right. This father has not taught his son to be filial and therefore the guilt really rests on him.'

Although he collected the poetry and preserved the history of the country, Judge Kung did nothing toward codifying the laws which he enforced, and in fact vigorously opposed all attempts to reduce laws to a written form. A statesman from one of the neighbouring principalities had perpetuated the text of some laws by having them cast in iron, and Judge Kung thoroughly disapproved of this act. In fact nearly all the statesmen and philosophers of the day rejected the idea that written laws could be drawn up which would provide for all the contingencies of life and establish a scale of punishments suitable to every occasion. Instead of a formal code of laws providing for penalties and punishments regulated with mathematical precision, there were simple commands which were issued as occasion arose, used as a guide of conduct, and forgotten on the disappearance of the evil they were designed to remedy. When the money-lenders became too avaricious or the merchants became too prosperous the king or one of the ruling princes would issue a mandate:

'You usurers must not be too hard on the farmers,' or 'You merchants must not wear silk gowns.'

Details of the enforcement of the mandates were left to the magistrate who was free to deal with each individual case on its own merits. Among the many laconic laws which were constantly repeated were:

> 'Do not hoard grain!'
> 'Do not displace legitimate heirs!'
> 'Do not obstruct waterways!'
> 'Do not marry your concubines!'
> 'Do not allow women to meddle in state affairs!'

The people, Judge Kung and many others contended, should be taught a sense of their moral obligations and provided they had this teaching and were set a good example by the princes they would do what was right of their own volition for they belonged to the school of philosophers which believed that all men were born inherently good. On the other hand, if an attempt were made to control them by laws they would merely try to evade the law and avoid punishment; they would have no sense of shame for any un-discovered misdemeanours or other offences for which they managed to escape punishment. Under a properly organised state no laws would be necessary, because the people would follow the good example of the princes and there would be no incentive to commit crime. With prophetic vision of the later developments of the legal profession, he pointed out that once laws were reduced to written form those of evil mind would soon find ways of evading them, or, if they did not have wit enough to do so themselves would employ clever men to do it for them. Regarding his own judicial activities he said:

'I am like others in administering justice. I apply the law to each case as a separate problem; sometimes it is necessary to slay one person in order to avoid having to slay more. The ancients under-stood prevention of crime better than we do now; at present all we can hope to do is to avoid punishing unjustly. The ancients strove to save a prisoner's life; in these corrupt times we can only do our best to prove his guilt before punishing him. However, better let a guilty man go free than punish an innocent one.'

Thousands of Chinese living in foreign lands have been in con-tact with the practical administration of Western laws for several generations and other thousands who attended schools abroad have returned to their homes with some knowledge of the cold machine-like justice of the foreign criminal courts. In harmony with their programme to modernise all the institutions of China, their present legal system is being revised so as to bring it more in line with Western practice and more laws are being written in China each year than the experience of ten centuries had produced at the time of Judge Kung. Chinese are adjusting themselves to adoption of this new legal procedure but in their hearts their affection is still for the old system in which the human element played a predominant part and men's weaknesses and temptations were fully and sympathetically considered. There is to them something very cold and strange in foreign ideas of punishments. They find it difficult, for example, to understand why it is as great a crime for a poor man to steal from a rich man as for a rich man to steal from a poor one; why it is not a much greater crime for a man to kill his father than to kill a stranger. These old-fashioned ideas are so deeply ingrained in Chinese thought that it is difficult to believe that they will ever be entirely eradicated.

In sifting the evidence in the trial of cases Judge Kung introduced an innovation which anticipated modern legal procedure by many centuries for he was the first to make use of the jury system in determining the guilt or innocence of the accused. There was nothing about this jury system any more fixed or formal than there was about the code of laws which he administered. Every trial would attract the usual crowd of curious or interested spectators and at the conclusion of the hearing it was his custom to ask the opinion of those who had heard the evidence. In most cases he deferred to the views expressed by the majority of the spectators and said, 'I decide the case in accordance with their opinion.' Judge Kung may have felt that the opinion of others might be of aid to him in preventing a miscarriage of justice but the reasons for his adoption of this procedure went deeper. He did not ask the opinion of others in order to escape or to divide the responsibility of making decisions but to educate the people to a clearer sense of right and wrong.

CHAPTER XI

*How by means of clever diplomacy Master Kung at
a treacherous peace conference succeeded in foiling
the murderous plots of the ministers of the State of
Tsi and regained some stolen territory.*

I N the spring of the year 500 B.C., while acting as chancellor or
premier, Master Kung was instrumental in concluding a treaty
of peace between his native state of Lu and the neighbouring state
of Tsi. It was to this state that he had several years before followed the former duke into exile and had been thoroughly snubbed
by the local dignitaries when the Marquis of Tsi proposed adding
him to his official family. The treaty was designed to settle a series
of petty disputes and put an end to border raids and military incur-
sions which had entertained the politicians and harassed the people
of the two states for several generations. Any treaty of peace which
might be concluded between Tsi and Lu was obviously to the
advantage of the latter which, as the weaker of the two contestants,
had almost invariably come out second best in every trial of strength.
A considerable part of the territory now held in the southern part
of Tsi had formerly belonged to Lu but had been alienated from it
by a series of military aggressions.

Except for its first few years of prosperity Lu had at all times
been considered a state of negligible political or military importance, and the neighbouring rulers had never treated very seriously
any of the pacts entered into with the smaller principality. In fact,
the military enterprises of the state had been so unimportant that
for eighty years no duke of Lu had led an army into the field, and
what fighting had been done was conducted under the direction of
officials. The situation was quite different in the other more militant states where the feudal rulers took an active interest in the
thrilling game of warfare and enjoyed the prerogative of leading
their troops to battle, though they usually remained at a discreet

distance from the actual fighting. Having no power with which
to gratify any political or military ambitions of its own, or to defend
itself against the aggressions of others, Lu had invariably adopted a
policy of *laissez faire* with other states, and attempted only to keep
out of trouble by means of compromise or evasion. This was not
always easy of accomplishment, for a cowardly gesture toward one
state aroused the jealousies and suspicions of its neighbours and Lu
was continually in hot water with one neighbour or another and
had to make sudden and often disgraceful shifts in policy. The
other states were, of course, equally shifty and ignored or violated
their covenants as often as it appeared to be to their advantage to
do so but they were not so often compelled to change by reason of
threats or because of groundless fears.

The rather innocuous peace treaty had been negotiated only a
few months, when the Tsi statesmen came to a sudden realisation
that events had been moving fast and that they were confronted
with an entirely new set of conditions which required a wholesale
readjustment of their policy toward Lu. Master Kung had been
making very rapid progress in his administration of the state, and
for the first time in generations Lu was beginning to present some
kind of strength and solidarity. The heads of the three great families still held their high-sounding titles, occupied the principal
ducal offices and wore their symbols of authority but it was obvious
to everyone that they no longer carried much weight in state affairs,
and that through the wise administration and clever politics of
Minister Kung, power was being restored to its rightful place, in
the hands of the duke. In the past Tsi had on all occasions counted
on its ability to stir up controversies between the three great clans,
or to make the winning of diplomatic or military battles easy by
bribing one or more of the clan leaders. With all power becoming
consolidated in the person of the duke these tactics would no longer
be possible, and it was easy to conceive of Lu as a strong state which
would dominate her neighbours instead of being subservient to
them.

Another factor which made a realignment of policy necessary
had been brought about by the rapid rise of the semi-naval power
of Wu, one of the so-called barbarian states with its capital near the
modern city of Soochow. With the guidance of able advisers from
the highly-civilised states, and spurred on by fear of invasion and

conquest from two other semi-barbarian quarters, the state of Wu, in less than a half-century, had lifted itself from the position of an obscure barbarian state of no culture and little power, to a place where it was demanding equality of treatment from the Yellow River people on the north and beginning to enforce their demands with threats of invasion. Living on the flat marshy land around the lower Yangtsze River, with access to many lakes and waterways, the Wu people were accomplished boatmen and by the use of their craft were able to transport troops and carry supplies with an ease unknown to others. They thus introduced to their northern neighbours a new, and at the time highly successful technique of warfare. In a more or less experimental way they had made several forays north of the Yangtsze and had recently inflicted a smarting humiliation on the Marquis of Tsi by compelling him to affiance his daughter to the heir of the Wu throne. The princesses of the house of Tsi had supplied many consorts for Lu and other orthodox states, and the marriage of one of them to a prince of the jungle barbarians was looked upon as being an abhorrent mixture of blood. The fact that the marriage alliance had been forced on the Tsi ruler was a matter of common gossip throughout the feudal states and made him the laughing-stock of the country. At the same time there were well-founded rumours that Lu and Wu were negotiating an alliance. It was known that Wu had proposed an alliance and it was only a question of whether or not Lu would have courage enough to brave the displeasure of the other feudal states by accepting it. A political partnership between these two states would have presented Tsi with a very menacing situation. With the acquiescence of Lu, whose territory would have to be crossed, Wu could throw her barbarian armies into Tsi with no difficulty, and be tolerably sure of an easy victory. With its great wealth and resources of iron and salt, Tsi was a prize toward which any ambitious statesman would turn his attention. With this threat hanging over their heads the Tsi statesmen came to the conclusion that the situation was so desperate as to demand desperate remedies.

It goes without saying that the question of whether the method of accomplishment of their purposes were to be by foul means or fair did not enter into consideration at all and the means the Tsi statesmen proposed to adopt were especially foul. Using as a pretext the ceremonial ratification of the treaty of peace which had been negotiated, it was proposed to invite the Duke of Lu to a supposedly friendly conference which would be held across the border in Tsi, far removed from any armed force that Lu might be able to muster at short notice. Once they got the visiting ruler into their territory the programme was to create an altercation by hired and captive barbarians in which the Duke of Lu would be captured or killed, and Master Kung disposed of in any manner that seemed appropriate at the time. In convincing the marquis of the feasibility of the scheme the Tsi plotters laid great stress on their statement:

'This fellow Kung knows all about ceremonies, but he has no courage, and by threatening him we can get him to agree to anything.'

By kidnapping, or possibly killing, the duke and doing away with Master Kung they thought to throw the state of Lu into such confusion that Tsi would be able to gain the upper hand and take control of the affairs of the state before any alliance with Wu could become effective. With Lu in their power they would find it an easier matter to withstand the attacks of Wu and the other political rivalries which threatened them. They felt the plan to have the criminal acts actually performed by a band of barbarians was particularly clever in its technique as in that way they would have a plausible explanation ready for any of the other feudal rulers who might become inquisitive. However, if the scheme succeeded and they added Lu to their own territories they believed that their strength would be such as to make it possible and safe to ignore interrogations and criticism. To detail all the plots and counter plots by which political movements of the day were actuated would be tedious and profitless, but an idea of their ramifications may be gathered from the fact that at the time the Tsi statesmen were hatching this plot to strengthen their state, they were also laying plans to divert the rule of their own state to a rival family by, on his accession, killing the son of the Tsi ruler, a programme which was a few years later successfully carried out, but at the expense of three murders instead of one.

Duke Ting of Lu had at this time been in power for several years, and should have enjoyed enough political experience to know that when a rival ruler suggested anything there was always a good deal more behind the proposal than met the naked and unsophisticated eye, but he was stupidly trustful and unsuspicious. When the diplomatic envoys from Tsi proposed the visit he accepted the invitation in good faith and planned going to the meeting-place in a simple chariot, without an armed escort, as one would go on a visit to a friend and neighbour. Minister Kung, who was to act as master of ceremonies or acting chancellor at this meeting had spent less than two years in Tsi, but he knew the treacherous ways of their politicians and was suspicious both of the men and their policies. He advised the duke:

'I have heard that when a prince has peaceful business to transact, he must make warlike preparations for it, and when he has warlike business to transact he must employ officials and diplomats. When a prince leaves the boundaries of his territory he must take with him his entire official retinue so that there can be no misunderstanding among his hosts as to his rank. So I beg you also to take your two chief military officers, together with their aides, as well as your civil officials.'

The duke agreed to these suggestions and so went to the conference with a rather imposing retinue.

For what was intended to be a treacherous and brutal assault there were very elaborate and deceitful preparations. It was typical of politicians of this period to sugar-coat the most atrocious lies and examples of bad faith with the most virtuous statements of principles and the most urbane behaviour. According to this code, it was quite in order to stab an unsuspecting enemy in the back, providing always, that the proceeding was carried out with the utmost decorum and politeness. On the ground set apart for the meeting-place, almost in the shadow of the great sacred mountain of Tai Shan a special terrace with a staircase of three steps had been built. The terrace was actually nothing more than a platform of pounded mud but it answered the purposes of the plot and provided the proper setting of ceremonial usage. The two rulers met at the bottom and each went through the polite pretence of offering the other the precedence of being the first to mount the steps. This matter having been settled, they sat together on the terrace and drank toasts to each other, and to their respective states. In the meantime the plotters of Tsi had grown somewhat nervous over the situation. They had not counted on the ducal visitor arriving with all of his officials and armed retainers, and decided they had better hurry on with their programme before something happened to upset their plans. With rather impolite haste one of the Tsi officials advanced to the terrace and said:

'I beg your graces to allow the performance of music from the four quarters of the earth.'

It was customary to introduce musical entertainment at all cere-monies of this character, though the music was always of classical nature consisting of compositions recounting historical episodes which would have some bearing on the matter under discussion. It was not unusual for a conference to be opened by the singing of one of the ancient songs and other songs would follow thus creating an atmosphere suitable for a discussion of the business on the agenda. One of the tests of the scholarship of an official lay in his ability to select the proper songs which often gave a hint of the message he proposed later to deliver. In this way important points of procedure or policy were often considered and decided upon before the actual verbal negotiations began. But the proposal of the Tsi official was quite unorthodox for he was referring to the barbarous or semi-barbarous music of the coast tribes who were looked upon as foreigners by the river people. The Marquis of Tsi agreed, as it had been arranged that he should, and without waiting for the assent of the guest of honour the barbarous crowd appeared. Many of them were prisoners of war who had been captured in the raids which were periodically made into barbarian territory and others had been employed for the event. Their usual grotesque appear-ance had been exaggerated for this occasion. Their heads were covered with strange bonnets of feathers, their faces and bodies were painted in gaudy colours and, to complete their savage costuming, they had ox tails tied on their rumps. Carrying well-sharpened spears, lances, swords and stout shields, they advanced rapidly to-ward the terrace to the accompaniment of beating drums and loud cries. If the noise they created could be called musical it was music of a particularly offensive kind, for the clamour was calculated to arouse tremors in the hearts of the timid and could not be pleasing even to the boldest. This pseudo-musical entertainment was sup-posed to be the prelude to the tragic climax; in the uproar and con-fusion, the visiting duke, according to plan, would be kidnapped or killed and such of his retainers captured or slaughtered as

173

opportunity afforded. In this connection, special attention was to be given to Master Kung. The barbarians would be blamed for the whole affair and once the political objective had been accomplished, the incident would be closed with the execution of a few of them.

Chancellor Kung had been anticipating some treachery on the part of Tsi but had no inkling of what form it would take until the barbarians appeared. Then the Tsi plotters had their calculations upset the second time for he did not live up to the character for cowardice which they had painted for him. As the uncouth visitors crowded around the place of ceremony where the two noblemen were sitting, he pushed his way through them and rushed to the steps leading to the terrace. It is significant of the importance attached to minute details of decorum that all Chinese historians who recorded this incident are careful to point out that Chancellor Kung, in spite of his natural anxiety and possible excitement did not commit the impropriety of mounting the top step of the terrace. This action would have been extremely impolite as it would have placed him on the same level as that of the two rulers. To have mounted any higher would have been, in the minds of sticklers for ritual, an offence as grave as to leave his defenceless duke to his fate. Instead of committing this breach of decorum, he stopped and stood still on the next step below them.

'Our two princes are here for a friendly meeting,' he cried to the host, but in a voice loud enough to be heard by all the assembled officials. 'What business has the music of barbarians at a peace conference? Weapons have no place at such a meeting as this! It is not right as between man and man and it is not polite as between the two princes! I beg that instructions be given to officers of the day to scatter these musicians!'

His emphasis on the fact that the music was barbarian, was striking rather close home for although Tsi was not a barbarian state, it was located on the barbarian borders, and as a matter of practical politics, some unorthodox practices had been introduced and countenanced by the Tsi statesmen. The Tsi officials were not only secretly ashamed of this barbarian contact, but their consciousness of inferiority was aggravated by the fact that the state of Lu, though weak and unimportant from a military point of view was admittedly the most cultured of the feudal states and its leaders could speak

Master Kung acted as master of ceremonies for the Duke of Lu at a treacherous peace conference arranged by the rulers of Tsi.

with an air of authority on all matters pertaining to propriety and ceremonies. Here they had given Master Kung an opportunity to accuse them of barbarous behaviour which they could neither deny nor condone.

The Marquis of Tsi hesitated and changed colour but took no action. To drive away the ruffians was not according to programme, and in his ceremonial isolation on the terrace he had no opportunity to consult with those who had engineered the plot and were managing the details. He was as embarrassed and helpless as an actor who has lost his cue and cannot get the eye of the prompter. In the meantime, Chancellor Kung's request had made an appeal to the spectators who had the human weakness of wishing to appear to do the polite and proper thing, and they turned their accusing eyes on the marquis. According to one Chinese historian, the marquis was inwardly ashamed and he caused the musicians to be removed. Parsimonious old Yen Yang the hunchback minister of Tsi was present at the conference and the spectators glared disapprovingly at his mis-shapen back. Chinese historians, in their anxiety to protect the reputation of a man whose brilliant and liberal statesmanship they all admire point out that there is no evidence that the hunchback statesman had anything to do with the murderous plot. This negative statement, of course, means nothing, as it can be taken for granted that whatever part he may have played in the plot he would be clever enough to conceal the evidence. It is only surprising that a man of such brilliance should lend himself to a stratagem so stupid.

The expulsion of these disguised warriors enabled the two rulers and their attendant ministers to carry on the formalities of the conference with at least an outward semblance of cordiality and politeness, and the two noblemen resumed their exchange of compliments and meaningless tittle-tattle. But the scheming plotters of Tsi were not to be so lightly thwarted. After an interval a second officer of ceremonies came forward with a request that he be given permission to order the performance of the palace music. It was appropriate, in fact almost essential from the standpoint of ceremonial usage that there be music and this music was the most appropriate kind, and it was as different from plots and military stratagems as daylight is from dark. It would appear, from the way the matter was presented, that the official was seeking an opportunity to atone for the previous performance and erase the bad impression it had created. There could be no objection to this suggestion and when the Marquis of Tsi assented it was with the tacit approval of all who were present including the visitors from Lu. They believed that the hosts were ashamed of their former disgraceful exhibition and were trying to make amends for it by a polite and harmless performance of their very finest musical entertainment. Nothing could have been more pleasing to Master Kung himself than a concert of this kind, for it was this ancient music as heard in Tsi which on the occasion of his former visit had made him lose interest in food for three months. The court usher gave the signal and in a moment the terrace was surrounded by a crowd even stranger than the barbarians with painted faces and ox tails who had preceded them. This was a crowd of dwarfs and acrobats, and armed men dressed as actresses, none of whom had any more pretentions to musical ability than the ruffians who had preceded them.

When the strange crowd approached the terrace Chancellor Kung again protested in the same terms as before. He gave no hint, of course, that anyone suspected the existence of a plot which was now transparent to the most stupid, but protested solely on the ground of propriety, a subject on which he as the master of ceremonies for the Duke of Lu was privileged to speak. He turned his gaze fixedly on the Marquis of Tsi and also on the hunchback minister, Yen Yang. Again he had the moral support of the crowd with him for even the Tsi partisans were anxious to disassociate themselves from the disgraceful proceedings and turned reproachful eyes on the marquis. The latter, seeing that his crafty advisers had let him down rather sadly, lost no time in ordering this second lot of disguised ruffians and fake musicians out of his sight.

The Chinese chronicles describing this event say that 'arms and legs went flying' which some historians believe is meant to describe the haste with which the acrobats somersaulted away from their ruler's wrath, while others think that in order to hasten them on their way the soldiers, aided by anyone else who happened to have a sword at hand, chopped off arms and legs and so added to the interest of what for a peace conference was really becoming a most exciting party. As a matter of fact, either interpretation would be plausible enough. The barbarian acrobats were quite capable of turning somersaults and cart-wheels and, on the other hand there would have been nothing extraordinary about soldiers and spectators hacking off a few arms and legs for the fun of the thing. Men were mutilated in this and in more revolting ways for rather trivial offences. Cutting off feet in all the feudal states was a popular way of exhibiting princely displeasure. Yen Yang himself had waggishly justified the amputation of feet by explaining that wooden feet were cheaper than leather shoes.

When he ordered the second lot of musicians away, the Marquis of Tsi realised that the stupid plot had failed, so he told some very adroit lies, blamed the undisciplined barbarians for the disturbance and the two noblemen drew their mats a little closer together to conclude the real business of the conference, which was to put their signatures to the treaty of alliance which would implement the treaty of peace. They were about ready to sign this agreement when it was discovered that the wily statesmen of Tsi had slipped into the written document a new paragraph which had not been included in the discussions. This clause provided that any time Tsi went to war no matter with whom or for what cause the state of Lu would provide for its support three hundred armed chariots, representing about one-third of the total armed strength of the state. Chancellor Kung was as much surprised as any at the discovery of this third piece of duplicity which now threatened to break up the conference and cause a resumption of hostilities. Instead of allowing the question to come to an issue he seized on the opportunity to endeavour to negotiate some astute diplomatic bargaining. He had no opportunity to consult the duke or any of his fellow-ministers and on his own initiative and responsibility immediately took action. Lu would agree to this, he proposed, but in return Tsi must consent to return certain specified territories which had been seized from Lu in the past. This was a good deal more than the Tsi politicians had bargained for and was a very high price to pay for a promise – even if that promise could be taken at its face value, which it certainly could not. But the presence of the duke's military escort, the failure of the two felonious plots, followed by the discovery of this tampering with the treaty left the Tsi statesmen with weakened morale and no stomach for an argument. There was nothing for them to do but accept this proposal with the best grace they could and so the treaty was amended and signed.

So far it had been a disastrous day for the Marquis of Tsi. He had expected to abduct or kill a neighbouring duke and steal all or a generous part of his realm. He had been foiled at every move and instead of adding to his territories had been compelled to surrender a few stolen counties. Nevertheless, he put the best face he could on the matter, did what etiquette demanded and invited the visiting duke and his ministers and retainers to an official banquet. The rules of politeness (rules which still prevail) provided that such an invitation must unquestionably be accepted. But Master Kung who by this time was in complete charge of the Lu delegation never allowed strict adherence to rules of etiquette to outweigh the dictates of sound common sense, and was as courageous about defying dangerous conventions as he was insistent on upholding useful ones. It had been a successful day for his duke and nothing more was to be gained by delaying their departure. It was getting late in the afternoon and the shadows of Tai Shan were growing long. The hosts had been treacherous enough in broad daylight and if visitors spent the night in the neighbourhood no one could foretell what further unexpected dangers might confront them. He pointed out that through an oversight they had not brought their ceremonial cups with them. With what might have been a touch of irony, he also remarked that they had failed to bring their musicians and musical instruments with them and so could not play their proper part in the ceremonial of the banquet. On behalf of his duke, he begged to be excused. The farewells were hurried through and before nightfall the Lu entourage had crossed the borders and was safe behind its own frontiers.

CHAPTER XII

During the able guidance of Master Kung the posi-
tion of the duke became so strong that fears of Tsi
were renewed and they brought about his downfall
and the exile of Master Kung by means of a gift to
the duke of dancing girls and well-groomed horses.

THE successful outcome of the peace conference, thanks to the courageous initiative of Master Kung, constituted a distinct and important political victory for the state of Lu which had, at no expense, established peaceful relations with a powerful and dangerous neighbour, regained possession of a very valuable piece of territory and emerged from the conference with a great deal of increased prestige. Many feudal rulers at the expense of the lives of their soldiers had fought long and bloody battles in attempts to accomplish much less than this. In parenthesis it may be stated that the promise on the part of Lu to supply Tsi with chariots in the event of the latter going to war did not eventually impose any burdens, for Lu at the first convenient opportunity, ignored the treaty and joined forces with the semi-barbarian state of Wu in an attack on the neighbour with whom she had a few years before made an alliance. Master Kung, however, had nothing to do with his breach of faith for when it occurred he was no longer connected with the administration of the state. The peaceful conclusion of the conference with the cession of territory by Tsi was almost unique for the state of Lu had been victorious without the shedding of one drop of blood on either side, unless account is taken of the rude blood that may have been spilled at the expense of the barbarian acrobats. It had been what is often rather ineptly described as a moral victory. In this instance the description is apt, for the news of the peaceful diplomatic victory of Lu spread throughout the ducal states and created some consternation among the militant princes who looked on statecraft as a bit of by-play

which added to the fascination of the game of war. The conception
of a bloodless victory which had been won by superior mentality
rather than by force of arms was strange to them and created new
doubts in many minds, turned thoughts back to the fabled age of
their country when it was ruled by virtue and wisdom, and soldiers
were of such small account that no prince boasted of the number
he possessed. A single scholar had in a day accomplished more
than a militant prince could accomplish with a thousand chariots.
One authority who summed up Master Kung's accomplishments at
this period said of him:

'He strengthened the authority of the duke and weakened that
of the powerful private families. He exalted the sovereign and
depressed the scheming ministers. A transforming government
went abroad and its influences were felt in many distant places.
Dishonesty and dissoluteness were ashamed and hid their heads.
Loyalty and good faith became the characteristics of the men, and
chastity and docility the characteristics of the women. Strangers
came to Zigzag Hill from other states to express their admiration
and to learn the rules of good government. Master Kung became
the idol of the people and was the subject of songs of praise in every
mouth.'

The neighbours of Master Kung, when they composed ballads
and sang them in his honour were doing no more than pay, by
means of their customary method of expressing sincere praise, the
genuine debt they owed him. While other neighbouring and distant states may have benefited indirectly by the heightened moral
tone injected into the conduct of political affairs, the residents of
Lu profited in a practical way, directly and immediately. With
each increase in official and political power he had gone further in
ameliorating the condition of the people and they had much to
thank him for but still more benefits were to come. The successful
result of the peace conference had definitely removed any immediate threat of aggression from the state of Tsi and for the first
time in several generations the ministers of the state of Lu, under
the leadership of Master Kung, were able to concentrate their
attention on domestic affairs without the customary fear that rival
states would take advantage of the first opportunity to encroach on
their territory. Under these favourable circumstances, the reforms
which Master Kung had accomplished as governor of a township

were duplicated here and extended over a wider area. Injustices in the collection of taxes were abolished, crime and punishments decreased and the people of Lu enjoyed more of the blessings of peace and prosperity than their predecessors had enjoyed for many generations.

Though Master Kung had never been given the actual title of premier or chancellor, he was to all intents and purposes, the principal minister, and, by common consent, took the lead in all matters of government. Even if the duke had desired to elevate him in rank and the other members of his official family had concurred, which is extremely improbable, the appointment would have presented some practical difficulties. Here, as in most of the other feudal states this, and other important offices were, by old custom, hereditary and, except under some unusual circumstance, descended from father to son irrespective of whatever abilities the new incumbent might possess. Thus the head of the Chi family was almost invariably the premier and the heads of the other great families held other positions of potential importance. To replace one in the line of succession would have been, to say the least, inexpedient and embarrassing, so it appears that while another held the office, Master Kung by reason of his superior ability exercised the actual powers. Although these powers were delegated from another, he had direct contact with the duke and it was not necessary for him to deal with any intermediaries while a number of lesser ministers were his official servants. Although the records are obscure on the point it appears that the highest actual title he was ever awarded was that of Minister of Crime.

Confident of his authority, he now undertook and partially succeeded in a very daring enterprise which was nothing less than the reduction of three castles which proud and haughty heads of the three clans had set up for themselves in defiance of the ducal authority. They were fortified in the strongest possible way and certainly could not under ordinary circumstances be reduced by any armed forces at the command of the duke. These strongholds were comparatively new developments in the political encroachments of the great families, as all of them had been built during Master Kung's lifetime. The status of each was illegal for the mandate of the king under which the feudal states were established made it a criminal offence for anyone except the ruler of a state to maintain a city with walls more than 3,000 feet long or to keep stores of weapons or military supplies. It was the boldness and effrontery of the powerful families as typified by establishments such as these, which had made it possible originally to undermine the authority of the ruler and had led to the involuntary exile of the former duke after the incident of the cock-fight.

Master Kung's success in his scheme for the reduction of these baronial strongholds has been given very high praise by Chinese historians because, like his victory at the peace conference, it was accomplished by moral suasion rather than by force of arms. There was some loss of blood but very little when accounted for in comparison with the results accomplished. In the case of at least one of the three fortified cities he is recorded as having convinced the baron concerned that he should voluntarily raze his castle and give up the military powers his grandfather had seized. On the face of it this appears to be a much more important moral victory than it actually was. The grandfathers of the barons of that day had built the castles for their own aggrandisement but, as the power of the succeeding disloyal barons had grown weaker and been usurped by their ministers, the latter had turned the treasonable equipment against the grandsons of its baronial creators. The powerful and ambitious ministers, like the redoubtable Dictator Yang Hoo and his predecessors, manned the castle walls with soldiers who were their own adherents, the powerless barons were ignored, and the structures were used to consolidate the political stranglehold of the ministers on the barons. At this time all three of the castled cities were held by ministers who defied the powerful families and were in more or less open rebellion. Under the circumstances, when the barons agreed to the razing of the castle walls, they were actually co-operating in a movement to destroy the powers of the ministers who tyrannised over them and were not giving up any powers or destroying any property they actually possessed. The genius of Master Kung's accomplishment lay in the adroitness with which he seized on this complicated political situation and used it to make a long step forward in the achievement of his programme to re-establish the centralisation of authority in the hands where it theoretically belonged.

The head of the Shuh-sun family was the first to fall in with this plan for the reduction of the cities. He had fought several

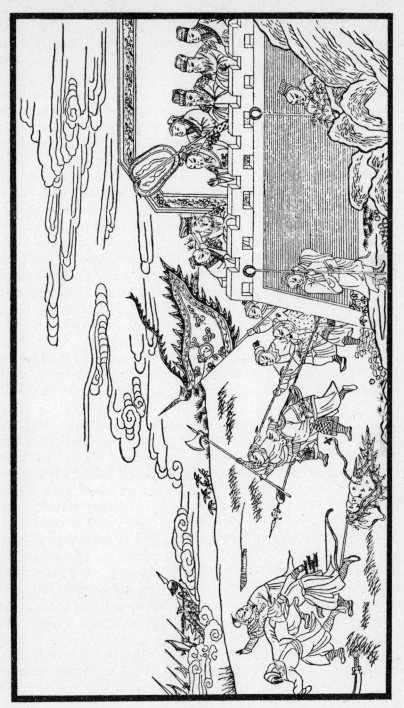

As acting chancellor, Master Kung advised Duke Ting to raze the walls of fortified cities which had been erected by the powerful barons.

unsuccessful battles to regain possession of the place and in desperation was negotiating with Tsi to trade it to that rival state. Aided by the ducal soldiers, he led the attack on his own city of How, easily drove out the cavalry commander who was holding it, disarmed the soldier and destroyed the fortifications. Following his example, Baron Huan of the Chi family agreed to raze the walls of their city of Pi and commenced actively to carry the plan into effect. Four years before this period when Yang Hoo's revolt had failed, his fellow-plotter, Commander Pieu New, it will be recalled was then in possession of the city of Pi and Master Kung had at the time seriously considered joining him in the administration of the place, had even suggested the possibility of founding a new dynasty. The commander still held the city which he ruled as a separate and independent fief in defiance of Baron Huan. The latter having been unable by his own efforts to regain possession of the place, was quite willing to accept the aid of the forces Master Kung could command in dispossessing the usurper. This was not so easily accomplished as the reduction of How had been. The citizens of Pi presented an unexpected opposition to this programme, for they preferred the rule of Commander Pieu New to that of Baron Huan and under the leadership of the former attacked not only the ducal army but the forces of the allied barons who were aiding Baron Huan in the enterprise. For a time the citizens of Pi were successful and made such advances against their foes that the duke and his ministers, including Master Kung, were compelled to take refuge in an auxiliary fortress of the Chi family. When matters reached this crisis, Master Kung took a hand in the direction of the troops and ordered additional forces of the duke to participate in the attack which was eventually completely successful. The citizen army was routed and annihilated, Commander Pieu New fled to Tsi where his colleague Yang Hoo had preceded him, and the city walls were razed and stores of war material seized.

There was but one baronial castle left, that of the Meng family whose ministers had been instrumental in foiling the Yang Hoo plot. This had been the least important family of the three, but their successful coup in connection with the Yang Hoo plot gave them a vastly increased prestige and aroused new ambitions in the minds of the usurping ministers. They watched with satisfaction and approval the destruction of the walls of How and took an active part in the razing of the walls of Pi. But as is not unusual in present-day problems of disarmament, they found that their own case presented extraordinary conditions. The territory they occupied lay in the northern part of Lu and was perilously near the borders of Tsi and for that reason required special consideration in spite of the fact that Tsi and Lu had recently concluded a pact of peace which was presumed to end all war between them. For many generations the Meng family had borne the brunt of the Tsi attacks and could not reasonably be blamed for taking a very practical and utilitarian view of the matter in hand.

'If the walls of our city are razed,' said one of the powerful ministers of the family, 'the people of Tsi will surely invade us. This city is different from the other two because our fortress is not a menace to Lu, but a protection against our common enemies in Tsi. I do not propose to allow the walls to be razed.'

There was general agreement with this presentation of the case and defences of the city were strengthened instead of reduced. This of course shifted the balance of power for the weak Meng family was now the only one with a fortified city. They had on many occasions compromised with the people of Tsi in order to divert their attacks to other parts of the state and the two other barons were naturally indignant at their failure to carry out the explicit or implied agreement to reduce the fortified cities. The forces of the duke and the indignant rival barons beleaguered the place but the people of Meng put up a stubborn resistance and they could not take it. Eventually the attack was abandoned and the Meng family remained in possession of their stronghold. The plan to destroy the castles had been only partially successful, but, from Master Kung's standpoint it had been more than satisfactory. The power of the barons and of the usurping ministers had been broken and the duke had more authority than any of his predecessors had enjoyed for several generations.

About this time Master Kung by a very simple act added still more to the ducal prestige. It will be remembered that when Duke Chao died in exile and his body was brought back to Zigzag Hill for burial, Baron Ping, the father of Baron Huan, showed his petty spite by having the body of the duke buried with a road separating his burial-place from that of his ancestors. This created an anomalous situation which was very difficult of adjustment. To allow the grave to remain wher it was perpetuated an insult to the duke, while to move it not only presented great ritualistic and ceremonial difficulties but might well be calculated to affront Baron Huan since his father had arranged the burial-place. Every ritualist knew that the location of the grave was wrong but none of them could devise a way to rectify the error without disturbing the spirit of the dead duke or offending Baron Huan or both. Master Kung cut the tangled knot and united the grave of Duke Chao with that of his ancestors by the simple but clever expedient of blocking the road which separated them and encircling the burial-place of all the deceased dukes with a ditch or moat.

The weakening of the power of the baronial officials and the increased power of the duke created a great deal of renewed apprehension in the neighbouring state of Tsi, for it removed factors which had been of supreme importance to the Tsi statesmen. They had always carried on intrigues with the barons and ministers and meddled in Lu's affairs, using bribery and other oblique and questionable methods to accomplish their aims. The change in the political machinery of Lu placed affairs on an entirely different basis and was especially disconcerting to them for another and more surreptitious reason; they were busily plotting to rob their own ageing marquis of his powers and usurp the government either for themselves or for a powerful rival family which had been nursing this plot for four generations. The reduction of the baronial castles and strengthening of the ducal power in Lu was a development they had not counted on and sent the Tsi statesmen in frantic search for some new formulae of procedure. From every point of view, their situation was fraught with dangerous possibilities. If Lu continued to make such progress as at present, it would soon be the most important of all the feudal states, even without an alliance with the powerful military state of Wu, and would demand room for expansion. In that event the first to be encroached upon would undoubtedly be Tsi, which lay directly to the north and had in the past unscrupulously purloined territory from Lu whenever a favourable opportunity presented itself. With all power in the hands of the duke and a centralised military command, reciprocal encroachments on Tsi by Lu would not only be easily accomplished, but help to satisfy many an ancient grudge. Some of the ministers of Tsi, in more or less of a panic, proposed to anticipate the event and compromise the matter by a voluntary cession of territory which had been illegally seized by them in the past. It was argued that by doing this they would strengthen the friendly relationship already existing in theory and possibly avoid the forcible seizure of a larger area. This suggestion of a voluntary cession of territory exhibited a point of view which was most unusual for them, and illustrated the seriousness with which they viewed the situation. A crafty old courtier who did not agree with the wisdom of this procedure argued against any precipitancy in making a generous move which might later be found to be unnecessary and so be the cause of future regrets.

'Let us first try in every way possible to hinder their progress,' he said, 'and if that fails then it will be time enough to talk about returning to them a piece of their territory.'

His advice prevailed and with this idea in mind they conferred together to devise a scheme which would weaken the power of the Duke of Lu and be proof against interference by Master Kung. Some genius for wicked but effective stratagems hit on a plan which would by means of the same paraphernalia take advantage of the duke's well-known amorousness and Master Kung's equally well-known disregard for women. The latter had been in Tsi during the entire period that Duke Chao had spent there in exile while the former had been there for a year or two and the Tsi politicians had plenty of time to observe the weakness of the one character and the idiosyncrasies of the other. Though the plan was conceived by one man, it was too expensive and too elaborate to be carried out single-handed and doubtless all the responsible ministers of Tsi played a part in it, including Yen Yang the hunchback who was then nearing the end of his brilliant earthly career. Baron Huan of Lu may or may not have been a party to the plot, but if not he fell into it with almost unbelievable credulity.

The plot was as elaborate, as carefully planned, as difficult of execution, as hazardous of success as a spectacular theatrical production. With great care they selected eighty of the most beautiful courtesans in the country and gave them an intensive training in singing and dancing. Tsi was the state which has been mentioned in an earlier chapter as having established government houses of prostitution in order to encourage traders to visit the place and to

The Duke of Lu was completely captivated by the present of beautiful dancing girls.

despoil them of their profits. This scheme had prospered and, as a result, in the selection of the eighty girls they had the finest talent in the country to choose from. The courtesans were provided with the richest and most stylish costumes obtainable and all the dye-pots of the country were searched for pigments to make their raiment gay and unusually colourful. Equal care was taken in the selection, training and caparisoning of thirty fine teams consisting of four horses each. When the whole magnificent show was ready, the enticing bribes were sent to Zigzag Hill and quartered near one of the city gates, where they would be sure to attract attention and create comment. The whole affair was handled with a great deal more ability and finesse than the Tsi officials had displayed on the occasion of the treacherous peace conference.

Baron Huan, whose town residence was at Zigzag Hill, was one of the first to see this luxurious display. Without making his presence known, he kept an eye on the girls and the horses for three days and, when everything was in readiness for a dress rehearsal, he invited the duke for a drive, taking him over a route where the girls and the horses were disposed to the best advantage. At the first glance, the duke was captivated, with an enthusiasm that would have been excusable as adolescence in a younger man. He was then approaching forty-five, but it must be said as a rather weak defence for his weakness that he had never before seen so much feminine beauty. There were no women like these in his inner-court or as a matter of fact, in any part of the territory over which he exercised sovereignty. Even if there had been, the rigid conventions of Lu would have modified or concealed their charms. Nor were there in his state any horses to compare with these which came from the barbarian north where the finest of their kind were bred. Whatever qualms he may have had about the acceptance of a present of this magnificence from a rival ruler, whose heart he knew to be filled with evil designs, did not weigh very heavily against the intriguing smiles of the girls and the graceful beauty of the horses. The carriage drive ended when they came in view of the display and he remained all day, fascinated and unable to tear himself away. The gift was somewhat hastily accepted and girls and horses were removed to more appropriate and convenient quarters in the palace of the duke for whom they were intended.

The day after the gifts were sent to the palace, Minister Kung went as usual to the court to confer with the duke regarding matters of official importance, but his amorous sovereign was in the inner-court, occupied with other matters. The beautiful and accomplished damsels engrossed his attention, and, with plans for the care and training of the horses, took up the time he should have been giving to the affairs of state. The next day and the next Minister Kung presented himself at the ducal court in conformance with the usual routine of duty. He was aware of the existence of the new occupants of the palace enclosure and of the thoroughness with which they engrossed the attention of the ruler, but could not believe that the edifice of state he had so carefully and successfully erected was going to be wrecked through the silly infatuation of the middle-aged duke for pretty girls and handsome horses. The idea was absurd. During the centuries since the foundation of the Chow dynasty there had been encroachments on the powers of practically all the feudal rulers and no one of them had been able to regain any of his lost prestige. The Duke of Lu, ruler of one of the weakest of any states had been the only exception. The diplomatic victory at the peace conference had made him famous in all of the feudal states. The partial success of the plan to raze the castles and circumscribe the power of the ambitious barons had added to that fame and made him the envy of all the other princes, for most of them were menaced by similar problems which they were helpless to solve. With peace at home and abroad and renewed prestige throughout the country there was no limit to the progress the duke might make. Through the force of his example and the authority he could exert it was possible that the salvation of the country, which Master Kung so greatly desired, could be accomplished.

When he returned after the third day of fruitless waiting at the palace, one of his disciples, the hot-tempered and outspoken Tze Loo, who was deeply incensed at the turn events had taken, advised him:

'Master, it is time for us to go.'

Tze Loo was at this time employed by the Chi family, and though he had no personal concern with the turn affairs had taken his loyalty compelled him to throw in his fortunes with those of his master who, he felt, was being treated very shabbily. The scholar knew that the situation was rather hopeless, but he would not so easily give up his successful career and postponed his departure as long as his dignity would allow. He told his anxious disciple:

'To-morrow the duke will celebrate the sacrificial feast in front of the open space before the city. If the feast is properly observed and the dignitaries are given the customary gift of sacrificial meat, I can remain in spite of what has occurred.'

He was referring to an annual ceremony at which, in conformance with ancient rites, the duke honoured all his principal ministers by sending them, as presents, portions of the meat which had been offered before the sacrificial altars. The sacrifice constituted the most important religious ceremony of the year and Master Kung was justified in believing that if anything would bring the erring duke to his senses it would be his more or less priestly responsibility for carrying out this ritual. It was at this ceremony that the duke, as the spiritual representative of his people, took the leading part and sacrificed to the supreme spirit. The gift of the sacrificial meat from the duke to his ministers was an essential part of the ceremony, typifying the unity of the government with the benign spirits which cast a mysterious influence over all the affairs of men. The day appointed for the sacrifices passed and the duke was still so engrossed by his new-found pleasures that he forgot even to attend to this highly important ceremony which in his absence was muddled through as best they could by the ritualists. Master Kung could bear no more and he adopted the final expedient of thwarted and disappointed statesmen; he sent in his resignation. The duke had so far abandoned himself to the charms of the girls that he did not even take time to consider Master Kung's letter. Perhaps it was never delivered to him. More than one courtier was in the pay of the Tsi plotters who were anxious to see the philosopher shorn of his power or exercising his abilities in some more remote state where his activities would not work to the detriment of Tsi.

Reluctantly the disappointed scholar turned away from his home in Zigzag Hill and prepared to cross the borders and leave his beloved native state. Most of his disciples were attached to him in various forms of official employment but many gave up their positions and left with him. He did not depart hastily as one might be expected to do while smarting under the affronts and disappointments which he had suffered. He travelled slowly and with many backward glances. He was hoping that the duke would become repentant and send a messenger to recall him but in this hope he was disappointed. There was never any occasion for him to retrace his footsteps and he continued on his way toward strange places.

.　　.　　.　　.　　.　　.　　.　　.　　.

When the Master left Zigzag Hill it was with a very sad heart. He was fifty-five years old, had taught and worked for more than thirty years in his attempts to save his country from ruin and restore it to the idyllic period – the fairy-story period of the golden age. He had first hoped to accomplish this by his teachings, which he thought would inspire the princes of the country to walk in the paths of virtue and thus set the people an example which they could follow. He had achieved nothing that could be set down as a practical accomplishment until he became an official and was able to augment moral suasion with some well buttressed and wisely exercised authority. There could be no doubt about the importance of his accomplishments during his brief period of official life. His first practical opportunity had been signalised by a brilliant success which was overshadowed and now wrecked by the moral surrender of the duke following the arrival of the fine horses and the beautiful girls. His loyal disciples were not the only ones who sympathised with him in his disappointment and felt very keenly the injustice which he had suffered. He was escorted part of the way by some of the courtiers of Lu, including the blind music master who was as devoted as one of his own disciples and did his best to convince him of the devotion of the people and their sorrow over the turn events had taken. Deeply grieved, the music master assured him:

'Master, no blame attaches to you.'

In reply Master Kung improvised a ballad which he sang:

> These women with their silly songs,
> Symbolise the country's wrongs,
> And drive me from my home.
> Death and ruin are in their faces,
> Virtue flies to distant places,
> Thither I must also roam.
> A lifetime work is gone for naught,
> Forgotten is all I ever taught,
> Homeless must I wander to the end.

When the music master returned to Zigzag Hill, Baron Huan sought him out and inquired anxiously about the circumstances of Master Kung's departure and the comments he had made. When he had heard the complete report he sighed deeply and said:

'The Master will ascribe to me the blame for these silly female slaves.'

On their journey the Master and his disciples halted for the night at a frontier town and the local magistrate asked to be introduced to the scholar of whom he had heard so much, saying:

'I have never failed to obtain an audience with any sage who has visited this remote part of the country.'

The two talked together all night and Master Kung found an intelligent and sympathetic listener. When they came out of the magistrate's house at daybreak, the official noted the woebegone expression of the disciples who were despondent in their grief. With a prophetic vision of the enormous and lasting influence the teachings Master Kung was to have, he reassured them.

'My sons, why do you grieve over your master's fall from power? The country has long been lying in evil ways but now Heaven is going to use your master as a bell, whose clear tones will serve as a herald to arouse the land.'

After the first shock of departure from Lu had been softened and the approach to new scenes suggested new opportunities the more ardent disciples who went with him shared Master Kung's belief that in some neighbouring state a duke would be found who would give him employment and an opportunity to work out his ideas of political reforms, or that the duke of Lu would repent and recall him. As the days passed and they got farther away from Lu with no message from the duke, some of the disciples returned to their homes. The master gave up hope of his recall and sang a ballad expressive of his grief:

> Through the valley howls the blast,
> The summer rain falls thick and fast,
> From my home I thus am driven,
> Through strange lands my way I trace,
> Without a certain dwelling-place.
> Dark, dark, the minds of men!
> Virtue in vain comes to their ken!
> Thus hastens on my term of years,
> Old age, desolate, now appears.

CHAPTER XIII

*The disciples who gathered around him followed
Master Kung through all his misfortunes learning
from him and by their eager questionings providing
him with mental stimulus.*

Some of the disciples who accompanied Master Kung when the
presence of the singing girls drove him from Lu went with him
only part of the way but others followed him on what eventually
developed to be a long, and in some ways completely fruitless period
of wandering in strange states. Among those who accompanied him
was the impulsive and venturesome Tze Loo, who though among
the least brilliant of his followers was the most devoted and became
the best known. He was only nine years the junior of his master
and because of the slight difference in their ages presumed on an
intimacy of speech which would have been an unheard of impertin-
ence on the part of the younger disciples. Through the years they
spent together he rebuked the master when he thought the occasion
warranted it and was as often rebuked in return. On their first
meeting Master Kung, who was always searching the characters of
others, asked Tze Loo in what he took the greatest pride.

'In my weapons,' he replied, 'in my long sword and stout bow.'

'Your ability with the sword and the bow are well known,' said
the scholar. 'But don't you think that if you added culture to your
attainments you would be a much superior man?'

'Of what good could learning be to me?' Tze Loo asked sceptically.
'On the southern slope of yonder hill is a bamboo, grown straight by
nature and needs no bending. If I cut it down and make an arrow
of it, it will pierce the hide of a rhinoceros.'

'Yes,' said the Master, 'but if you notch and feather it, barb and
sharpen it, will not the arrow penetrate much deeper?'

Tze Loo bowed low in admiration and reverence and thereafter
followed the master's teachings, serving him with a faithfulness

198

which stopped at no personal sacrifices. The method by which he demonstrated to the sceptical Tze Loo how education could improve archery was typical of the method of instruction Master Kung gave to all of his disciples on a wide variety of subjects. He was not a teacher of text-book learning – but a teacher of ethics and morals and an exponent of the ancient rites, ceremonies and songs. Those who came to him for instruction were properly called disciples, rather than pupils, for learning had not yet been formalised and he was a moral leader rather than a schoolmaster. That they began following his teachings before he was twenty years old is a tribute to the maturity of his youthful mind, as well as to the knowledge of the history and classic literature which he had acquired at a remarkably early age. He was by no means the first scholar of his country who had attracted schools of disciples and the relationship was well established. As in the case of the schoolmaster who had taught him, there were no fixed fees. The disciples brought him gratuities, if they could afford them, nothing if they could not. In any event the young tithe-collector had abandoned his distasteful work even before his disciples were numerous enough to promise a fairly steady supply of food and clothing, and from that time to his death a half-century later he was, through brief periods of prosperity and longer and more constant periods of adversity, always a master surrounded by groups of devoted disciples who treasured his words and sought to model their lives after his example. His rigid code of honour, his blending of sternness with urbanity, his dignity and unfailing courtesy all made a deep impression on his disciples who idolised him as a teacher and loved him as a man.

All instruction was verbal and the disciples, unlike the student of to-day, received little if any aid from books. The only writing was inscribed on slips of wood, and mechanical difficulties made characters of generous size necessary. The Chinese became great scholars many centuries before they invented printing, centuries in fact before they invented paper. In the absence of a convenient method of writing students performed prodigious feats of memory. The lists of presidents and kings which the average American and British schoolboys are required to learn were infantile scholastic accomplishments as compared with the things the schoolboy of Master Kung's day were required to memorise. These feats of memory – this profound scholarship which was achieved with only minor aid from writing – established a tradition and Chinese of all classes have memories which are amazing to the foreigner. If the sacred books of China were again destroyed, as they were in the second century B.C., there would be no difficulty about reconstructing them from memory by any one of a number of groups of scholars, certainly the task would be easier and much surer of accomplishment than would be the reconstruction of the text of the Bible under similar circumstances.

The strict curriculum of Chinese learning was to come much later and was founded in fact on the teachings of Master Kung himself. Each scholar learned from the teachings of older scholars and improved on his learning according to his talents, opportunities and industry. What learning he was able to acquire he handed on to his pupils, tinctured by his own interest in a variety of subjects. There were, however, certain broad divisions of learning such as ethics, history, music, literature and two gentlemanly sports, archery and charioteering. Except that it had to do with the management of horses and the driving of the heavy carts which are for literary purposes courteously denominated as chariots, little is known as to exactly what constituted the art of charioteering. We do know that Master Kung did not hold it in very high esteem. Archery, however, is mentioned frequently in all the ancient literature and is described in some detail. One famous archer is said to have spent six years in acquiring his proficiency. For three years, so the story goes, he lay under his wife's loom with his eyes wide open and watched the shuttle flash back and forth across the sunlight. With that training he learned to gaze with unimpeded vision into the sun without blinking. He then hung up a louse in his room and gazed at it for three years until it looked the size of a plate. After this period of training and self-discipline, he could, it is said, unerringly shoot a louse through the heart. Master Kung though never famous for his skill, taught archery to his disciples and was so skilled that he could bring down birds on the wing. Though he had nothing but contempt for mere feats of strength he constantly taught the rigid self-discipline which involved training of the muscles as well as the mind.

There was no formality about his teaching, no set academic lessons to be learned, no fixed hours of study. His instruction was more like that of a wise and affectionate father attempting to solve the problems of life for his sons. The disciples hung on his words and after his death those who survived him gathered the sayings into a book known as the *Analects of Confucius* which is the most important of the so-called *Sacred books of China*. His miscellaneous sayings, as collected in this book are not arranged in any chronological order and with few exceptions it is impossible to ascribe any of them to any particular period but most of them are attributed to the period of wandering which followed his departure from Lu. With no logical sequence, but set down as the disciples remembered them, the *Analects* are always disappointing to the reader on his first introduction to them for they appear to be but little more than a collection of disjointed commonplaces. What makes them all the more puzzling and disappointing to the casual reader is that they were written in a style so concise as to be almost cryptic and presuppose a knowledge of men and events of that ancient period. The contents of the *Analects* may roughly be divided into two parts, his advice to princes who brought their political problems for solution and his remarks to his disciples. In both there was a mixture of concrete advice covering certain specific and often personal problems, and aphorisms of general application. A number of the latter, such as 'The cautious seldom err', have become a part of the great heritage of common knowledge which is embodied in the world's great proverbs. Another, 'learning without thought is labour lost, and thought without learning is dangerous' may be placed in the same category. It is naturally the fate of great proverbs to become hackneyed and after they have been quoted for centuries it is difficult to realise the revolutionary and startling effect they had when they were first heard.

His disciples asked him questions about all manner of things and always received good advice. His answers were always full of unexpected and delightful surprises for he had no preconceived ideas. His consistency did not come from stubborn loyalty to opinions already expressed but to his child-like ideals of simplicity and purity. One said he had come into possession of a precious stone which was of no practical value to him and asked the master for advice as to whether he should keep it or sell it for a good price.

'By all means sell it,' said the Master, and then added: 'But I would wait for someone to offer the price.'

While, by advice like this, he taught them the first principles of shrewd trading which he had learned from his experience as a tithe-collector, he laid much greater stress on teaching them the principles of good sportsmanship, to fish like gentlemen with a hook and line and look with contempt on the use of a net; to shoot an arrow at birds only when they were on the wing; never shoot them when they were perching in apparent security. Indeed much of his teachings both to princes and to disciples was presaged on the idea of inculcating gentlemanly conduct in which he was careful to set them the most meticulous example. The 'superior man', who is mentioned so often in the translation of his works and the subsequent works of his followers, is nothing more nor less than a gentleman in the true sense of the word who, except for some minor and harmless idiosyncrasies of manner, would serve as a model of gentlemanly deportment in any land. Under every conceivable circumstance of life there are certain things a gentleman would do, certain things he would not do. His obligations were so broad as to include all human relationships.

With all of these rules and examples of gentlemanly conduct went an absorbing love for faithfulness and sincerity, and a profound hatred for any kind of show or ostentation and he was especially suspicious of eloquence. He despised the half-truths and sophistry which lurk in catch phrases and for that reason one searches rather unsuccessfully for any of the sparkling phrases which are generally presumed to indicate genius. On one occasion he said:

'Fine words and an insinuating appearance are seldom associated with virtue.'

His literary style was a perfect exemplification of this idea for it is a marvel of clarity and conciseness. There could never be any doubt about his meaning and there was never a word that could be omitted. In spite of the fact that he loved the poetry of the country in which there was a great amount of poetic imagery, he detested flowery language as simply another form of insincerity and said:

'In language it is simply required that it convey the meaning.'

No one ever made more relentless attacks on the shams and insincerities of life and this in a country where most of life was made up of shams and insincerities. A disciple asked him what a man must do in order to be considered distinguished and the following conversation took place:

Master Kung predicted a shower of rain, not by the use of magic, but by observation of the climatic conditions.

'What do you mean by the term "distinguished"?'

'I mean one who is so famous that his name is known not only to his own family and associates but throughout the state at large.'

'That is notoriety, not distinction,' replied Master Kung. 'The man of true distinction is simple, honest, and a lover of justice and duty. He is careful to weigh men's words and at the same time to observe the expression of their faces. He does not force himself upon others. Such a one is truly distinguished in his private and public life. As to the man who is merely much talked about, he puts on the appearance of charity and benevolence, but his actions belie it. He is self-satisfied and has no misgivings. Neither in private nor in public life does he achieve more than mere notoriety.'

Teaching of science was not included in the instruction he gave his disciples. That was among the mysteries possessed by the physicians, necromancers, magicians and astrologers and not an essential part of scholarship. The average schoolboy of to-day knows a great deal more about science than all the scientists of that day put together. The men of the period who did have any rudimentary knowledge of science used that knowledge to give themselves the reputation for magical powers and so prey upon the ignorance of their superstitious fellow-countrymen. Master Kung was interested in the sciences and learned what little there was to learn. In urging his disciples to study the odes he pointed out that in that way they would learn the names of beasts, birds and insects, and it may be said that the only knowledge possessed to-day about the animal life of China of that period comes from the source to which he referred his disciples. One morning when they were starting for a walk in the country, Master Kung told the disciples to bring their umbrellas with them. A little later a heavy rain began to fall and they were ready to give him credit for some supernatural knowledge. He only laughed at them and pointed out that anyone by observing the sky and taking into consideration the season and atmospheric conditions could make a fair guess as to the probabilities of a shower. On another occasion he is reputed to have foretold a deluge of rain which flooded the neighbourhood by reason of the migration of a strange bird.

He kept his disciples under rigid mental discipline. He was careless or indifferent regarding their gratuities of fees, or food or clothing but would waste no time with a stupid pupil. A few for that reason gained a questionable fame for they are known to history only because of the humiliating reproofs the Master gave them. According to his own statements he made no attempt to sugar-coat the pill of learning. He once said in effect that in his teachings he would present one corner of a proposition and if the student could not from that construct the other three corners he bothered no more about him. No doubt that was his theory but his disciples were warmly attached to him and he was warmly attached to them and some of the least brilliant followed him for years, so in his teachings he was not so strict as this theory would indicate. He had no charity for sloth and laziness which he looked on as a contemptible weakness. He caught a lazy disciple asleep in the sun and cried out to the others:

'Rotten wood cannot be carved, a wall of dirty earth will not receive the trowel! What is the use of my trying to teach this fellow!'

He was by no means an ascetic and enjoyed a good meal and the glow of alcohol as well as any man but these were trivialities as compared to the more important things of life. But he was constantly impressing on his disciples the sacrifices that must be made in the name of scholarship and told them:

'The scholar who cherishes the love of comfort does not deserve the name of scholar.'

While he was quick to rebuke his disciples for silly questions and stupid comments, their unquestioning acceptance of his teachings brought equally prompt condemnation.

'Hui gives me no assistance,' he said of one of them. 'There is nothing that I say in which he does not delight.'

The Master was probably as fortunate in his involuntary selection of disciples as they were in their carefully considered selection of a master. Many of them were men of but little less than his own age who proved, by their later careers, the brilliancy of their minds and the soundness of their characters. The questions they put to him were not the idle inquiries of immature schoolboys but the earnest questionings of men who were able to feel a serious concern over the troubled period in which they lived and by their urgent questioning stimulated the mind of the Master. It is significant that his most notable and most discussed sayings are embodied in his informal conversations with his disciples and not with his more formal

The appearance of a strange bird enabled Master Kung to foretell a deluge of rain which flooded the neighbourhood.

discourses to dukes, viscounts, barons and others who often asked for his advice.

One day a disciple approached him with an inquiry regarding a strange new ideal of human conduct which Lao-tsze, the philosopher he had met at Loyang, had proposed and was being seriously considered in some quarters.

'What do you say,' asked the disciple, 'about the idea that injury should be recompensed by kindness, that one should return good for evil?'

To Master Kung's logical mind there could be but one answer to a theory of this kind, which he rejected at once as vain idealism.

'If you returned kindness for injury, and good for evil,' he replied, 'what would you return for kindness and what for good? No! Recompense injury and evil with justice! Recompense kindness with kindness, good with good!'

A disciple on another occasion asked for a word which might serve as a general rule of conduct throughout life. The Master selected the word which has been translated as 'altruism' and then amplified its meaning by saying:

'Do not unto others what you would not have others do unto you.'

That this phrase is put in the negative form rather than the more familiar positive form of Christ's 'golden rule' is due to the idiosyncrasies of Chinese phraseology rather than to any difference in the meaning of the two sentences. When Christian missionaries first came in contact with Chinese teaching they were surprised, and some of them a little chagrined, to learn that some of the teachings of Master Kung so closely paralleled the teachings of Christ in the matter of human relationships. Indeed a great many Christian sermons fit neatly and accurately around Confucian texts.

His philosophy did not embrace the theory that poverty and distress in this life might be compensated for in the glories and joys of a life to come. With most philosophers of that time the future life was hoped for but was not taken for granted. The spiritual world was one about which there was a great deal of speculation but it was a subject which Master Kung would not discuss. Whatever opinions he may have had, were not definite enough to be transmitted to others. His disciples questioned him about these matters but he gave them enigmatic answers, such as:

'Heaven does not speak and yet the four seasons come with regularity.'

He and his disciples were seldom long in one locality and travelled about from place to place even when there was no particular occasion or necessity for them doing so. Each new scene suggested some new problem and Master Kung appeared to find a text in each one. When they approached the banks of a river they all unconsciously paused and watched the water.

'Why do gentlemen always stop to look at a flowing stream,' asked a disciple and Master Kung replied:

'It is because a river, like truth, flows on for ever and will have no end.'

One spring day he was in the country with four of his disciples and there was the usual lesson made up of questions and answers. The question which the sage asked was:

'What would you do if you were given either a position of authority or were free to do exactly as you liked?'

The first disciple to answer was an ambitious and self-confident young fellow who in reply to this query set himself a most difficult task and then solved it brilliantly with complete satisfaction to himself. He said he would like to be appointed premier of a weak state threatened by revolutions within and by invasions from enemies without. Confronted by this difficult situation he would, he boasted, in three years' time pacify the rebels, vanquish the invaders and set the state on its feet. As this coincided with the aims and teachings of the Master, the disciple sat down feeling sure of approval, perhaps of praise.

The second disciple, more modest or less imaginative than the first, followed the same fancy but carried it to a more indefinite conclusion. As the premier of a state beset by these troubles he would, he said, in three years' time so arrange affairs that the people would be fed and comfortably clothed but said that he would have to leave the more difficult problems of politics and military victories to men who were older and wiser than himself.

The third disciple had no interest in such practical affairs. If given his choice he said he would spend his time as an acolyte in the state temples and so become letter perfect in the rites and ceremonies.

In the meantime the fourth disciple had been sitting on the

'A river, like truth, will flow on for ever and have no end.'

grass in the sun idly strumming on his lute and paying but slight attention to the conversation that had been going on. The Master had to repeat the question to him:

'It is now near the beginning of spring,' said the disciple. 'I would like to take off this winter clothing, join a crowd of young men and boys and bathe in the River Yi, dance on the grass, enjoy the spring breezes and come home singing.'

His more austere comrades looked their shocked disapproval at this frivolity. They felt sure he was in for the sharp, incisive rebuke which the Master could administer so effectively. When the fourth disciple sat down the Master was silent for a moment. He looked at the sunlight on the grass and felt the warm spring breezes; all nature was calling to the new life of spring. For a moment he forgot the heavy cares and duties of his leadership. He sighed and said:

'That is just the way I feel.'

It would of course be possible to fill several not uninteresting pages with quotations from the wise common-sense advice which Master Kung gave to his disciples but a few examples will suffice:

It is bootless to discuss accomplished facts, to protest against things past remedy, to find fault with bygone things.

Men's faults are characteristic. It is by observing a man's faults that one may come to know his virtues.

The scholar who is bent on studying the principles of virtue, yet is ashamed of poor clothing and coarse food, is not yet fit to receive instruction.

When you see a good man, think of emulating him; when you see a bad man, examine your own heart.

Without a sense of proportion, courtesy becomes oppressive, prudence degenerates into timidity, valour into violence, and candour into rudeness.

Though in making a mound I should stop when but one more basketful of earth would complete it, the fact remains that I *have* stopped. On the other hand, if in levelling it to the ground I advance my work by but one basketful at a time, the fact remains that I *am* advancing.

A great army may be robbed of its leader, but nothing can rob a poor man of his will.

To take an untrained multitude into battle is equivalent to throwing them away.

It is harder to be poor without murmuring than to be rich without arrogance.

Hopeless indeed is the case of those who can herd together all day long without once letting their conversation reach a higher plane, but are content to bandy smart and shallow wit.

The serious fault is to have faults and not try to mend them.

Men's natures are all alike; it is their habits that carry them far apart.

Men who are of grave and stern appearance, but inwardly weak and unprincipled – are they not comparable to the lowest class of humanity – sneak thieves who break into the house at night?

Your goody-goody people are really the ones who are the thieves of virtue.

These are only desultory fragments of his conversations with his followers. To review with anything like completeness the teachings to his disciples would involve a discussion of Confucian philosophy which has formed the subject of thousands of volumes in many languages. It is said that if a young Chinese should as soon as he learned to read devote his entire waking hours to a perusal of the books of his own country on the subject which foreigners refer to as 'Confucianism' he might live to be a very old man without having read all the available books on the subject. The Japanese literature is almost as voluminous. British authors have been foremost in their translations and studies of the Chinese classics and the English language books on the teachings of the sage would form a large library in themselves. This book is only an attempt to tell the story of the life of this great man. With the many excellent and authoritative existing books concerning his philosophy, it would be both idle and presumptuous to attempt to add anything to what has already been written.

One of his human vanities which has been shared by most men was a conceit that he could appraise the character of men – not only of the great men of the past but of living men of lesser importance, including his disciples. He was constantly studying the characters, not only of the people about him but of historical personages, and his appraisals were in most cases surprisingly accurate. He was rather dogmatic about this and like all others who try to accurately calculate such an uncertain and variable factor as human character, he sometimes went wrong. With experience he grew more discreet.

'At first,' he said, 'my way with men was to hear their words and give them credit for their conduct. Now my way is to hear their words, and look at their conduct.'

He did not believe that a man could conceal his character. One of his disciples was of such an unprepossessing – not to say stupid appearance that the Master did not expect even mediocre achievements from him yet he turned out to be one of the most brilliant of the band and later founded an important school of disciples of his own. Another disciple who gained great fame and who is accorded high honours in the Confucian temples was distinguished for little except his own unswerving loyalty and the Master's favouritism. When the high honours which had been heaped on this disciple were called to the attention of a dour old scholar, the latter made a remark over which other Chinese scholars have chuckled for centuries.

'It only goes to show,' he said, 'how far a horse fly can travel on the tail of a horse.'

CHAPTER XIV

After his departure from his native state the scholar and his disciples sojourned in Wei where he was embarrassed and humiliated by the beautiful but wicked and notorious duchess Nan Tze was mistaken for the former dictator Yang Hoo and left Wei to sojourn in other states.

THE introduction of the dancing girls and the horses to Zigzag Hill and Duke Ting's absorption in them had been entirely unexpected; the incident had come to its tragi-comic culmination with dramatic suddenness. One day Master Kung had been in effectual charge of the affairs of state, honoured by his country-men, famous in distant places, and making rapid progress in the congenial task of successfully putting his political theories into practice. He had brought about the regeneration of Lu by repair-ing the ravages of generations of corruption and misrule and he had enjoyed visions of similar accomplishments covering a much wider field of activity. Less than a week later he had become a homeless wanderer, leaving the borders of his native state to travel new and difficult paths and to exist on the hospitality of strangers.

His voluntary exile had been occasioned by events of which he had been given no warning and his plans to seek other fields of activity were very hastily made. However, there was very little choice as to the route he could take. To the south, which would have led him towards the site of the present capital city of Nanking, were inhospitable marshes surrounding the territory of Wu, half barbarous and wholly occupied with military and naval affairs. This was to Master Kung a foreign country with whose people he felt little sense of kinship. They followed strange customs and spoke a strange language. To the east, on the coast near the modern port of Tsingtao were barbarians of a much lower degree. He had become uncomfortably well acquainted with them when they threatened the duke and himself on the occasion of the peace conference. To the north was the state of Tsi, where the dancing-girl plot had been conceived and where he had previously followed the refugee duke into exile. Naturally these three points of the compass were out of the question.

The one remaining direction he could take was to the north-west and led to the small state of Wei, a principality of about the same size and importance of Lu. The Duke of Wei, it is true, had ambitions to make his state a great military power but it was only an idle fancy as he was too weak to carry out this or any other projects he might have in mind. Though he talked a great deal about war and fought many battles over the wine-cups the state enjoyed a vicarious reputation for peace and the civil officials, as in Lu, were not completely dominated by the military factions. The duke was actually twelve years younger than Master Kung, but his life had not been a wholesome one and he was prematurely aged. The legal wife of the duke's father had borne no sons and the crippled son of a favourite concubine was first declared to be prospective heir but when a second son who was sound of limb was born, the crippled son was set aside in his favour. In this way Duke Ling ascended the ducal throne at the age of five and was brought up in the companionship of his father's concubines and eunuchs with the effect on his morals that might easily be imagined. He never escaped the domination of ministers and eunuchs which had surrounded him as an infant ruler, though the ministers he had were above the usual in ability. The political conditions in his state were very similar to those prevailing in Lu, and there was no doubt but that he could make good use of the services of a scholar and practical statesman like Master Kung. There was still other reasons why Wei was the logical place toward which the wanderers should turn their steps. The wealthy brother-in-law of the disciple Tze Loo lived there and offered the scholar and his band of followers a hospitable home. Finally, the reigning ducal family of Wei had some ancient genealogical connection with the reigning family of Lu, so that Wei was not entirely as strange a country as any other state would be. Because of this remote relationship, the two states were joined in a kind of sentimental alliance which appears to have been stronger and more permanent than any of the numerous formal alliances which the various states had entered into with each other.

In all the shifting feuds and political deals of the feudal states Lu and Wei were seldom at loggerheads and had never fought against each other. This could not be said of either Lu or Wei and any of their other neighbours.

When they finally arrived in the capital of Wei, Master Kung had nothing to complain of, so far as the amenities were concerned. Dissolute Duke Ling received him, not like the unemployed scholar that he was, but like a visiting official and made him an honoured guest of the country. One of the duke's first inquiries was as to the emoluments he received as an official of the state of Lu and when told that he received annually 60,000 measures of grain, promptly gave instructions that he be given the same amount from the ducal storehouse. It was the custom, when a great officer changed his residence from one state to another, to accord him certain rank and perquisites, but both in lesser degree than those held before. By giving him the same amount as he had received when employed in Lu, the duke was displaying unusual generosity. There is some doubt as to just what constituted the measure of grain referred to but the allowance was certainly generous enough to provide the scholar and his disciples with a great deal more than they needed to support themselves comfortably. Master Kung's first inquiries were concerning the government of the country and he was not satisfied until he had thoroughly familiarised himself with political alignments in Wei and knew the strength and weakness of everyone who played any part in the affairs of the state. While many other critics and reformers were keenly aware of the weakness of the political system as a whole, he was the only one who familiarised himself with the details of each feudal government with which he came in contact and could diagnose the individual ills of each particular state. His political theories were broad and general in principle but he endowed them with a specific and practical application in each problem he encountered. The duke gave the philosopher every opportunity to expound his views, listened to him politely if not understandingly and appreciatively but that was as far as matters went. Master Kung's reputation as a philosopher and a statesman had preceded him and he was well known to the officials of Wei as he was in fact to the prominent officials of all of the ducal states who had heard of his brilliant success in Lu. He was not liked by this envious class, but he was a popular idol with the peasants because of

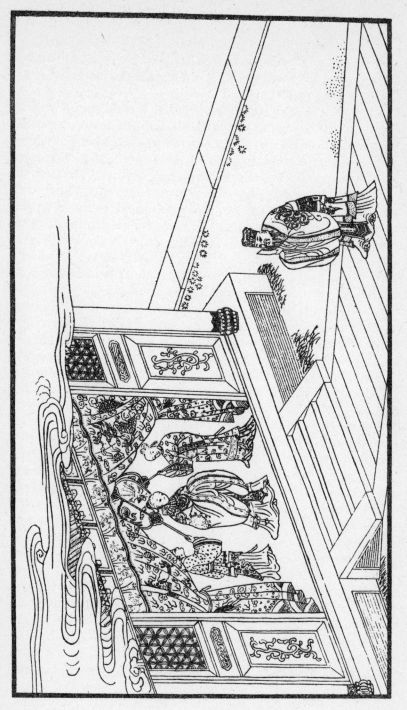

Master Kung was compelled, very unwillingly, to pay his respects to beautiful Madame Nan Tze, Duchess of Wei.

the burdens he had lifted from their fellow-sufferers in Lu through reforms which they hoped might be duplicated here. There was plenty of need for improvement in the state of Wei where conditions of life were no better than in the other feudal states, but so far as the duke was concerned his liberal allowance of grain ended the matter. He gave the philosopher no official powers and though he often asked for his advice he paid no attention to it.

It was during his sojourn in Wei, after a brief excursion outside its borders, that the Master had his famous encounter with the duke's notorious but beautiful consort, Madam Nan Tze. Though the incident was trivial enough in itself it created quite a little gossip at the time and a great many scholarly pages have been written about it. Chinese historians are unanimous in referring to Madam Nan Tze as a woman of well-known wickedness. She was accused of having committed incest with her own half-brother as well as many other less shocking lapses from virtue. The half-brother, it may be remarked, was reputed to be the handsomest man in the country. All the stories about Madam Nan Tze were of a nature that any filthy-minded gossip could easily allege, but could not substantiate and they may or may not have been true. There is no doubt, however, about the fact that she was a very beautiful woman, high spirited and uninfluenced by the narrow prudishness of her time. Much more talented than the duke, she had very early in their married life gained a domination over him which made her the real head of affairs; and officials, much as they disliked women's interference in politics, found it to their advantage to be subservient to her or pretend a compliance with her wishes. The ministers had enjoyed almost supreme power before she arrived on the scene, with her strong personality, for the weak duke would agree to anything so long as the ministers humoured him in the matter of making elaborate military plans which never came to anything. These facts alone were enough to give her a bad reputation with the fusty old historians who might be notorious libertines themselves but insisted on a very strict observance of the proprieties so far as women were concerned. The fact that she was born in a neighbouring state from a princely family with a colourful family tree made the fabrication of gossip concerning her all the easier.

Madam Nan Tze had heard a great deal about the famous philosopher whose flight from Lu to Wei was the talk of the town and had a natural desire to meet him. She was probably curious to see if he was as huge and as grotesque in appearance as he was generally reputed to be. She sent him several invitations to call on her, not neglecting to point out that even when visiting princes were in Wei they invariably paid their respects.

'The lords of the land,' she instructed her messenger to say, 'who come here to conclude pacts of brotherhood with our prince, are always accustomed to call to see my insignificant self. My insignificance desires also to see Master Kung.'

For a famous scholar or, for that matter, for any man not a near relative to call on a woman, even a duchess, was not customary but Madam Nan Tze was an unusual woman. As her father had been one of the princes of the royal house, the rank of her family was really superior to that of any of the feudal dukes and she was not the sort to allow them to forget this fact. Master Kung was well aware of her rank and of the power she wielded through her influence with the duke, but to call on a woman, especially a woman of a questionable reputation, was so contrary to his strict ideas of propriety that he tactfully avoided an acceptance of the invitation. Being a proud and wilful woman his refusal made her all the more determined to have her own way. She repeated her invitation and Master Kung was at length forced to forgo his ideas of propriety and pay her a formal call. The visit was not a clandestine one but was made openly and with a certain show of ceremony though this was incomplete in a minor detail.

He drove to the ducal palace and entered the courtyard of Madam Nan Tze's quarters where he bowed ceremoniously toward the north, thereby making acknowledgment of the superiority of her rank. Madam Nan Tze, with her two maids of honour, made her appearance, partly concealed by a curtain of flax and acknowledged his greetings by bowing twice. It does not appear that any words were exchanged. Even if he had been bold and impolite enough to try to look at the beautiful face of the lady, the flax screen would have formed a partial barrier. According to his account of the meeting he did not look at her at all and the only impression he carried away was supplied by the musical jingle of the jade rings and ornaments she wore. Having in his own mind some doubts as to the propriety of this visit, he took upon himself the sole responsibility for it and made the visit alone, unaccom-

panied by any of his disciples, who were usually inseparable from
him. According to the strict rules of etiquette he should have been
accompanied by attendants and undoubtedly the proud duchess
noticed this omission and remembered it later when plans concerning Master Kung came up for discussion. She was sedately chaper-
oned by two of her court ladies. Everything that Madam Nan Tze
did was the subject of gossip around the ducal capital and soon the
town was buzzing with news of the visit. His disciples were horrified at the idea that their beloved and respected master should
comport himself in such an apparently dissolute manner. They
reproached him bitterly and it appears that for one of the few
times in his life he was put on the defensive and felt the necessity
of explaining and justifying his conduct. He insisted that in paying this visit to the notorious beauty he had nothing improper in
his mind.

'I really did not wish to see her,' he exclaimed. 'Now I have seen
her, and she returned my greeting with proper decorum.'

His disciple Tze Loo whose brother-in-law's house gave them
shelter persisted in his criticism and the Master with a half-guilty
conscience assured him:

'Whatever I have done that is wrong, heaven forced me to do,
heaven forced me to do!'

If this unsolicited meeting with the duchess had developed into
the clandestine intimacy which the gossips of the capital thought
to be the logical and natural culmination, it would not have constituted an incident that would have been very exceptional in the
state of Wei. The women of this state had a reputation of loose
morals which caused considerable gossip over several neighbouring
principalities and, although there was the usual amount of fancy
and exaggerations in these stories told by travellers, the cold and
unadorned truth was not especially savoury. While the marriage
ritual was not ignored and the domestic virtues not unknown, virtuous maidens and faithful wives did not exist in Wei in such large
proportion as in other states. A ruler who lived several generations
before this period had encouraged the rearing of children in order to
restore the population which had been decimated by war. Because
of the number of men who had been killed in the fighting there
was a surplus of females and the ruler removed the conventional
obstacles which might prevent the mating of the marriageable

girls and encouraged the loose relationships which in other places were severely frowned upon. As a result, Wei had marriage customs different from those of other states. Boys and girls, instead of leaving the selection of mates to their parents, took the initiative themselves and even participated in some of the curious betrothal ceremonies which in itself constituted an important part of the marriage rites. The result had been a looseness of conduct which persisted for generations after the population had been restored to something like a normal balance and the conditions which had brought it into existence had disappeared. The visitors from Lu had heard all the stories concerning the dissolute conduct of the women of Wei, and were properly shocked. In sharp contrast with Wei, Lu had a reputation for strait-laced virtue which has probably never been excelled in any country or at any time. One of many stories may illustrate it. A bachelor of Lu lived alone. One stormy night his neighbour's house blew down and the neighbour's beautiful young daughter spent the night alone in the bachelor's house, the only place of refuge she could find. Here was a situation fraught with many possibilities and redolent with scandal. The bachelor was equal to the occasion and solved the problem of current and future gossip by sitting up all night with a lighted candle in his hand. Afterwards he boasted of his gallant and circumspect conduct, and so became a character in history. At the period under discussion he was one of the heroes of the punctilious lads of Lu who looked on him as an example to be followed. So far as Master Kung was concerned, the meeting was just the sort of incident that any gentleman might get into quite innocently and at the same time have difficulty explaining to his wife. Master Kung was not faced with this necessity, but his envious detractors who were growing in number made the most of their opportunity and more than a hundred years later his followers were often put to the trouble of denying silly gossip about the incident.

After a stay of some months in Wei, the Master found that he was accomplishing nothing in his attempts to influence the duke, so he and his disciples left for the still smaller state of Chen. They were approaching the city of Kwang, capital of Chen, when trouble for the band of scholars was precipitated by the fancied resemblance between Master Kung and Yang Hoo, the ambitious politician who had usurped power and authority and maintained a

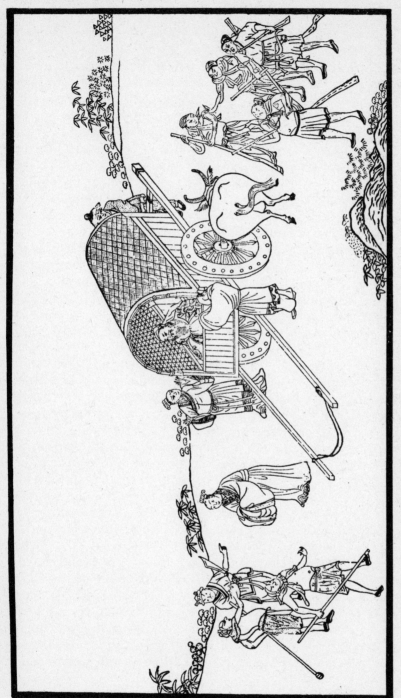

Mistaking him for a hated enemy, the people of Kwang made an attack on Master Kung and his disciples.

dictatorship in Lu. Unlike most other politicians of that period, Yang Hoo's ambitions had not been confined by feudal boundaries and his influence, which did not disappear with his exile from Lu, extended over a number of states. After his exile first from Lu and then from Tsi, he became a military officer in Tsin, a state which for several generations had been strong enough to bully its neighbours especially Chen which was one of the smaller states on which all of its neighbours alternately imposed their will. On one of his military expeditions Yang Hoo had torn down a part of the wall of Kwang by which means his soldiers had entered the city and inflicted severe punishments on the inhabitants. One of the soldiers who had taken part in this expedition was acting as guide for Master Kung and his disciples and was driving the Master's carriage. As they came to the city walls, the guide, his mind full of recollections of the exciting events attending his last visit, pointed with his whip, and said to Master Kung:

'The last time I was here, we entered through a breach in yonder wall.'

The remark was overheard by some of the natives and was repeated and distorted. Master Kung and Yang Hoo were both homely men of very generous proportions and soon the news spread among the townspeople that their old enemy had returned with a band of ruffians to scourge the city again. It looked to the citizens like a heaven-sent opportunity for revenge against the massive man in the cart, whom they thought to be Yang Hoo. He was unaccompanied by a guard and was surrounded only by a small group of men who were obviously unarmed. With this convenient opportunity at hand they surrounded the lodgings the Master had taken and set about to pay off their old enmity with any warlike implements they could find at hand. According to stories the disciples proudly related, the Master forbade their defending themselves by force but led them in song and after the third song the attackers dispersed. Whereupon the scholars sought another residence farther away from the city. The disciples were inclined to ascribe some psychic influence to the song but the more logical explanation seems to be that the context of the song revealed the identity of the scholarly band and disclosed their peaceful mission.

During the excitement following their flight one disciple, Yen Yuan, was found to be missing and the Master was very much

concerned because Yen Yuan, a brilliant student, was weak in body
and for that reason had not been able to keep pace with the others
when they ran away to a safer place after the siege was lifted.
When he finally rejoined the others after an absence of five days
and the Master told him of his fears the disciple made himself
famous by his loyal and affectionate reply:

'While you, Master, are still living, how could I dare to die?'

While foreign critics can see in this little more than a neatly
turned phrase, Chinese scholars look on it as the most perfect
expression of filial devotion.

The disciples were terrified at the turn events had taken and
especially apprehensive lest some new attack might bring harm to
their beloved Master but he reassured them and for the first time
expressed his belief in the divine character of his mission.

'Since the death of King Wan of our present dynasty,' he said, 'has
not the cause of truth lodged here in me? If heaven had wished to
let this cause of truth perish, then I who am doomed to die like other
mortals, would not have been entrusted with that mission. While
heaven does not abandon the cause of truth, what can the people of
this city of Kwang do to me?'

Although there had been no casualties, this incident was not
auspicious and their further stay in the state brought them no
encouragement. The people of the city made no further attacks on
them, but they were not received hospitably and were objects of such
suspicion and were kept under such strict surveillance that it was
only by the aid of a friend from Wei that they were able to escape
from the neighbourhood of the town. No one even wanted to listen
to the Master so after an unpleasant stay of a little more than a
month, he was again in Wei. Relatives of his loyal disciple Tze Loo
lived here, he had several scholarly cronies, the questionable friendship of the duke and with all of these connections, he was always
sure of a home. In spite of his many wanderings to distant places
over a period of years, the Master, so long as the dissipated duke was
alive, came back to Wei after each disappointment and made one
long final visit after the duke's death.

While *en route* to Wei he passed a house where he had been hospitably entertained a few months before and was shocked to find
that the head of the house, his former host, was dead and that the
funeral ceremony was in progress. He went in to condole with the

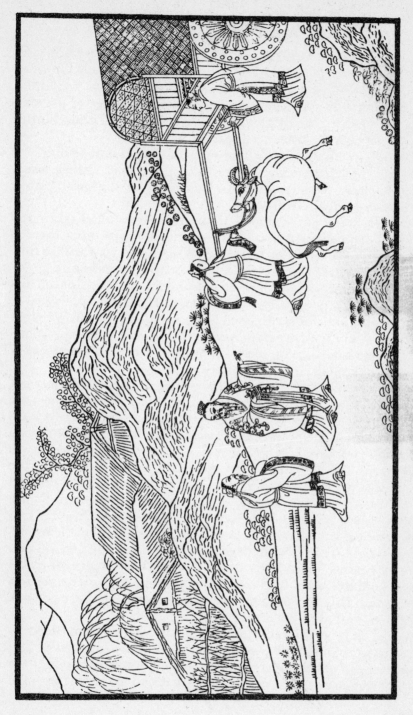

On learning of the death of his former host Master Kung gave one of his horses to help defray the funeral expenses.

mourners and when he came out gave orders to one of his disciples to take the extra team of horses from his carriage and give them as a contribution toward the expenses of the funeral. The disciple remonstrated with him:

'You have never before done such a thing at the funeral of any of your disciples! Is this not too great a gift on the death of one who, after all, was only a host?'

'When I went into the place of mourning,' replied Master Kung, 'my appearance brought forth a burst of grief from the chief mourner, and I joined him with my tears. I dislike the idea of my tears not being followed by anything more substantial. Give them the horses, my child!'

Soon after his return to Wei Master Kung had his second rather unfortunate experience with the beautiful, talented and troublesome Madam Nan Tze. The duke had invited the philosopher to accompany him as his guest on a formal official call and Master Kung had, as a matter of course, accepted the invitation. When he went to meet the ducal carriage he was mortified to find that the notorious woman was riding beside her consort in the place of honour he had taken for granted would be occupied by himself, while he had been relegated to a position which was not only inferior but humiliating, for he was seated with the eunuch who drove a second carriage. He did not discover the arrangement until it was too late to decline without creating an embarrassing scene, so he took his place in the cart with the eunuch and the plodding ox. To add to his chagrin and indignation the eunuch, who was secretly powerful in state affairs, impudently asked him to help drive. Pictures depicting this incident, which may or may not be historically accurate, show the duke and the duchess seated in a large four-wheeled and rather ornate carriage drawn by horses and caparisoned with outriders, while the philosopher's conveyance was a humble two-wheel cart, drawn by a single ox. The route of the journey lay through the market-place, the duke and the duchess riding proudly ahead in their magnificent equipage while the philosopher followed humbly behind in the lumbering ox-cart. Every idler in the capital was out to see the ducal procession pass by, and this open affront to the famous and popular philosopher created a sensational scandal. Some of the people, on seeing the procession pass, called out:

'Lust rides in front and virtue trails behind!'

We may be sure they did not call out loud enough for the duchess to hear them or there would have been a few toes and noses chopped off. The affront was no doubt a result of the scheming of this artful and ᵛitious woman who in this way revenged herself on the scholar for the grudging and unwilling homage he had paid to her. The incident of the dancing girls was fresh in his mind and he with a great deal of justice blamed the beautiful Nan Tze for his failure to make any progress in his programme of reform he had hoped the duke would adopt. He was thwarted again by the influence of feminine charms and told his disciples bitterly:

'I have never known anyone who will work so hard on behalf of virtue as for a beautiful face.'

He felt so humiliated over this incident that he left Wei at once. More than a century later his detractors used this incident as the basis for new attempts to steep his reputation in scandal. They said he seleced the seat in the ox-cart himself because he was really cultivating the friendship of the eunuch on account of the influence the latter had with the dissolute duke and hoped in that way to get a profitable appointment.

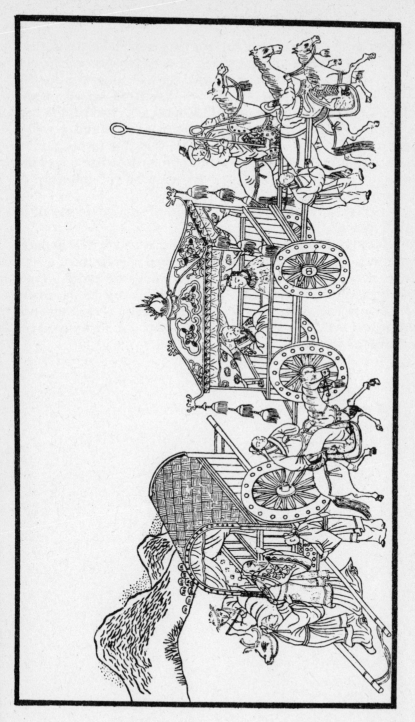

Duke Ling of Wei and his consort rode in the first carriage and assigned Master Kung an inferior carriage.

CHAPTER XV

*Further disappointments and dangers were met with
in the travels from state to state in search of official
employment. The War Minister of Sung makes an
attempt on his life. Held in custody by a rebellious
officer Master Kung is released under oath that he
will not go to Wei, an oath which he promptly violates.*

FOLLOWING the humiliating carriage ride behind the notorious
duchess Master Kung and his disciples crossed the borders and
stopped in the state of Sung, the state from which his ancestors had
migrated to Lu. In order to reach Sung from Wei they had to travel
very near to Lu but they did not cross its borders. Here the Master,
as was usual during these scholastic pilgrimages, taught his followers under the shade of a tree. When they were travelling from
place to place these scholarly discussions were held almost daily, for
the new scenes of each day's journey brought up new ideas for discussion, and suggested to the disciples new problems to bring to the
attention of the Master. It is hardly necessary to explain that the
country was not then so thickly populated and covered with farm
lands as at present and that there were plenty of rustic retreats that
could serve for purposes of instruction in the absence of school-
rooms. They had not been in the state of Sung very long before
their presence attracted the resentful attention of one of the powerful ministers of the state. The Sung Minister of War, whose brother
was one of the disciples, for some reason which has not been clearly
explained, fell into a murderous rage against the Master, the disciples and even the tree which was affording them shelter from the
sun. Some have thought his rage might have been a survival of the
family feud which had led to the flight of Master Kung's ancestor
from Sung and the establishment of the family in the state of Lu. In
this day it sounds preposterous that a family feud should be perpetuated over so many generations but with their cult of reverence for

235

ancestors, family feuds were bitter and lasting for feuds did not die with the birth of a new generation. The fact that the minister's brother was one of the disciples makes his rage all the more puzzling though if the facts were known it might possibly supply a plausible explanation. Whatever may have been the occasion, the Minister of War was very determined to carry out his attacks. He sent a squad of soldiers to the meeting-place with instructions to pull down the tree, capture or scatter the disciples and kill Master Kung. As events developed, nothing serious happened, but the incident is made much of in all Chinese histories of that period. As the soldiers approached and threw ropes over the tree in a futile attempt to uproot it, the disciples were very much disturbed over the threat against their Master's life, but he was calm and reassured them as he had on the occasion of the attack at Kwang:

'Since heaven has produced the virtue that is in me; what can this man do to me?'

When the soldiers set about pulling down the tree the Master and the disciples scattered and fled in several directions and later rejoined each other at a point some distance away but the Master was missing and his followers rushed around anxiously looking for him. A countryman told one of them of seeing a stranger standing alone near the city gates describing with unflattering accuracy the Master's unusual physical appearance, his huge size, prominent eyes, projecting teeth, pendulous ears and ridiculous nose adding:

'He stands there alone looking as sad and cast down as a stray dog in a house of mourning.'

The disciple hurried to the city gate where he found the Master and excitedly told how he had found him, relating in rather impolite detail exactly how the countryman had described him. The scholar with hearty good humour forgot his cares and anxieties, laughed joyously and said:

'The description of my outer form is a secondary matter, but the description of a stray dog in a house of mourning, that fits me exactly!'

During the remainder of his brief stay in this unfriendly state the Master took no chances and went in disguise. They did not remain there long but moved south to the small border state of Chin and remained there for a year or more as the guest of a military official, the warden of the city wall. This officer as well as many others

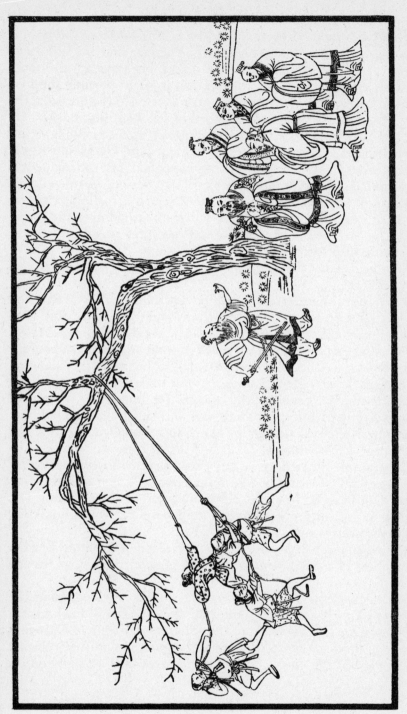

The Minister of War of Sung attempted to pull down the tree under which Master Kung was giving instruction to his disciples.

ardently supported Master Kung but he made no progress with those who were in power. Conditions here were not favourable for his employment or for the reception of any change in methods of administration. The state was in turmoil for it was being attacked by Wu, the barbarian power south of the Yangtsze which a few years before had humiliated the state of Tsi by its easy victory. The King of Wu was then rapidly advancing in power and was finding it a comparatively easy matter to harass the more highly cultivated but less warlike states clustered along the Yellow River. He had captured and held three cities of Chin, then abandoned them only to return later and plunder a large part of the country. The rulers of Chin were too occupied with military troubles and too terrified by the threatened raids of the savage barbarian soldiers to have any time for the teachings of a philosopher.

Again the band of travellers turned towards Wei. The duke was weak and dissolute, his consort's reputation scandalous and the state reflected its rulers and was notoriously immoral, but at any rate it was hospitable. When hunger threatened elsewhere, they could always return to the allowance of grain granted by the duke. Aside from this practical consideration of the ducal granaries, there were other circumstances which made Wei appear like a second home to them. While the Master's attempts to influence the duke had come to nothing, many of his disciples had been more successful in a smaller way and were employed in various official capacities. Though they came from different states and different classes of society and temperamentally were as different as any body of highly cultivated and intelligent men could well be, their common scholastic interests and loyalty to their Master created in the band a sound and lasting brotherhood. The homes of the former disciples who were now officials of the state were always open to their unemployed brethren. The Master also had his friends among the scholars of Wei so that whenever the wanderers returned there they were always sure of food, shelter and a hospitable welcome.

They were approaching the borders of Wei when they had the ill luck to be captured by a rebellious officer who had taken possession of that part of the country and had some ambitious political and military projects in mind. This time they did not run away nor did they submit tamely to capture, though threatened by soldiers who were armed with spears and swords. Among the newer disciples was a man of mature years, great wealth and more than the usual amount of physical courage. He was travelling in a state which must have been in marked contrast with that of his fellow-disciples for he had five chariots and about sixty attendants with him. As charioteers and their assistants were also soldiers and acted as body-guards to their employers, this band of attendants constituted a well-disciplined fighting force of some strength. This disciple does not appear to have been present on the occasion of the murderous attack by the war minister of Sung but had been among the disciples on the earlier occasion when the Master was mistaken for Yang Hoo and besieged by the irate citizenry of Kwang. He had in that instance been compelled to stand helplessly by and felt very much humiliated that a man with his courage and resources should be placed in this helpless and defenceless position. He afterwards provided himself with this guard in order to meet future emergencies of this nature and it was probably while away on this enterprise that the attack in Sung was made. He was now in a state of military preparedness and when the armed forces of the rebellious officer threatened their little band, he rushed between the soldiers and Master Kung.

'When I formerly joined the Master,' he cried impetuously, 'we met with difficulties in the city of Kwang. To-day we again meet with difficulties here. That is fate. But I will fight and die rather than see the Master again placed in danger.'

With that he disposed his chariots and guards to the best advantage for purposes of defence and with his own sword made a way for the passage of the Master to a protected place. Fortunately the issue did not develop into a decisive conflict. As soon as the rebellious officer learned that the party consisted of the renowned philosopher and his band of disciples, he had no wish to detain them, and agreed to release them at once if they would promise not to go to Wei, where he did not want his rebellious military plans disclosed. Wei was, of course, their destination but Master Kung gave his oath not to go there and the officer withdrew his forces leaving them free to travel. With a pretence of keeping his promise, Master Kung set off in a different direction, but as soon as he was safely out of sight and in no fear of recapture, he changed his course and hurried on to Wei by the quickest possible route. Disciple

Master Kung became separated from his disciples and wandered about, a bystander said, 'like a stray dog'.

Tze Loo, who partly by reason of the fact that he was only nine years younger than the Master and partly because of his impetuous honesty was usually outspoken in his criticism of the Master's acts, protested against this breach of faith but the Master made light of it.

'It was a forced oath,' he said. 'The spirits do not hear such oaths.'

It is not to be presumed from this rather questionable conduct that Master Kung held an oath in light regard, for on the contrary he on several occasions impressed on his disciples the sanctity of simple promise and agreements. He specified as one of the qualifications of the complete man, 'one who does not forget an old agreement, however far back it may extend'. To discuss the matter at this late date would only lead to idle speculation but it is worth while to record that Master Kung's action has had a lasting effect on the attitude of his countrymen in their appraisal of the sanctity of promises. This does not necessarily mean their endorsement of a code of lower standard, but of a code different in an essential detail from others. Before the advent of foreign traders to China acquainted them with the convenient loopholes provided by legal technicalities by which the consequences of unfavourable contracts could be escaped there was an often quoted saying to the effect that the word of a Chinese was as good as his bond. This was undoubtedly true as far as it went but the degree of faithfulness with which the Chinese traders stuck to their contracts never exceeded the sincerity of the circumstances under which the contracts were entered into. With a higher regard for the spirit of the covenant than for the letter of the law, they have paid slight regard for the sanctity of contracts entered into through trickery or *force majeure*. It would be impossible to determine how far Master Kung's explanation to Tze Loo affected this point of view but it was not without its influence which was undoubtedly of far-reaching effect. More than two thousand years later Chinese diplomats quoted Master Kung's remark as justification for the violation of a treaty which they had been compelled to sign by force of arms, and his example had previously qualified many a promise. This contention that a forced oath had no sanctity was not originated by Master Kung though he is generally given credit for its authorship. About forty years before this, one of the ministers of China, justifying himself under similar circumstances, had said: 'At a forced covenant where there is no sincerity, the spirits are not present. They are present only where there is good faith.' He was merely quoting very ancient authorities.

Back in Wei, the duke received the philosopher with even more hospitality than before. In fact, when he heard of his approach he went out to the city gates to meet him, an honour that would usually be paid only to a visiting ruler and a very high honour even for a dignitary of ducal standing. In a neutral and detached appraisal of this incident the fact must be set down that the duke, with his senile obsession for theoretical warfare was very curious about the movements of the rebellious officer who had first detained and then released Master Kung and his going to the city gate to meet the scholar may have been dictated by curiosity rather than courtesy. The scholar not only gave the duke all the information he had about the military situation but some military advice as well. However that was not the only reason the duke was glad to welcome the returning scholar. He was at this time very much in need of the friendly help of an able administrator for he had lost the services of some of his most important officials, and troubles he was too weak to cope with without the aid of stronger men were beginning to pile up about him. Most if not all these troubles centred around the beautiful but wicked Madam Nan Tze who was as thirsty for power as she was unscrupulous in the means she employed to further her ambitions. She had just made the best of a political opportunity which had unexpectedly fallen at her feet. The wealthy old prime minister of the state, in order to preserve his riches from confiscation and avoid the jealousy of others had maintained a humble attitude toward all who were in power and had refrained from giving offence to anyone. When he died and his son succeeded not only to his wealth but to his powerful office, the son adopted a bold policy and attempted to exile the partisans of the Madam Nan Tze, who undoubtedly constituted a troublesome and dangerous political element. The duchess struck back quickly and effectively, for she accused the young prime minister of treason and he was compelled to flee for his life and take refuge in the state of Lu, accompanied of course by many of his adherents and minor officials who had been associated with him in his bold but unsuccessful coup. A short time after that another important official suffered the same fate for a similar reason and Madam Nan

While en route to Wei Master Kung was seized by a rebellious officer and released on his promise not to go to Wei, which promise he did not keep.

Tze assumed as complete control over the affairs of Wei as dictator Yang Hoo had gained over the affairs of Lu, though by strikingly different methods. A Chinese historian summed up the situation as follows:

'Duke Ling of Wei gave ear implicitly to what was told him in the inner-court. It was because of this that he sent out as fugitives the hereditary servants of the state together with all of their friends. The state was in fact placed at the disposal of the inner-court and governed by the ladies of the court, the eunuchs and the concubines.'

This shift in authority from officials of ability to the concubines and eunuchs of the inner-court had occurred just prior to Master Kung's arrival and the duke may have had in mind offering him one of the official positions which had been vacated only a few months before in the hope that the scholar might be able to rescue him from the utterly ridiculous position in which he was now placed. He may have hoped that the scholar would be able to manage the duchess which was certainly something he did not even have the courage to attempt. Though they had no tastes and few interests in common, and were in most respects the direct antithesis of each other it appears that the duke not only admired and respected the philosopher, but held for him an affection as genuine as was possible for one of his weak character. His dissolute life had told on him and though not an old man in years he was old and tired in body and mind; with the new problems facing his state he was, apparently, ready for the help the philosopher was so willing to give him. The Master following his first interview with him, was much encouraged and confided to some of his disciples.

'If there were any of the princes who would employ me, in the course of twelve months I would accomplish something considerable. In three years the government would be perfected.'

But in his premature dotage, the duke's mind was engrossed with military affairs. He had always had an ambition to become a great and powerful war lord though he had never progressed beyond the toy-soldier stage of drawing up ambitious plans of conquest of neighbouring states which his ministers were diplomatic enough to discuss with him and wise enough to ignore. He was now more absorbed than ever in military ventures, perhaps because

247

it was one function of the government in which he would have the least interference from Madame Nan Tze and the inner-court. He asked all kinds of absurd questions which irritated and annoyed the philosopher. In the midst of a discussion regarding the arrangement of the ceremonial vessels at a sacrificial ceremony, he would ask whether footmen with bows and arrows or horsemen with lances should lead an attack. It may here be remarked that his wanderings and disappointments had not improved Master Kung's temper; he was, for a man of his equanimity, getting crotchety and crabbed and easily offended. One day he had the duke's rapt attention while he was expounding his political ideas and thought he was making progress. In the middle of a sentence he looked up and saw that the duke instead of listening to his sound advice was observing the flight of some wild swans. The incident was trivial but it came as the climax to many others of a similar nature and the Master, deciding that further effort here was futile, again abandoned the hospitality of Wei.

The odyssey of the further wanderings of the Master and his disciples is a confused one with much jumbled and uncertain chronology and equal uncertainty as to the exact location of the spots they visited. Local historians made no comment on the comings or goings of the unemployed scholar who a few years before had made a reputation of sorts in Lu but was now beginning to be looked upon as an impractical politician who had been wandering here and there for years looking for a position but without success. He was half forgotten in his home state, where important local affairs engrossed everyone's attention, so that the story of his wanderings can only be reconstructed from the fragmentary and imperfect recollections of his disciples who did not know that historians for many centuries would be trying to trace their footsteps. They wandered from state to state, sometimes remaining for years and sometimes for only a few months always with the one main object of serving some ruler and by that means accomplishing the rejuvenation of the state. It is to be noted, however, that though they approached it several times they did not go to Loyang, the national capital and theoretical seat of the government. The king still lived there and held his colourful but powerless court, surrounded by powerless officials with imposing titles, ritualists, astrologers, historians, musicians, concubines, eunuchs and court fools. The court

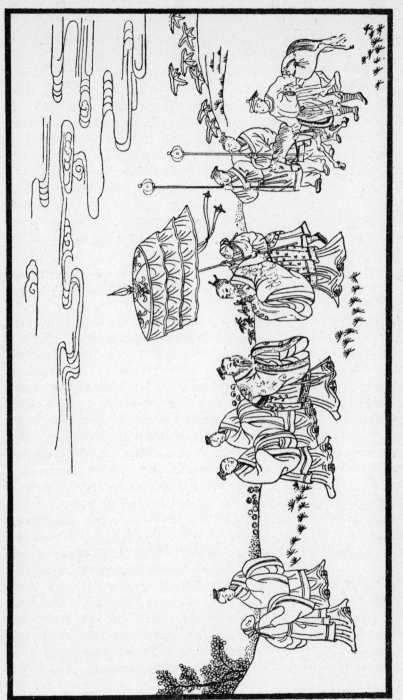

Duke Ling of Wei received Master Kung very graciously at the city gates after the latter's return from Chin.

at Loyang of that time has been described as an extinct volcano which occasionally rumbled and sent forth smoke or noxious fumes but never flames. All power was in the hands of the feudal rulers and only through them could anything in the way of reform be accomplished. Wherever in any of the feudal courts there appeared to be a promise of employment Master Kung journeyed thither, always accompanied by his disciples who were as tireless as he and as indifferent to discouragement.

While waiting for this hoped-for opportunity, Master Kung studied the political affairs of every state, made himself familiar not only with the historical traditions and legends of the state but also with the practical current politics, the characters, the weaknesses and the ambitions of everyone who had a finger in the political pie and conjectured shrewdly as to how he could make each one of them play a part in his scheme of things if he should be given the direction of affairs. No greybearded politician who had grown old in official service was more familiar with the intricacies of the sophisticated political game played in his own state. Master Kung was able, at any time, to solve the problems of any state he had visited, not alone because of his profound scholarship and highly trained mind but because of his knowledge of practical politics in which he was the equal if not the superior of any politician in the land. He did not get an opportunity to use this knowledge to full advantage, but it was not entirely wasted. When he visited various rulers, dukes, viscounts, barons and others, it was customary for them to ask his advice regarding problems of government. Usually these were nothing more than polite inquiries couched in general terms, and in most cases the inquirer probably expected replies in similar general vein, possibly flattering and certainly innocuous, the kind of mental pabulum on which officials fed the vanity of their princely employers. In Master Kung's answers to their polite inquiries, they usually got a good deal more than they asked for. With his accurate and detailed knowledge of the problems of each state and his familiarity with the weakness of each ruler and official he was able in his reply to offer very sound and practical advice and he never hesitated to take advantage of his opportunity. Thus, when in his early contact with princes the Marquis of Tsi asked him about good government and he replied that it meant being careful in expenditure, he was hitting at the principal weakness of the state for while Tsi, owing to its monopoly on iron and salt, was potentially the richest of the states it was usually in financial difficulties owing to the carelessness with which the marquis and the officials squandered the public money and enriched themselves at the expense of the people.

His disciples who were in official employment afforded him an indirect opportunity to put his theories into practice for they brought their problems to him and relied on him for instruction and advice. When his disciples came to him with their problems of personal conduct he gave different and sometimes contradictory answers to identical questions, always taking into consideration the personality of the individual. In the *Confucian Analects* which record the sayings of Master Kung, a great deal of the advice given to the rulers appears on a casual reading to consist of a collection of general platitudes which might be incorporated in any copybook maxims and government. But with an understanding of the local political problems of the day and the character of the questioner it becomes quite clear that the advice he gave was always practical and specific, that he invariably diagnosed the ills of the state and with one or two apt phrases indicated the remedy.

While he received little encouragement from the feudal rulers on whom he tried to impress his ideas, rebellious rulers were more appreciative of his talents. Years before this in Lu, two of the usurping ministers had invited him to join them and a similar invitation came to him shortly after he left Wei for the third time. A rebellious officer of the Duchy of Tsin was holding a part of his state against his duke and sent Master Kung an invitation to join him. The scholar was considering the invitation. Tze Loo, the same disciple who had intervened on many previous occasions to keep his Master in what he believed to be the straight and narrow path, protested:

'Master, I have heard you say that when a man in his own person is guilty of doing evil, gentlemen will not associate with him. This man is a rebel; if you go to him what will be said about you?'

'Yes, I did use those words,' admitted Master Kung. 'But is it not said that if a stone is really hard it may be ground without being made thin; that if it be really white it may be steeped in dye without being made black? Am I an empty gourd? Am I to be hung up out of the way of being eaten?'

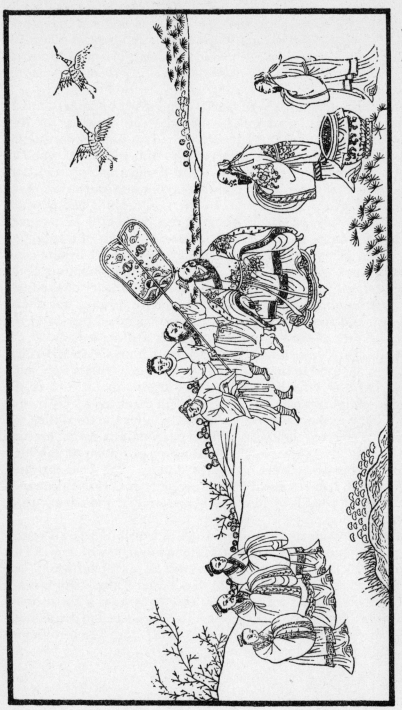

While giving Duke Ling advice regarding governmental affairs, Master Kung noticed that the duke's attention was focused on a flight of wild swans.

The matter ended there and he did not go. Some commentators on his life have expressed regret that he should even have considered employment by the rebel as they have expressed similar chagrin and explanations over the fact that he had considered helping Commander Pieu New found a new dynasty.

CHAPTER XVI

*Fearing that if he joined the ministry of the King of
Chu some of their chicaneries would be revealed the
ministers of two small border states captured Master
Kung and his disciples and held them without food
for a week after which they escaped and ended another unsuccessful venture by returning again to Wei.*

IN the year 489 B.C. Master Kung's wanderings which had begun
seven years previously carried him further from his birthplace
than he had ever been before. This was to a point very near the
boundary of the present provinces of Hupeh and Honan which
was at that time the approximate boundary between the orthodox
feudal states of the Chow kingdom and the rapidly growing domain
of the King of Chu. The latter was one of the barbarian jungle
states which, without very much aid from the culture of the river
people, had grown rapidly in military power and was now threatening its northern neighbours just as the other barbarian state of
Wu was doing from its domain on the Lower Yangtsze. The original
capital of the country of Chu had been located on the famous
Yangtsze Gorges above the present port of Ichang, but the colonisa-
tion of the increasing population, as well as the subjugation of the
more barbarous but less powerful tribes followed the lower courses
of the Yangtsze with the result that the capital was moved to the
east from time to time for political and administrative reasons.
It was at this time near the present treaty port of Shasi on the
middle section of the Yangtsze River about a hundred and twenty
miles above Hankow. For many centuries these two main divisions
of the Chinese peoples, the cultured ones who had settled on the
banks of the Yellow River, and the barbarous ones who lived on
the Yangtsze Rivers, were separated entirely from each other, and
for a long time after the spreading population of each part of the
country had brought them into fairly close contact with each other,

256

their political isolation remained complete. To the Yellow River
people the territory around the Yangtsze River was a jungle inhabited by incoherent savages who had strange customs and knew no
written language. They were contemptuously referred to as barbarians and no attention was paid to them until they grew strong
enough to send their soldiers across the borders in successful raids.
The other barbarian state of Wu on the Lower Yangtsze had gone
through a similar period of growth and development with the result
that at this time the existence of the cultured Yellow River states
was threatened by the semi-barbarian states of the Yangtsze. That
this menace did not develop any more rapidly was due to the
rather frequent battles between Chu and Wu whose jealousies of
each other delayed and ultimately prevented the conquest of the
feudal states which it appears that either of them might easily have
accomplished.

The earlier rulers of Chu accepted the distinction of barbarism
with healthy good humour. 'I am only a barbarian savage and do
not concern myself with Chinese titles,' said one of them who
boasted that the founder of his family had been suckled by a tigress.
It was about the time he made this remark that the duke of one
of the feudal states sent two diplomatic envoys to him and he, in
excessive humour, proposed to his ministers that they castrate one
of the envoys and make a palace eunuch out of him; and cut the
feet off the other thus making him a dwarf who could be used as
a slave to open the palace doors. This would at once show his
robust barbarian contempt for the little princeling whom the
envoys represented, and provide him with the enjoyment of a good
practical joke during the entire lifetime of the two victims. The
ministers, while admitting the intriguing possibilities of the idea,
dissuaded him from it, on the grounds that it would cause dangerous complications and take a lot of difficult explaining to the
princes of the feudal states who had different ideas about the lati-
tude allowable in practical jokes.

With each generation the cultured states on the Yellow River
grew weaker whilst barbarian states on the Yangtsze grew stronger
and about a century before Master Kung's birth Chu had begun a
consistently successful programme of annexing the petty civilised
states located directly to the north of the middle Yangtsze. The
Chu rulers as well as their ministers were not sophisticated enough

257

to indulge in the intrigues, stratagems and diplomatic deceptions of their highly cultivated neighbours, but their bearded warriors were numerous and fierce and accomplished more by force of arms than the orthodox states could accomplish by means of their ritual, their ceremonies, and their cunning diplomacy. For a long time these aggressions were confined to the small buffer states placed like pawns on the extreme southern fringe of Chow domains, and did not materially affect the more important feudal states. As they progressed from the barbarous to the semi-barbarous, then to the half-civilised state, the Chu rulers grew socially and politically ambitious and made vain attempts to attain treatment on the basis of political equality with the orthodox states. While in their jungle strongholds they were far more secure from interference than the strongest of the feudal states they were willing to sacrifice some of this independence for the privilege of being admitted to membership in this exclusive and aristocratic family. They made no progress in these ambitions. While the Chu rulers, in the pride of their sovereignty and power called themselves kings, the feudal states patronisingly referred to them as viscounts, placing them on a scale lower than that of barons. Finally, with their rather easy conquests and growing appreciation of the weakness of the entire Chow political machine, Chu began to entertain imperial ambitions, and pushed the conquest of adjoining states even more vigorously than before, attacking the large as well as the small and gradually coming to take an active part in feudal politics. It was while engaged on one of these military expeditions with a political object in view that the King of Chu camped near where Master Kung and his disciples were staying. One reason for the continued military success of the Chu rulers lay in the fact that they were lovers of war for the game's sake and fought their own battles instead of leaving the conduct of military strategy to underlings who might be intimidated or bribed.

Learning that the famous philosopher was in his neighbourhood, the king sent him an invitation and Master Kung started at once to pay a visit to the ruler who, though a barbarian, might be made the vehicle for carrying out reforms. Invitations like this from a sovereign to a man who was a scholar and former minister meant only one thing, that it was a ceremonial preface to an invitation to join his ministry. It may have been possible that Master Kung had been hoping for this opportunity for he had remained several years in this unpromising neighbourhood for no apparent reason.

There were plenty of spies in all the camps and courts and it was only a matter of a few hours before the politicians of the two small neighbouring states knew of the negotiations that were in progress which might result in Master Kung joining the official family of the King of Chu. The prospect of the scholar-politician putting the weight of his talents into the balance with this great barbarian military state threw terror into the ranks of the local dignitaries. Master Kung had for several years been trying to give their rulers his services and as had happened in many other places the ministers had seen to it that he did not receive an appointment and was kept safely in the background where he had spent his time leading his disciples in studies which included a careful analysis of local politics with all of its manifold and corrupt ramifications. The prospect of his employment by this rival military power introduced an entirely new factor into the situation and brought forth new and undreamed-of complications. The officials of Chu, while they had abilities at military strategy, were simpletons at diplomacy, and it had been an easy matter for ministers of the small neighbouring states to throw dust in their eyes. With the help of this Lu scholar as a councillor Chu would be able to win diplomatic as well as military victories. There was the further possibility that his activities as a minister would lead to the exposure of some of the political trickeries they had been indulging in. The most practical bit of diplomacy the Chu ministers had learned was that by promises to prevent or delay threatened attacks it was possible to extort rich bribes from the small states and this had led to the development of a highly-profitable system of blackmail in which the ministers of Chu profited most but the ministers of all the small states who acted as go-betweens shared in a lesser degree. The officials of the two petty states who were most concerned forgot their own rivalries for the time and held a conference at which the following statement of facts was agreed to:

'This scholar from Lu is without doubt considered by many to be a sage and whether he is or not, he is in any event a very troublesome fellow. He has many criticisms to offer concerning the faults of the feudal princes and especially of the conduct of their ministers such as our humble selves. Now he has been living for almost three years in the neighbourhood of our two states and is thoroughly familiar with everything that has been going on including many things that were attended to in strict secrecy and should never have been disclosed. Many of our acts have not been in accordance with Mr. Kung's fancy ideas as to how affairs should be conducted. Chu is a large and powerful state and now its barbarian ruler extends an invitation to the Lu philosopher. If this garrulous amateur obtains influence in Chu, he will have an audience for his theories will probably tattle about past events which do not concern him and conditions will not be very pleasant for us dignitaries. We must at all odds prevent his becoming an official of Chu.'

To circumvent this threatened danger required instant action for Master Kung was even then preparing to set out to pay his visit to the military camp which was the headquarters of the king. The problem faced by the scheming ministers was further complicated by the fact that the visit of the king to this part of the country was a friendly one, for he had left his capital and established his camp here in order to defend one of these two small states against the aggressions of the other growing Yangtsze River powers, the state of Wu. To openly affront this invited and powerful guest would have been a proceeding fraught with rather dangerous consequences. They could not as a result employ the soldiers who were at their command for their identity would possibly come to the knowledge of the king and bring about reprisals and troublesome diplomatic complications. Whatever they did would have to be done under cover of a secrecy so complete as to defy detection but they were adepts at such clandestine stratagems. The dignitaries got together covertly and employed a band of their own servants who under pledge of secrecy as to their own identity surrounded Master Kung and his disciples in a wild and desolate part of the country. They not only cut off the progress of Master Kung toward the royal camp but with unnecessary and cruel zeal stopped all their supplies of food. The bitterness with which the disciples complained about this hardship would indicate that though they had travelled for years in many parts of the country and under varying conditions they had never missed regular meal hours. During the days they were detained by the bullies they had no cooked food, and existed on what wild berries and other forest food they could find. Those who have lived in China know the supreme importance of food

Master Kung and his disciples surrounded by hired bullies who prevented his visit to the King of Chu.

provided at customary intervals and can appreciate the fact that unless these ancient progenitors of the Chinese race were of hardier stuff than their present-day descendants, their suffering must have been intense. No other people can endure pain and sorrow more stoically or a fast less cheerfully. Chinese commentators have recognised this and have been outspoken in their admiration for the Master in that he could exist on a diet of wild berries and other raw food for a week and still keep his temper and maintain his philosophic calm. Like the capable captain of a ship which is in difficulties, he did not allow the routine duties to be disturbed. He continued with his lessons, played his lute and sang his ballads as if they were comfortably housed and the food bowls were full of hot cabbage and barley. The hungry disciples were not so philosophic and Tze Loo, who had taken his Master to task on many previous occasions, acted as spokesman for the other disciples, all of whom were much younger. His speech had the churlish and complaining tone of the hungry man who feels that he has been deprived of his food through no fault of his own and is looking for someone on whom he can place the blame for his discomfort.

'I have learned,' said Tze Loo, quoting from Master Kung's own words, 'that providence will bestow blessings on those who act rightly and punish wrong-doers accordingly. Why is it that you are still living in retirement, in spite of your high standard of moral behaviour and the years you have devoted to learning?'

Coming from a disciple to his master, this was a rather rude speech and under other circumstances Master Kung would doubtless have answered him and sent him on his way with the kind of rebuke he could administer so cuttingly. But to him, his disciples no matter what their age, were always children, and when they were in difficulties he treated them with the kindness and sympathy of an outwardly stern but inwardly indulgent father. Instead of rebuking Tze Loo he delivered one of the longest speeches he is ever recorded to have made and for the first time expressed his scepticism and hinted at the fallacy in his fairy-tale theory of the ultimate triumph of virtue over wrong.

'You do not realise the situation,' he said, 'and I will tell you why.

'Do you believe that the talents of a man of knowledge are sure to be used by the ruler of his country? If that were true, then why have so many wise statesmen been subjected to cruel punishments and heart-breaking disappointments?

'Do you believe that a loyal man will always be trusted by his ruler? Then why have good and brave men been executed simply because of their loyalty?

'Do you believe that a statesman who dissuades his ruler from doing a wrong thing should win the trust of his sovereign? Then remember the able and loyal statesman whose head was recently cut off and displayed at the Soochow city gate.

'From these and many other examples it is definitely made known that whether or not a scholar has an opportunity to serve his ruler depends, not on himself alone, but on the time in which he lives. As for the natural talent of a man, that is an endowment from heaven. To be a gentleman one has only to be well-versed in learning and serious-minded in thought. Do not concern yourself about the good fortune or the distress that may befall him. Before I was born there were many men of scholarship and virtue who were destined, as I may be, to live and die in obscurity.

'We find parallels for this in nature. Take a plant for example. You know that orchids grow in the deep forests where their beautiful blooms give off a rich and marvellous fragrance, though few people ever go to the forests to enjoy it. In the same way, when a gentleman becomes an accomplished scholar, it is not because fortune and honour are his main objects. He is not looking for material rewards and only depends on the satisfaction of scholarship to safeguard himself against distress and worry. In a word, no misfortune can belittle a man of learning. He will neither be distressed nor beguiled by the temporary vicissitudes of fortunes or worldly affairs. We are now threatened by hunger but this is predestined. With our learning and our virtue as weapons against adversity, we have only to wait for the right time to come. History shows us that many who have swallowed the bitter pill of defeat have by perseverance and determination turned defeat into victory.'

Following this lecture there was no more dissension on the part of the disciples and they soon escaped from their predicament. One of the prisoners, Tze Kung, managed to elude the cordon of guards, gained the presence of the King of Chu and laid the situation before him. The king promptly dispatched some soldiers who sent the bullies flying and so the little band was released.

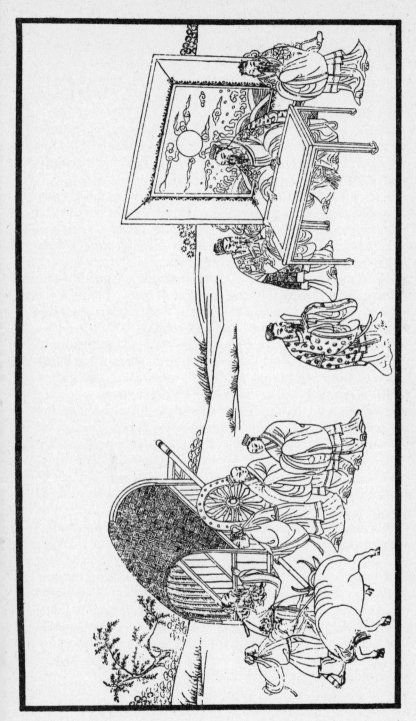

His principal minister dissuaded the King of Chu from his proposed appointment of Master Kung to high position.

As matters turned out the frightened dignitaries of the two small states had worried themselves without cause and by their crude stratagem had given Master Kung and his disciples quite a lot of unnecessary discomfort, for the king's plan to employ the philosopher was foredoomed to failure without the aid of their clumsy interference. The Chu statesmen were just as anxious as they were to keep this fussy reformer out of an official position where he might be counted on to upset precedents and make trouble for unprincipled politicians. The release of Master Kung and his followers brought matters to a head, for the King of Chu announced to his ministers his plan, which was to induce the Lu scholar to become a permanent resident and official of his state by giving him a fief of territory consisting of about 700 square miles. Since most of his domain was mountainous a grant of this area was not so rich as it might appear to be though generous enough by any calculation. The Chu ministers were aghast at the idea of a princely gift like this which would settle the scholar and his followers on them definitely and permanently and they set about to defeat the plan. This presented some difficulties. The power of the King of Chu had not been attenuated by the usurpations of powerful barons, great families and clever ministers, as was the case with the petty feudal rulers and threats would have no weight with him. The only way in which he could be dissuaded from this project was by clever argument. One of his ministers proved equal to the occasion. He said to the king:

'Among the ambassadors whom you send to the princes, is there any, Your Majesty, who is the equal of Tze Kung, the disciple of the scholar who visited you regarding his release from capture?'

The king was compelled to agree with the minister's self-deprecatory comparison of the abilities of himself and his fellow-statesman. The wily politician was quick to follow up this advantage.

'Then consider, Majesty, the abilities of his other followers! Is there among Your Majesty's counsellors any who is the equal of the youthful but grey-headed Yen Hui? Is there among Your Majesty's generals any who is the equal of the brave Tze Loo? Is there among Your Majesty's officials any who is the equal of Tsai Yu? all of whom without pay and without hope of reward faithfully serve Master Kung?'

The king answered in the negative for he had no illusions

regarding the abilities of his own uncultured and poorly-trained officials. The minister then pressed his point to a decisive conclusion. In his speech, he of course did not forget that he was speaking to his own sovereign and so its text was full of sly allusions which concealed its bluntness but stripped of its diplomatic subterfuges the plain purport of the message was as follows:

'The original ancestor of the house of Chu started as an unimportant land-owner with a fief of about fifty square miles and this has been extended until it encompasses mighty rivers and great mountains and covers thousands of square miles. But the expansion has not been by methods which would meet the approval of this fellow Kung, who is very old-fashioned in his ideas and is always holding up as an example the visionary and altruistic ideas of the old dead rulers of past dynasties. If Your Majesty should appoint him he would insist on his policies being carried out and how then would it be possible for the kingdom of Chu to continue its present successful methods of expansion, proud and prosperous, from generation to generation, over many more thousands of square miles? No! This ambitious fellow would stop your present progress and sap the strength of Chu for his own personal benefit! Remember that King Wen in Fen and Kung Wu in Hao (referring to two ancient rulers) were originally princes with fiefs but a fraction the size of the territory you propose giving to this man from Lu, and yet they dominated their neighbours and finally became rulers of the whole world. If Mr. Kung receives this fief on which he can rely, his able disciples will become his ministers, he will have a superb political organisation, much better, by Your Majesty's own admission, than any Your Majesty now possesses, and there will be no way to quench the fires of his ambition or to hinder his progress. No, to use his services in any way will not redound to the good fortunes of the Kingdom of Chu.'

The king was convinced and abandoned the idea for the time being. The proposal never came up again for a few months later the king died while still in military camp.

The court of Chu, like the more pretentious ducal courts farther north boasted a court fool, whose wit and persiflage would in idle moments relieve the tedium of the king and his courtiers. This jester was a unique personage, for he was a scholar of great talent and attainments, a native of Chu, who feigned madness in order to

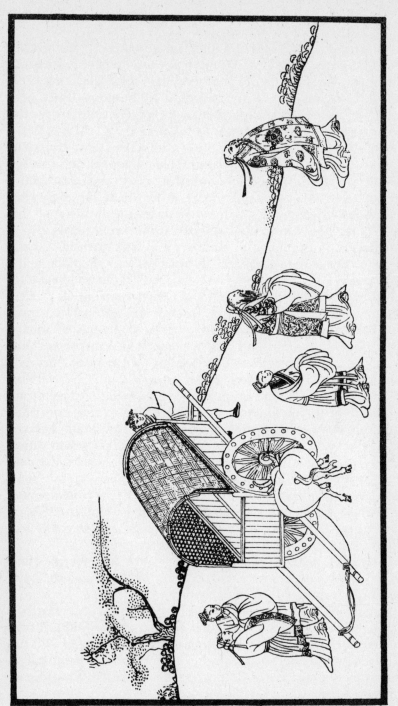

The court fool of the state of Chu warned Master Kung against taking office.

avoid the king's importunities to enter public office just as other men of high character became hermits or recluses for similar reasons. While Master Kung was still tarrying in the neighbourhood of the Chu court the fool came near his carriage singing:

> O, phoenix bird of ancient fame,
> What present virtues can you claim?
> The past is gone beyond recall,
> What may the future have in thrall?
> Peril waits those in princes' pay.
> Forsake your vain and futile way.

Master Kung alighted from his carriage and wanted to converse with the jester but the fool had delivered his message and fled. Disappointed and disillusioned again he departed with his disciples for their one hospitable haven of refuge, the state of Wei.

CHAPTER XVII

*Master Kung's theories of government and his
attempts to reform the world aroused the opposition
of some and the derision of others who sought to make
him ridiculous by exaggerating his theories to the
point of absurdity inventing the story of the lad who
was able to confound the Master's arguments.*

WHILE he was constantly surrounded by a crowd of disciples
whose adulation almost amounted to worship and while many
of the common people sang rude but heartfelt songs in his praise,
it is not to be supposed that Master Kung was universally admired
as a man, or that his scholarly and highly moral teachings were held
in anything like universal respect. As a matter of fact, during his
entire lifetime, he was the subject of criticism and attack by very
active and capable enemies, mostly made up of the educated classes.
While not exactly an hereditary guild, most of the scholars were
sons and grandsons of scholars and they looked on themselves as
persons of superior breeding as well as superior attainments. No
matter how sound his scholarship might be, Master Kung was, after
all, to them, only the son of a poor common soldier. They ignored
the existence of his eminent ancestors and looked on him as an interloper, someone who did not belong to their exclusive circle. His
policies, involving as they did certain fundamental readjustments
in the relationships between different classes of society, they
denounced as vain and visionary. His success as an administrator
in Lu convinced none of them that he would really be able to accomplish the nation-wide reforms he talked so much about and only
added to the energy and bitterness of their attacks. The strength
and effectiveness of their opposition is shown by the fact that even
after the outstanding success he had achieved in the administration
of the state of Lu, he never succeeded in securing another opportunity to serve the state. Many of the rebuffs he received were

administered by the princes, but they had been instigated by the jealousy and envy of the scholars.

When the parsimonious old Yen Yang, ambitious minister of the state of Tsi, by his sophisticated objections, put an end to Duke Ling's plans for Master Kung's employment, he was voicing very accurately and convincingly the objections held by the orthodox contemporary scholars to the pretentions of this brilliant upstart, and they never changed their opinions. In order to protect their own positions from this interloper, it was necessary that the scholar from Lu be discredited and this they endeavoured to bring about by the clever expedient of exaggerating his well-known ideas to the point of absurdity, just as Yen Yang had done. To the scheming, self-seeking, and utterly conscienceless politicians who held the balance of power in most, if not all, of the states, Master Kung's views on what he held to be necessary social and political reforms were visionary and absurd to the point of being humorously ridiculous. The scholars were not the only ones who thought the philosopher with his highly-developed idealism was carrying things too far and overlooking the practical realities of life. Even the farmers, with an eye to the practical exigencies of stock raising, must have enjoyed many a ribald laugh over the regulation that cattle on the way to market should not be watered.

During the lifetime of Master Kung there is said to have lived a very precocious youth, who according to tradition, was, at the age of seven, profoundly versed in the ceremonies and rituals and a past master in the arts of disputation. Probably the shadow of such a boy did live, although only his doubtful name is recorded in history and no one ever set down the date of his birth or of his death. But even the rumour of his existence was enough to give the old orthodox scholars an inspiration, and so as a bit of a literary diversion they created the satiric fiction of a precocious youth who while a mere infant was clever enough to confound the theories of the scholar of Lu and show him up in a ridiculous light. The name of the author of this fiction is unknown, and for the very good reason that the clever satire was not the work of one man or of one year but was added to and improved upon from time to time as various wits thought of new quips which would round out and complete the narrative.

One day, according to the story of the precocious youth, Master

Kung, followed by his disciples, went out to travel through the country and came across several children at their sports; among them was a youngster of seven who did not join in with the other children. Master Kung, stopping his carriage, asked him:

'Why is it that you alone do not play?'

'All play is without any profit,' the lad replied. 'One's clothes get torn, and they are not easily mended; by playing I disgrace those above me including my father and mother; among those below me, even to the lowest, play results in fighting and altercation; with so much toil and no reward, how can idle amusement be considered a good business? It is for these reasons that I do not play.' Then turning his head, he began building a toy city wall out of pieces of tile.

'Why do you not take your tiles out of the way of my carriage?' said Master Kung, reproving him.

'From ancient times till now,' the boy replied, 'it has always been considered proper for a carriage to turn out for a city, and not for a city wall to be torn down to make way for a carriage.' Master Kung was so impressed by these precocious replies that he got out of his carriage to talk further with this remarkable boy.

'You are still young in years, how does it happen that you are so quick in your answers?'

'A human being at the age of three years, discriminates between his father and his mother,' replied the lad. 'A hare, three days after it is born, runs over the ground and hides in furrows of the fields; fish, three days after their birth, wander far from home in rivers and lakes; what heaven thus produces naturally, how can it be called unusual?'

'In what village and neighbourhood do you reside, what is your surname and name, and what your nickname?'

'I live in a mean village and in an insignificant land; my surname is Hiang, my name is Toh and as yet I am too young to have a nickname.'

Master Kung according to the apocryphal narrative saw here an exceptional opportunity to add to the galaxy of talent comprised in his band of disciples and said:

'I would like to have you come and travel with me; what do you think of the idea?'

'A stern father is at home, whom I am bound to serve,' the youth

replied. 'An affectionate mother is there whom it is my duty to protect and cherish; a worthy elder brother is at home, whom it is
proper for me to obey, with a tender young brother whom I must
instruct; and an intelligent teacher is there from whom I am
required to learn. How under these circumstances can I have
leisure to go travelling idly about with you?'

'I have in my carriage thirty-two chessmen; what do you say to
having a game together?' said Master Kung, thinking to tempt him.
This paragon of a youth was proof against anything of this kind
and said rebukingly:

'If the king loves gaming, the country will not be well governed;
if the nobles love play, the progress of the states will be impeded; if
scholars love idle diversions, learning and research will be lost and
thrown by the wayside; if the lower classes are fond of gambling,
they will fail utterly in the support of their families; if servants and
slaves love to game, they will get to quarrelling and fighting; if
farmers love it, they miss the time for ploughing and sowing; for
these reasons I shall not play with you.'

Master Kung, according to the story, was by this time even more
impressed with the character and talents of the lad and even more
anxious to make a disciple of him, so his next proposal was of a very
different nature for he said:

'I wish to have you go with me, so that we, by our joint efforts, may
solve the problems which are distressing the people and fully
equalise the country, what do you think of this?'

'The country cannot be equalised,' replied the boy emphatically.
'There are high hills, there are lakes and rivers; either there are
princes and nobles, or there are slaves and servants. If the high hills
be levelled, the birds and beasts will have no resort; if the rivers
and lakes be filled up, the fishes and the turtles will have nowhere
to go; do away with kings and nobles, and the common people will
have much dispute about right and wrong; obliterate slaves and
who will there be to serve the prince! If the country be so vast and
unsettled how can it be equalised?'

Master Kung, trying to trip him up asked: 'Can you tell, under
the whole sky, what fire has no smoke, what water no fish; what hill
has no stones, what tree no branches; what man has no wife; what
woman no husband; what cow has no calf; what mare no colt; what
cock has no hen; what hen no cock; what constitutes an excellent

man; and what an inferior man; what is that which has not enough, and that which has an overplus; what city is without a market, and who is the man without a name?'

'A glow-worm's fire has no smoke,' said the lad, 'and well-water no fish; a mound of earth has no stones, and a rotten tree no branches; genii have no wives, and fairies no husbands; earthenware cows have no calves, nor wooden mares any colts; lonely cocks have no hens, and widowed hens no cocks; he who is worthy is an excellent man, and a fool is an inferior man; a winter's day is not long enough, and a summer's day is too long; the imperial city has no market, and little folks have no name.'

Master Kung inquiring said: 'Do you know what are the connecting bonds between heaven and earth, and what is the beginning and ending of the dual powers! What is left, and what is right; what is out, and what is in; who is father, and who is mother; who is husband, and who is wife? Do you know where the wind comes from, and from whence the rain? From whence the clouds issue, and the dew arises? And for how many tens of thousands of miles the sky and earth go parallel?'

The youth answering said: 'Nine multiplied nine times makes eighty-one, which mystic figure is the controlling bond of heaven and earth; eight multiplied by nine makes seventy-two, the beginning and the end of the dual powers. Heaven is father, and earth is mother; the sun is husband, and the moon is wife; east is left, and west is right; without is out, and inside is in; the winds come from the heavens, and the rains proceed from wastes and wilds; the clouds issue from the hills, and the dew rises from the ground. Sky and earth go parallel for ten thousand times ten thousand miles, and the four points of the compass have each their station.'

'Which do you say is the nearest relation, father and mother, or husband and wife?'

'One's parents are near; husband and wife are not so near.'

'While husband and wife are alive, they sleep under the same coverlet; when they are dead they lie in the same grave; how then can you say that they are not near?'

'A man without a wife is like a carriage without a wheel; if there be no wheel another one is made, for he can doubtless get a new one; so, if one's wife die, he seeks again, for he also can obtain a new one,' the boy replied. 'The daughter of a worthy family must certainly marry an honourable husband; a house having ten rooms always has a plate and a ridgepole; three windows and six lattices do not give the light of a single door; the whole host of stars with all their sparkling brilliancy do not equal the splendour of the solitary moon: the affection of a father and mother – alas, if it be once lost!'

Master Kung, sighing, said: 'How clever! how worthy!'

'You have just been giving me questions,' said the youngster, 'which I have answered one by one; I now wish to seek information; will the teacher in one sentence afford me some plain instruction? I shall be much gratified if my request be not rejected. Why is it that mallad and duck are able to swim; how is it that wild geese and cranes sing; and why are firs and pines green through the winter?'

'Mallard and duck can swim because their feet are broad,' Master Kung replied. 'Wild geese and cranes can sing because they have long necks; firs and pines remain green throughout the winter because they have strong hearts.'

'Not so,' the youth rejoined. 'Fishes and turtles can swim, is it because their feet are broad? Frogs and toads can sing; is it because their necks are long? The green bamboo keeps fresh in winter, is it on account of its strong heart?'

Again interrogating, he said: 'How many stars are there altogether in the sky?'

Master Kung replied: 'If you wish to ask questions, inquire about the earth; how can we converse about the sky with certainty?'

'Then how many houses in all are there on the earth?'

'Come, come, now,' the sage answered. 'Speak about something that's before our eyes; why must you converse about heaven and earth?'

The lad resumed. 'Well, to speak about what's before our eyes – how many hairs are there in your eyebrows?'

Master Kung smiled, but did not answer. He then got into his carriage and rode away.

Most of the opposition to Master Kung was secretly expressed and the jokes told at his expense were many, the story of the precocious boy being an elaboration of these quips. Most of them never reached his ears, but with his long and completely futile search for employment, many outside the exclusive class of scholars began to laugh at him more or less openly. They belonged to that perverse class which finds high humour in the futile endeavours of a fellow-man. With each fresh rebuff by princes or powerful ministers there were new jokes, and the wits of the day vied with each other in concocting stories which would make Master Kung appear in a ludicrous light. One day an old man who was full of these stories met Master Kung face to face and could not resist the temptation to take a verbal pot shot at him. Calling him familiarly by his first name, he asked:

'How is it that you manage to keep roosting about? Isn't it only because you are a glib and insinuating talker?'

Master Kung did not lose his temper, or if he did lose it, managed to keep his usual philosophical calm and made a reply which brought the conversation to a close without an opportunity for any further rudeness.

There were others who while reposing full faith in Master Kung's ability and sincerity did not think he would accomplish anything while pursuing his unbending policy. No doubt many of them thought of him as did the gatekeeper who inquired of one of the disciples:

'Is not your master the man who keeps on trying to accomplish what he knows to be impossible?'

Some blamed him for refusal to compromise with conditions and be satisfied with small accomplishments. These were principally the common people, who were not interested in grandiose schemes for the regeneration of the country but were suffering from cruel oppressions which Master Kung, as an official in a minor capacity could and would relieve. One day he was playing the musical stones when a man carrying a basket of weeds paused by his door to listen. The man, of course, knew the identity of the musician but after the fashion of the time worded his criticism so that it would appear to be directed toward an unknown person.

'The one who strikes the musical stone,' he said, 'is one with a very serious purpose in life. But why is he so obstinate? If no one knows the sufferings of the common people and no one will help us, let us give up and have done with it.'

In his years of wandering from state to state, Master Kung had received a great many rebuffs and very little encouragement and had no illusions as to the opinion in which he was held by his fellow-countrymen. He was too great to be affected by either praise or censure and plodded on the undeviating course he had set for himself. The flattery of his disciples, the rebuffs of the princes, the deceit and slander of the jealous scholars, the adulation of the common people, the petty treachery of the politicians were all without any effect on him. A disciple told him one day that a curious duke had made some inquiries about him and the Master said:

'Why did you not reply: he is a man who constantly studies to learn the truth, without ever growing weary at the task; who instructs mankind without becoming disgusted with ignorance and stupidity, whose zeal for self-improvement is such that he neglects his food, whose happiness in this pursuit is so great that he forgets all care, and so does not observe the gradual approach of old age.'

On one of their many pilgrimages the Master and his disciples approached a river it was necessary to cross and in a field near by he observed two men who were obviously not peasants hard at work weeding and hoeing. The ever-faithful disciple Tze Loo was sent to inquire about the ford and one of the recluses inquired:

'Who is that man sitting in the chariot?'

'That is Mr. Kung,' replied the disciple.

'Is it the Mr. Kung of Lu?'

'Yes.'

'And who are you?'

'I am Tze Loo.'

'Are you one of the disciples of Mr. Kung?'

'Yes,' answered Tze Loo, and the recluse continued:

'Disorder, like an uncontrollable flood, deluges the whole world, and who is there who can change it for you? Would it not be better for you, instead of following a master who merely withdraws first from this one and then from that one, to follow one, who, like myself and my companion, withdraws from the world entirely?'

He did not wait for an answer but took up his hoe and continued digging. Tze Loo returned to the chariot and reported his conversation. Master Kung said with a sigh:

'I cannot follow their example for it is impossible for me to associate with birds and beasts as if they were the same as us. If I do not associate with people – with mankind – with whom shall I associate? If order and right principles prevailed throughout the world there would be no reason, of course, for me to attempt to change anything.'

These encounters with hermits and recluses were by no means

uncommon. With the steady decline in civilisation, the constantly growing anarchy of the country, more and more of the followers of Lao Tze, the old mystic Master Kung had met on his visit to Loyang, had retired to rustic retreats and lost all interests in worldly affairs. One day Tze Loo met an old man carrying a basket and asked:

'Have you seen my Master?'

The old man looked at the scholar with some contempt and said:

'The muscles on your four limbs show that you are not fit to do any useful work. Your hands show that you cannot distinguish between the five kinds of grain. What does it matter who your master is or where he is?'

Master Kung accepted rebuffs and criticisms with the hearty good humour which had characterised him on the occasion that a country-man described him as looking like 'a lost dog in a house of mourning'. He was passing through a small side-street when a wit of the neighbourhood shouted for the benefit of all who might hear:

'Great is Master Kung, the philosopher! But in spite of his wide learning, he has not a single accomplishment that will bring him fame!' Master Kung heard this, as had been intended, and laughingly said to his disciples:

'What shall I take up in order to gain fame? Shall I take up archery or shall I take up charioteering? I have it! I will take up charioteering!'

Master Kung was even-tempered under criticisms, but he would not tolerate bores. A feeble-minded and unmannerly old acquaintance was always bothering him with stupid suggestions about religion, a subject the Master would never discuss. One day the old man was squatting on his haunches like a barbarian, waiting for Master Kung to approach so that he could pop a few more foolish questions at him. The latter did not give him an opportunity to start a conversation but as soon as he came up with him said:

'In youth not humble as befits a junior; in manhood doing nothing worthy to be handed down; and living on to a useless old age; this is to be a pest.' With this he hit the old man on the shank with his staff and walked away.

When his disciples inquired about the location of a ford, the hermit who was cultivating the field said:
'Master Kung knows the ford.'

CHAPTER XVIII

An attempt to murder Madam Nan Tze led to the exile of her stepson and the appointment of his son to the ducal succession. Master Kung and Yang Hoo played their independent parts in the affairs of the state of Wei.

A T least one familiar face was missing when Master Kung returned to Wei after his long stay near the Yangtsze River, for his old friend the duke had died, after a weak and inglorious reign of more than forty years, leaving to his state a heritage of confusion and disorder. His death brought to a head the political troubles which had their origin in his own weakness and had bred and multiplied through the years of his tenure of the ducal office. He had come to the throne at the age of five, his nursery and school-room had been the inner-court and his governesses and tutors were concubines and eunuchs. When he married the beautiful Madam Nan Tze, she soon dominated his thoughts and actions so that he had always been under inner-court influence with all the weakness, intrigue and wickedness that a harem environment implies. His loyal and capable ministers were restive under this interference by concubines and eunuchs and were looking for an opportunity to throw it off, which they thought they might do by the selection of a successor. Meanwhile, the plotters of the inner-court had their own ideas as to who should be selected and all had for years eagerly awaited the opportunity which the death of the duke would present. The ducal succession was the richest plum in the political pie of the feudal states and when, as in this case, a duke outlived the span of expectations, schemes for the selection of a successor grew with every year the plotters waited. It seemed to be the case in every feudal state that plots to interfere with the succession to the ducal power multiplied increasingly with each year that an incumbent lived, and the plots in Wei had been hatching forty years, for they had started the day Duke Ling was given the emblems of authority in the place of his crippled elder brother. With the numerous wives, concubines and 'court ladies' and the multiplicity of sons which might quite naturally follow their residence in the inner-court there were plenty of circumstances which gave encouragement to the plotters. The youngest son of the most obscure concubine might, by some turn of fate or by some carefully-planned administration of poison, become the heir. Every concubine with a son warmed her heart with these hopes and every eunuch sought to attach himself to one or more of the possible heirs with a view to the profit which might later come to him.

Madam Nan Tze played a prominent part in the plots as she did in all of the tangled political affairs of the state. If she had given birth to a son the question of a successor to the duke would have been simple, and there would have been no plots, for it is inconceivable that she would have then tolerated any pretentions from the sons of concubines or secondary wives. But she was childless or if she had any children they were unrecorded daughters and she had her own ideas as to who should succeed her husband. In order to make clear her part in some of the important events of the time, it is necessary to set down briefly and in broad outline a rather unsavoury story. At her insistence the duke invited her handsome half-brother from the state of Sung to visit them and he remained as an official employee, being charged with the agreeable duty of welcoming and entertaining official guests. The story that she and this half-brother had indulged in incestuous relations was well known to the gossips of Wei and the odorous speculations which the prolonged visit of the half-brother occasioned may easily be imagined. After he had been there for some time the people began singing ribald songs about them. One song which was supposed to be addressed to the duke had a refrain:

'Now that the heat of your sow has been allayed
Why not send the old boar home?'

The stepson of Madam Nan Tze, who was the legitimate heir to the ducal estate, heard the song being sung by the country people and was so overcome with shame that he decided his stepmother should die. Lacking courage to commit the crime himself, he induced a friend to help him carry out his enterprise and actually perform the murderous act. The details of the plot were very simple. The heir would engage his stepmother in conversation while his friend stood near at hand but back of her with a sharp sword. When the conversation reached an appropriate turn, and Madam Nan Tze's defenceless back was conveniently exposed, the heir was to give a signal and the friend would make the fatal thrust. But the friend was as cowardly as the instigator of the plot, and his courage did not prove equal to the occasion. Three times the signal was given but the would-be assassin stood in his place stupidly with his sword drawn but without the courage to use it. In the meantime Madam Nan Tze grew suspicious at the nervous and purposeless conversation of the heir and then with a glimpse of the sword saw through the plot. She ran from the room to the duke screaming that an attempt had been made to murder her. The duke, who never wavered in his infatuation, comforted her, removed her to a place of safety and took her part in the family feud which followed. The heir was banished, together with all of his followers who could be apprehended. Acquiescence of the ministers, in the banishment of the heir was not due to any moral indignation over his murderous plot but because it afforded one set of partisans a convenient opportunity to get him out of the way. This banishment which, after all, might have been the result of an exaggerated story by Madam Nan Tze, did not necessarily affect the ducal succession, and on the death of the duke the son should have been brought back and enthroned. This would have been the correct procedure even if he had been guilty of the murder of Madam Nan Tze. Some were in favour of this but a stronger party headed by Madam Nan Tze opposed it and when the duke died, his young grandson, the son of the banished heir, ascended the ducal throne and was given the symbols of authority. This had not been accomplished without the conception and abortion of many plots and counterplots in which all the politicians of Wei took a hand and these proved so serious that the funeral ceremony of the duke was delayed several months beyond the time prescribed by strict ceremonial custom. The grandson of the duke was little more than an infant and this circumstance added to the power of Madam Nan Tze and the intriguing ministers.

The name of Yang Hoo has occurred several times in this narrative and it will be recalled that the failure of his ambitious plots and his banishments from Lu preceded by several years the voluntary exile of Master Kung. Like the latter, exile in a strange state did not mean inactivity and did not quench the fires of his ambitions. His movements were shrouded in the obscurity that must necessarily guard the actions of all revolutionists but he appears here and there in various places where he always played a part which was a mixture of heroism and bravado and portrayed his contempt for smug constituted authority as he had done when he took Duke Ting's ceremonial bow with him as a souvenir of his dictatorship of Lu. He was at this time in the state of Tsin, which adjoined Wei on the north, attached to the military establishments of one of the local barons in a capacity which appears to have given him the freedom of individual action which was necessary to a man of his temperament.

There were naturally a great many people in Wei, a few because of the principles involved and more because of political considerations, who disapproved of the irregular way in which the grandson instead of the son had been given the ducal office. A great many of the subjects of the state would doubtless have looked on the successful conclusion of the murderous plot against Madam Nan Tze as a meritorious and public-spirited act and would have seen in it no occasion for banishing the assassin or interfering with the regular succession. Hundreds, or, more probably, thousands entertained these ideas but they held aloof from anything which might compromise and endanger them. Yang Hoo alone took action. He went to the deposed heir's place of exile and secured his approval of a plot whose success would give him his rightful place as the Duke of Wei. It is significant of the tangled state of affairs that the deposed heir should place himself under the protection of an alien and exiled adventurer, because he had no opportunity to entrust his fate to any men of his own state. Acting under instructions from Yang Hoo, the deposed heir put on mourning costume so as to show proper ceremonial grief for the death of his father. He clad some sympathisers from Wei in the same garb and with his own armed guard personally conducted the party across the borders to a town in Wei, where the deposed heir was in a better strategic position to carry out his plans to depose his usurping son. It was thought that with convenient rendezvous his supporters would rally around him. With this brave and generous gesture, Yang Hoo, who was then an old man, disappeared from the pages of history for the plot made no further progress and the deposed heir was never restored. It is interesting, though profitless, to speculate on how the history of the country might have been changed if Master Kung had accepted the first overtures of this man of ability and action, and joined forces with him when the dictator of Lu had asked him to do so.

As can well be imagined the hotchpotch of events which has been described above, together with the existence of many other factors, too detailed and complicated for enumeration here, had left the state of Wei in great confusion, and when Master Kung more or less unexpectedly returned they looked on him as one who had been providentially sent, and who might provide a solution to their problems. A great many of his disciples were now serving as officials of Wei in various minor capacities and they were quite active in promoting any movement which would add to the prestige of their master, give him the official position to which they thought his talents entitled him and which he had been unsuccessfully seeking for so many years. His age and fame would provide the state with the dignity and prestige which was so sadly lacking in the person of the youthful duke and would do a great deal towards quieting the outcry and unrest occasioned by his irregular succession. The officials of Wei remembered his success in circumventing the schemes of Tsi against Lu and thought the same talents might save them from the even more serious aggressions with which they were threatened. The rivalries of the feudal states, which had been acute at the time of Master Kung's birth, had grown in intensity. They were all at each other's throats and at the same time the existence of practically all of them was threatened by the growing power of Chu and Wu the barbarian Yangtsze River states. They were in such a panic that even the jealous scholars who under ordinary circumstances would have solidly opposed any plan for his employment were now ready to throw on his capable shoulders the problems which staggered them. It appears that even before Master Kung's arrival there was news of his impending visit and it had already been decided to ask him to serve the state.

Tze Loo, the impetuous and outspoken disciple whose name

occurs so frequently in any discussion of Master Kung, had now been in the service of the young duke for some time and probably took a very active part in promoting the appointment of the Master. He presumed that as the latter had made no objection to his serving the duke, he would not object to service himself. He anticipated this appointment and asked the Master what problem he would first take up when called upon to take charge of the affairs of Wei. The Master replied that nothing could be of greater importance than the correct use of the names by which everyone was called, from the ruler to the lowest servant. The rectification of the names in use in Wei would he said be his first undertaking. Tze Loo did not see the meaning behind this cryptic remark and presumed that the Master had grown conservative and was proposing to discuss some unimportant rules of decorum instead of the very serious problems of the state and, with his usual blunt frankness told him so.

'So indeed!' said Tze Loo. 'You are wide of the mark! Why should it be so important to rectify names.'

'How uncultivated you are!' said the Master. 'A superior man, in speaking about something he does not know, shows a cautious reserve.

'If names be not correct, then language is not in accordance with the truth of things. If language be not in accordance with the truth of things, affairs cannot be carried on successfully.

'When affairs cannot be carried on to success, proprieties and music will not flourish. When proprieties and music do not flourish, punishments will not be properly awarded. When punishments are not properly awarded, the people do not know how to move hand or foot.

'Therefore the superior man considers it necessary that the names he uses be spoken appropriately, and that what he speaks be carried out appropriately. What the superior man requires is just that in his words there may be nothing incorrect.'

This was his indirect method of pointing out in a sentence that the irregular ducal succession, together with the usurpation of power on the part of the ministers needed correcting before the confused affairs of the state could be untangled. It also answered the question of whether or not he would serve the duke for he could not do so while the latter was usurping the place of his father and was being referred to by a title which he did not rightfully possess. Master Kung's rectification of names would have relegated him to the position of heir.

What made his attitude at this time all the more inexplicable to his disciple was the fact that after cheerfully and even jovially accepting rebuffs for years, he had recently shown evidences of a complete lack of faith in mankind and in his own destiny. He was now almost seventy years old, had been ill and was reluctantly coming to the conclusion that the brief span of life left to him would not be sufficient to enable him to accomplish anything of importance. In his period of wandering which had now extended over more than a dozen years he had certainly received little encouragement, and the country was measurably nearer to moral ruin and political anarchy than it had been when he first began his teachings. In despair he composed a ballad which he sang to his disciples:

> 'We must climb the hill though the slopes are steep.
> Travel the road though the brambles are deep.
> What seems near at hand retreats on the way.
> And so lengthens our vain labour for another day.
> We must go on although in pain and sorrow,
> And expect no easier route to-morrow.
> There stands Tai Shan, a majestic height,
> Our symbol of wisdom, virtue and right.
> There is no axe to cut the thorns which multiply apace,
> When the way is blocked beyond recall, where will the
>   traveller face?
> Alas for a black despair so deep,
> That all one can do is sigh and weep.'

'My doctrines make no headway,' he declared. 'I will get on a raft and float about on the sea.'

Again he said:

'All is over. I have not yet seen one who could perceive his own faults and inwardly accuse himself.'

On previous occasions he had met the advances of rulers with a certain enthusiasm and had travelled toward any state which appeared to offer any opportunity. Now when office was urged on him he refused to accept it. The Wei statesmen were insistent but he refused to compromise with his principles. Aside from his age and illness he would under no circumstances countenance the illegal and irregular appointment of the young duke in the place of his father, and the only condition under which he could serve the state would be the impossible one that the rightful heir be restored to power. One of the disciples became insistent and asked him why he did not take office and he replied:

'The bird selects the tree; the tree does not select the bird.'

In the midst of their futile negotiations with him, one of the Wei politicians gave him great offence by asking his advice regarding a duel he proposed fighting. Irritated and discouraged beyond measure he ordered his ox-cart yoked and was preparing to resume his wandering when messengers arrived from the state of Lu. He had been waiting for them since he left his native state fourteen years before and he lost no time in hurrying on towards Zigzag Hill.

CHAPTER XIX

A brief résumé of the few facts known concerning the obscure family of Master Kung whose descendants constitute the great Kung clan the oldest and most numerous recorded family on earth.

IF little is said about the family of Master Kung, it is because the meagre facts concerning unimportant lives do not admit of anything but the briefest narrative. Of the nine half-sisters nothing is known beyond the fact of their birth which had proven so embarrassing to their father and led to his consorting with a concubine and then to a second more or less irregular union which resulted in the birth of Master Kung. If any one of them ever met her illustrious half-brother the fact was never recorded in a form permanent enough to survive the ravages of more than two thousand years. It is presumed that the nine girls eventually embraced the anonymity which was the lot of the married woman of China but it appears rather remarkable that none of their descendants ever escaped the obscurity into which they were born. It seems improbable that any of their sons or grandsons ever achieved distinction of any kind. Hundreds of devoted scholars, zealous to add to the glory of Master Kung by recording the achievements of everyone even remotely connected with him, have never found it possible to inscribe a single word about the family of his half-sisters.

The negative record of Master Kung's one son is comprised in a few phrases. One of the disciples, the one who had discouraged human sacrifices by suggesting that his sister-in-law immolate herself on her husband's tomb if she thought such an act necessary and desirable, was curious to learn whether or not there was any partiality shown in the teachings of the Master. He was not the only disciple, who out of his love for the Master, jealously feared that some other might be receiving an advantage in the way of private lessons. If anyone were to be favoured they quite naturally assumed that it would be the son. At a convenient opportunity he asked Carp Primus, the son of Master Kung:

'Have you heard from your father any lessons different from those which the rest of us have heard?'

'No,' replied the son, 'unless it might be the following. He was standing alone once, and I hurried through the hall hoping to avoid him when he saw me and called out: "Have you learned the odes" and on my replying that I had not yet done so he said, "if you do not know the odes you will not be fit to carry on a conversation with a gentleman." With that remark I retired and studied the odes.'

'On another occasion he was, as before, standing in the hall when I hurried by but he saw me and called out: "Have you learned the rules of propriety?" On my admitting that I had not yet done so he said: "If you do not learn the rules of propriety your character cannot be established." These are the only two things I have privately heard from him.'

The disciple was quite well-satisfied with the result of his inquiry and told the others:

'I asked one thing of Master Kung's son and I got three. I have heard about the importance of the odes. I have heard about the rules of propriety. I have also learned that the superior man maintains a distant reserve towards his son.'

On another occasion Master Kung said to his son:

'Give yourself to the study of the ancient songs. The man who has not studied these songs is like one who stands with his face right against the wall. Is this not true?'

Although the son assured his father that he would learn the odes and the rules of propriety there is not only no evidence but no indication that he ever did so. He is numbered among the list of distinguished disciples whose names are enshrined on the memorial tablets of all important Confucian temples, but this was undoubtedly an honour paid to his memory because of his relationship to the sage, for the same reason that old Kung the Tall, centuries after his death was posthumously created a duke and various other members of the Kung family were similarly honoured. While hundreds of young men eagerly placed themselves under the tutelage of Master Kung, his own son never became a genuine disciple and kept out of the father's way as much as possible.

At one of their very rare encounters Master Kung admonished his light-headed son to learn the odes and the rules of propriety.

There was one daughter who was given in marriage to one of the disciples. This was a generous gesture on the part of Master Kung for the man had a shady though unmerited reputation, and Master Kung showed his vindication of the character of the disciple by giving him his own daughter in marriage. It was only one of a number of gestures he made to show that though he was an ardent supporter of the ancient customs he was no blind adherent to the narrow conventional ideas of the day. This disciple had served a term in prison, and though it is not definitely known why he was given this punishment Master Kung was familiar with the circumstances and knew that he had not been guilty of any crime. One legend has it that he fell under suspicion of the authorities because of his knowledge of the language of birds. The imprisonment, in the minds of some of his strict fellow-disciples, was a definite bar to his marriage but Master Kung decreed otherwise and in order definitely to settle the matter gave him his own daughter. He rewarded another disciple by giving him to wife the daughter of his crippled half-brother. A second daughter of his own died before she came to marriageable age. There must have been some kind of a rift between Master Kung and other members of the family for though he had innumerable relatives in Lu not one of them, so far as is known, ever joined his numerous band of followers.

The wife is a figure even more shadowy than that of the son. There are stories that the two were divorced shortly after the return of the scholar from his visit to the Chow capital in Loyang, and one version of the story is that she, in rather unseemly haste, remarried; this time to a less erudite but more companionable husband. The weight of evidence, according to the historians of the Kung family, indicates that there was no actual legal divorce and no second marriage, but it is certain that they lived separate lives and that they probably never saw each other again after Master Kung's visit to Loyang. There was no practical reason why he should procure a divorce, for married life had no charms for him and with a son to carry on the family sacrifices there was no occasion for his taking a second wife. When she died the son mourned her with such excessive grief that Master Kung, for the third time, reprimanded him. He pointed out that to mourn so extravagantly for one parent while the other was still alive was contrary to the rules of propriety which the son had promised to learn and to observe. The son, who was then well past middle age, was obedient to his father's wishes and calmed his expressions of grief. When the son died, the conventional period of mourning was observed by the father but his grief found no necessity for further expression. In the burial of the son he did not err on the side of extravagance for he buried him in a coffin consisting of only one shell of wood instead of the customary two shells. This was not an act of parsimony. He was in straitened circumstances and in order to provide the extra shell it would have been necessary to sell his carriage, a sacrifice which he did not feel justified in making since the carriage was an essential part of his ceremonial equipment as a personage of official rank. This was another example of his indifference to the narrow conventions and opinions of the day, for many fathers impoverished themselves in providing elaborate funerals for their sons, not necessarily because of affection for them but because it was the customary thing to do. The manifestations of grief were quite different when Yen Yuan one of his favourite disciples died for then his usual self-possession deserted him and he grieved so excessively that some of the most outspoken of the surviving disciples remonstrated with him as he had done with his son for grieving so long over the death of his mother. He was quick to show them that there was a difference between the conventional grief prescribed by propriety and the genuine heartfelt grief over the death of a loved one.

'Master, is not your grief excessive?' inquired a punctilious disciple.

'If I do not grieve for this man, then for whom should I grieve?' he replied.

Yen Yuan was the disciple who, when there were fears that he had been killed, said to the Master: 'How would I dare to die while you are still alive.' He was grey-headed when in the early twenties. One of the most faithful and certainly the most brilliant of all of the disciples and he had in spite of his youth a better grasp of the Master's ideas than any of the others. Master Kung who at this time saw that death would probably overtake him before he had been able to carry his work to a successful conclusion looked on Yen Yuan as the one best fitted to carry on his mission. When the disciple died prematurely at the age of thirty-three, he felt that indeed his life had been a failure and cried: 'Alas! Heaven is destroying me!'

Yen Yuan's father begged the Master for an outer coffin for his

'You have split the firewood,' said Master Kung's grandson, 'and I will carry it in.'

son but his request was refused for the same reason as on the death of Carp Primus.

While Master Kung's son, on the evidence available, can only be set down as a light-minded and more or less colourless and valueless personality, the genius of the Kung blood did not perish with him. On the death of the son, his wife married again and Master Kung adopted his young grandson, who became the youngest of his followers. The grandson was entrusted by the sage with carrying out one of the most important of his literary legacies and wrote *The Doctrine of the Mean* which is one of the Chinese classics. The sage's declining years were cheered by the evident scholarship of the young man and his promise to carry on his work. The grandson was only a small boy when he learned of Master Kung's ambition to perpetuate his teachings and like a filial son he volunteered to carry on the work.

'You have split the firewood,' he said, 'and I will carry it in.'

For three generations there had been but one son and it appeared more than probable that the ancestral line of Kung the Tall would die out. But on the contrary with the marriage of the grandson the descendants of this attenuated line prospered and multiplied like fertile mustard-seeds and are now numbered by the tens of thousands. Without hope of reward or dignities which they might secure because of their descent, but solely out of respect and veneration for their great ancestor the descendants of Master Kung have proudly recorded their names in the voluminous records of the great Kung family. In the twenty-four centuries which have passed since the birth of the son of Kung the Tall the genealogy of thousands of royal or noble families has been lost or obscured. Even in China, where the family and family descent is of supreme importance it is impossible to trace the collateral descendants of comparatively recent emperors. But the Kung clan is intact and its roster fairly complete. Descent from the great sage is the only requirement, for membership-rolls have included many scholars, statesmen, prosperous merchants, and petty shopkeepers, farmers and wheelbarrow coolies. Though they have engaged in many occupations it is said that none has ever become a Buddhist priest.

CHAPTER XX

*The death of Baron Huan led to the employment of
one of Master Kung's disciples and indirectly to the
recall of the philosopher to his native state but after
the lapse of several disappointing years and on his
return he did not resume his assistance to the government of the state as everyone had expected him to do.*

FOR two years after the arrival of the dancing girls had caused
Master Kung to resign his position and leave his native state,
there was increasing evidence that heaven had ceased to exert a
benign influence over the destinies of the state of Lu. With his
infatuation for the Tsi courtesans and horses Duke Ting sunk to
even lower depths of sensuality and indolence and left the government of the state in the incapable hands of Baron Huan. The stratagem by which the Tsi politicians had planned to weaken the
rival state by the gifts of the girls and horses had worked even
better than they could possibly have anticipated for soon after
Master Kung's departure, Lu was in a position where it no longer
had the respect of its neighbouring states but would have fallen an
easy prey to any form of aggression. That it was allowed to exist
in comparative peace was due entirely to the fact that Tsi and the
other principalities were all involved in internal troubles of one
kind or another, and so had matters of more immediate importance
to occupy their attention. The deaths of several of the feudal rulers
had precipitated the usual scramble for power which might be
gained through a hand in the selection of successors and the plotters in Tsi, Wei, Sung and Tsin were busier on questionable enterprises of this kind than they had been for several generations.
There was no acknowledged leader among the states and the
strongest among them were striving for supremacy by aggressions
against the weaker ones.

The officials of Lu played a rather timorous part in these plots
but Duke Ting kept personally aloof from them, not so much

through caution as through sloth and indifference. He did not even maintain the ceremonial dignity of his rank. The ruler of the unimportant state of Choo came on an official visit to Zigzag Hill and on the occasion of the formal reception behaved in a ridiculously arrogant manner, either due to his lack of breeding or because of a desire to show his contempt for the state which he had been anxious to curry favour with only a few years before. He held his jade emblem unnecessarily high and threw his head back when looking at his host, Duke Ting. The latter, apparently over-awed by this arrogance, received the jade emblem too low and hung his head timidly in the presence of the other. The courtiers present were all indignant at the attitude of the visitor and deeply humiliated by the conduct of their duke. Tze Kung, one of Master Kung's disciples who had remained behind in the employ of Baron Huan was present at the meeting and said that the conduct of the two rulers showed that the minds of both were gone.

'Looking on at the meeting,' he said, 'I could only judge the affair by the rules of ceremony. Those rules are as a stem from which may grow life or death, preservation or ruin. We draw our conclusions from the manner in which the parties move to the right or the left, advance or recede, look up or down. We observe these things at court meetings, sacrifices and the occasion of death and war. At this meeting both princes violated the proper rules. The symbol carried high and the upturned look are indicative of pride. The symbol held low and the bent down look are indicative of negligence. Pride is not far removed from disorder and negligence is near to sickness. Both are doomed to die but as our ruler is the host, he will probably be the first to meet that fate.'

A few weeks after this meeting the people of Lu were very much disturbed by a strange event. An ox had, with the usual ceremonies of divination, been selected for sacrifice at an important approaching ceremony and was being fattened for that purpose. The animal was attacked by hungry fieldmice and injured so severely that it died. The fact that there was no famine which might have made the fieldmice especially voracious added to the mystery of this unusual occurrence which could only be regarded as an evil omen. It was necessary to await for the selection and fattening of another ox and this delayed matters so that the sacrifice could not be offered until after the proper time.

The sacrifice had just been completed when Duke Ting died. His death was so sudden and unexpected that there was no opportunity to place him in the state chamber where, by the rigid ritual of the time, all feudal rulers were supposed to be removed when death approached. In the state chamber, away from the contaminating presence and influence of eunuchs and concubines, the expiring dukes could give their final solemn commands to their ministers, announce the name of their successor and expire with decorum and dignity. The discreet chronicles are so obscure about the location of the Duke Ting's death-bed that it appears probable that he died in one of the many chambers of the inner-court. This was not the end of the calamities which beset the state of Lu in this year. While the preparations for the formal funeral ceremony of the deceased duke were in progress, there was an eclipse of the sun in the forenoon (July 16, 494 B.C.) the second solar eclipse in three years. For the moon to be eclipsed was looked on as a matter of ordinary importance which should cause no great alarm, but an eclipse of the sun was an event of very evil portent. Following this inauspicious occurrence, on the day set aside for the funeral, an unseasonable rain came down in such torrents that the ceremony had to be delayed. Obviously heaven did not regard the state of Lu with favour and Duke Gay who succeeded his father began his rule under what were believed to be very unlucky auspices. These ominous events created a profound impression on Baron Huan who was even more superstitious than others in that age of omens and portents. The decline in the fortunes of Lu had begun with the advent of the dancing girls and the departure of Master Kung, and it was easy to connect cause with effect.

Baron Huan had always been ashamed and, as far as it was possible for him to be, a little conscience-stricken over the part he had played in this scheme. To do him complete justice in the matter, he did not know the full implications of the plot and had no idea that matters would go as far as they did. He was filled with rather timorous regret as soon as he learned that the scholar had left his native state.

Two years after the death of the duke, the summer heat brought on an illness and Baron Huan, believing that this was an evidence of the further displeasure of heaven, had a premonition which soon proved to be correct that his death would not be long delayed. He was in fact then in a dying condition but he insisted that his servants dress him and drive him out in his chariot so that he might once again see the walls of Zigzag Hill. Sighing deeply he said to his oldest son, who accompanied him:

'Only a few years ago this state was enjoying a period of prosperity which was equal almost to that of the early days of the Chow dynasty, and it had an opportunity to reach the peak of that prosperous period. I am to blame for the fact that the state has not prospered because of my treatment of Master Kung.'

With this responsibility heavy on his conscience he turned to his son to make amends as many aged and guilty fathers have done since his time.

'When I die,' he said, 'you will undoubtedly be appointed by the duke as chancellor of Lu and when you are chancellor you must summon Chung Ni,' affectionately calling Master Kung by his boyhood name.

The old baron died only a few days after this carriage ride and his son automatically succeeded him as baron and was at the same time appointed chancellor. As soon as the funeral ceremonies were over and he could with propriety attend to official business, Baron Kang set about carrying out the dying wishes of his father and sent orders that Master Kung, who was then wandering in one of the other states, should be summoned to return and resume his official duties. As had happened so many times before, the suggested appointment of Master Kung was opposed by the professional politicians with specious reasoning. The old official to whom the young baron expressed his wishes at once produced arguments against it.

'Several years ago our sainted lord, the former Duke Ting,' he said, 'appointed Mr. Kung to an important position and advanced him rapidly in power but the affair was not carried to a conclusion because Mr. Kung lost his temper over a trivial incident and left the state. As a result our sainted lord brought down on himself the derision of the princes. Now if you appoint him again, and history repeats itself, and he again leaves the state in high dudgeon, the duke will become the laughing-stock of all the other princes.'

Baron Kang listened to these arguments and in the end weakly agreed to a compromise. He did not carry out his father's dying wishes by the recall of Master Kung, but instead summoned one of the disciples, Jan Chui, who was then wandering with the Master in the latter's vain search for employment. Jan Chui, who was at that time only thirty-one, was a native of Lu and his selection in place of others of greater ability was doubtless inspired by local political considerations. Master Kung was elated over this appointment, for although it was only an indirect approval of his teachings it was the first recognition of any kind he had received from his native state since he had left its borders four or five years previously. Other disciples had been employed in other states and some in more responsible positions than that given to Jan Chui, but they had been ignored in Lu. For some reason the appointment brought the Master a new and unusual satisfaction, probably because it meant the forging of a new link connecting him with his native state. The Master's affection for his birthplace caused him to look on its affairs as being of much greater importance than the affairs of the other feudal states, its actions fraught with a great significance. Full of pride in the success of his disciple and of hope for better days in his native state he said:

'This appointment of Jan Chui to an official position in Lu is not done for the accomplishment of small purposes, but as part of a plan for great accomplishments.'

The incident brought back a flood of old memories and he recalled the problems he had faced as an administrator, the adroitness and unscrupulousness of the Lu politicians, the petty but ruinous intrigues of the three great families, and his mind was clouded with doubt as to whether or not Jan Chui would be able to cope with the situation.

'I want to go home! I want to go home!' he cried. 'My young pupils are enthusiastic and undertake things on an ambitious scale. They are accomplished in the fine arts, in knowledge and theories, but they do not know how to restrict and shape themselves in the conduct of practical affairs.'

When Jan Chui left to take up his official duties, some of his comrades went with him a part of the way and urged him to use his official influence, as soon as possible, to see that the Master was invited to return. The admiring disciple kept this suggestion in mind and overlooked no discreet opportunity to sing his Master's praises and to suggest the advisability of his appointment. The professional politicians presented a solid wall of opposition it was impossible for him to break down, and with his own position at stake he did not push matters perilously far.

Jan Chui remained inconspicuously in the service of Baron Kang for seven years before a military invasion by the state of Tsi gave him an opportunity to distinguish himself and so carry out his obligation to secure the recall of his Master. Marquis Ching of Tsi after ruling for sixty years had died and in the sanguinary contest for the succession which followed, his numerous sons fled to other states for safety, four of them coming to Lu. Baron Kang, a political opportunist, betrothed his younger sister Ki Ki to one of the noble refugees, who shortly thereafter returned to Tsi and, following the murder of his predecessor, became the ruling marquis. He then sent for his affianced bride but she in the meantime had carried on an inner-court intrigue with a cousin, was no longer a virgin, and when questioned told the truth about her unfaithfulness. Under the circumstances Baron Kang was afraid to send her to the young Marquis of Tsi and put him off with excuses. The marquis finally learned what had occurred and with injured dignity became very angry over the turn events had taken and invaded Lu, easily taking possession of several cities. Jan Chui in this petty conflict had charge of the troops of Baron Kang. This affair eventually had a happier sequel than would be expected. The Tsi emissary who came to Lu to arrange the terms of peace took the erring Ki Ki back with him as a prize of war. Considering all the circumstances of her betrothal, her unfaithfulness and the bloodshed and other serious consequences which followed it might naturally be anticipated that her visit to Tsi and her encounter with the young marquis would not be very pleasant but it turned out quite differently. The out-raged bridegroom would have been quite justified in punishing her very severely – might even have given her as a soiled bride to a captive barbarian. Instead he forgave her, she joined his retinue of wives and became his favourite. She must have been not only fascinating but exceptionally clever for she persuaded him to give back to her father the cities for whose loss she had been to blame.

The fighting had been unimportant, and victory had gone against Lu, but Jan Chui by his part in it had shown great military skill and good judgment, and apparently got credit for a good deal more than he deserved. Full of admiration for the way his henchman had conducted himself and doubtless envisaging further and more important military victories, Baron Kang rather stupidly asked him: 'How did you acquire your military skill? Was it by study and learning or were you born with it?'

Jan Chui was quick to take advantage of the opportunity offered and replied:

'I learned of Master Kung.'

If he intended by this reply to infer that Master Kung knew or cared anything about the art of war, he was guilty of a wilful deception for the Master had never known anything about military affairs and had certainly never made any attempt to teach it or even to discuss it. But Jan Chui's statement had been general and was designed to interest the baron in the recall of Master Kung at what appeared to be an opportune moment.

'What sort of a man is this scholar Kung?' inquired the baron, giving the former disciple just the opening he had been waiting for.

'If any ruler makes use of his services,' he said with enthusiasm, 'that ruler will gain great fame. If one asks the people of this country about him, or even if it were possible to get the gods and the spirits to express themselves concerning him, one would on every hand hear no criticism, but only praise. His life has been devoted to attaining the highest pinnacle of perfection on the path of virtue. He is wholly without personal ambition and if you should give him a fief of a thousand square miles he would not regard it as gain.'

The avaricious Baron Kang was impressed by this testimonial from the former disciple, especially by his reference to Master Kung's indifference to wealth. As he had managed with Jan Chui's help to sequestrate nearly all the state revenue any rewards that were to be paid to distinguished officials would be at his expense and he was quite happy to think that the services of this famous scholar would cost him very little. Competent ministers were not unconscious of their worth and it was necessary to pay some of them very liberally in order to retain their services. He remembered the dying request of his father and was not unconscious of the aid this famous native son might give him. Lu was, as a matter of fact, in more desperate need of help than the state of Wei where Master Kung was now sojourning. The latter, as the result of Madam

The homesick scholar hastened back to his native state of Lu when he was finally invited to return.

Nan Tze's intrigues and personal feud with her stepson, had interfered with the succession, and precipitated controversies in which
the neighbouring states participated. In the meantime Lu was
faced by a much more formidable danger. About forty years before
this a prince of the strange and barbarous state of Wu had made a
tour of the orthodox civilised states in order to improve his learning
for the benefit of his king. He was received in Lu as in other states
with the same patronising and half-humorous condescension that
people in Europe and America bestowed on the patriotic young
Japanese who less than a century ago set out to learn the secrets of
greatness from foreign lands. The tremendous strides made by Wu
following the visit of her prince found a parallel many centuries
later in the progress of Japan under similar incentives and with
similar aid from foreign sources. A refugee from the north carried
with him to Wu the new knowledge of the strategy of war which
enabled commanders to discipline and dispose effectively of large
masses of troops, and the Wu rulers learned this lesson so thoroughly
that in a short time their practice was equal to the theory of their
teachers. While formerly barbarous Wu was advancing, the cultured orthodox states were growing weaker and just at this time Wu
was making humiliating demands on Lu. One of them had recently
had the effrontery to stipulate how many animals he should be
given as a present when he visited the Lu capital and had with difficulty been induced to accept without offence a present of reasonable
proportions. Less than half a century before Wu had been grateful
for any attention Lu might bestow, but now was attempting to
dictate terms even on matters of ceremonial. Duke Gay, Baron
Kang and their attendant ministers were in desperate need of help.

'I should like to summon him,' said Baron Kang. 'Can that be
done?'

Jan Chui remembered the bitter disappointment of his master on
the many previous occasions, when marquises, dukes or lesser dignitaries had planned to employ him and their plans had been nullified
by the jealous politicians.

'If you wish to summon him,' he said, 'you must not let your plans
be circumvented by inferior people. In that way it can be done.'

Baron Kang still temporised and it was not until the statesmen
of Wei had finally implored Master Kung to straighten out the
tangled and scandalous affairs of their state that he finally took

action with the consent and approval of Duke Gay. They appear to have leaned rather heavily on his anticipated help and expected to have the decks cleared for him to take charge of affairs for they dismissed three important officials whom they knew to be objectionable to him and so were ready for a complete change of administration. Baron Kang then sent a mission of prominent citizens of Lu to visit Master Kung with ceremonial gifts of silk and an invitation from the highest authorities for him to return to his native state. The invitation actually came from the duke and its urgency may be judged by the fact that the emissaries brought rich gifts with them. At the same time the officials of Wei tried to detain him with heavy bribes.

Fourteen years before this Master Kung had left the state slowly, reluctantly and with heavy heart, looking back in expectation of an invitation to return. The summons had finally been received and he hastened towards his home.

CHAPTER XXI

*Though the famous scholar had been brought back
to his native state to aid in its government these plans
did not prosper for very obvious reasons and he did
not take official employment but spent his remaining
years in literary work.*

IT was generally assumed at Zigzag Hill, and throughout the
ducal state of Lu, that when the famous philosopher returned he
would resume his office as a responsible minister of the state and
possibly restore and bring to completion the reforms he had inaugurated with little help from the authorities, carried on so successfully, and terminated so abruptly. Many people of the state still
remembered the blessings of his administrations, had hoped for his
return and were overjoyed when they learned that an invitation
had been sent to him. Baron Kang and Duke Gay had certainly asked him to return with the idea that he might aid in
an important way in the management of affairs but their point of
view was not the popular one. They were not interested in
alleviating the sorrows of the common people but looked for his
assistance along other, and, to them, more important lines. They
especially hoped that he might be able to extricate them from the
difficulties in which they were involved through their cowardly
and highly-dangerous policy of secret and deceptive alliances, whose
discovery had brought on them the wrath of powerful neighbours.
It was undoubtedly the intention of Baron Kang and of Duke Gay
to unload on him the sorry mess for which their cowardice, avarice
and stupidity were responsible and to place on his shoulders the
responsibility for straightening everything out. Though the problems were many and difficult he was well equipped successfully to
undertake their solution if he cared to forget his principles and
blindly serve his selfish masters which is what they stupidly expected
him to do. For this task he was superbly equipped. During his

years of wandering he had learned the history of the various states, had familiarised himself with their political secrets and was in expert knowledge as well as diplomacy and political strategy the superior to any other statesman in the country. His personal attainments did not comprise the only assets of which he was in command. Those of his disciples who were not already employed in other places, or detained by family ties, accompanied him to Lu, comprising a galaxy of scholastic and political talent unequalled before in any feudal state. It was because of the possession of this potentially valuable coterie of assistants that the King of Chu had been dissuaded from employing him a few years previously. They were ready and eager to help their master make a practical application of the theories of government they had been studying for so many years. Most of them were natives of Lu, and, like their master, had a sentimental interest in the affairs of the state and could give to it more loyal service than they could give to any other.

These selfish plans of the duke and baron and the ambitious and praiseworthy aims of the disciples alike proved vain. As an old Chinese historian put it:

'But it finally turned out that they could not make use of Master Kung in Lu. And neither did Master Kung strive for official position.'

His first contacts with the officials after his return were not under happy circumstances and forcibly reminded him of his humble and humiliating years as collector of tithes. Baron Kuan, who wanted to levy an increased tax on the land, sent Jan Chui, the former disciple who had been responsible for his return, to ask Master Kung's opinion or rather to get his approval of a measure he had already decided on. The scholar listened to his disciple present the proposal and the arguments with which it was supported by the baron but refused to make any comment. After he had listened three times to the involved and insincere arguments in justification of the extra tax and still remained silent Baron Kuan sent Jan Chui with a more urgent request:

'You are an old officer of the state,' Jan Chui reported the baron as saying, 'and I am waiting for your opinion before I act in this matter. Why is it that you will not let me have the benefit of your advice?'

Master Kung still declined to express any opinion for the guidance of the baron but he said privately to his former disciple:

'The conduct of a gentleman is governed by the rules of propriety and he does not need advice from anyone on questions like this. In his benefactions, a gentleman prefers to be liberal, in affairs of government he tries to pursue the course of justice, and in his taxation he tries to be light. According to this principle the contribution of the people as anciently established is sufficient for the needs of the state. If the actions of Baron Kuan are not governed by the rules of propriety but by his own covetousness and insatiable ambitions, then even though he enforce this new taxation on lands, still it will not be enough to satisfy him. If you and Baron Kuan wish to act according to law, then you may consult the statutes of the Duke of Chow which are still in force and effect. If you wish to act in an illegal and irregular manner, then why do you consult me about it?'

Nevertheless the increased land-tax was decreed by Baron Kuan, adding by its burdens to the distress of the people, and Master Kung was both ashamed and indignant that one of his followers should have taken any part in this unjust and illegal imposition. While giving his disciples great liberty of individual action in most respects, he would not countenance their subservience to the arbitrary and unjust use of power by the rulers of the country. The theory under which the machinery of government was conducted was that a capable and conscientious official should be able to prevent any foolish or shameful act his ruler proposed and if he did not do so the blame lay on his own head rather than on that of his superior. This was the progenitor of the theory that the king can do no wrong. The relationship between Master Kung and his disciples was that of a stern but loving father with numerous affectionate and loyal sons for whose conduct he was responsible. The many who had followed him and then left to take up employment elsewhere, did not by that act become independent entities but continued to look on him as one to whom they were accountable for all of their thoughts and actions. He was a spiritual father to all of them. He accepted and encouraged this point of view and looked on all of his present and former disciples, no matter what their age, as children who were subject alike to his rebukes and praise. The fact that many of them had grown old with him did not in the least change his paternal attitude. Jan Chui was now approaching forty, was an important officer of the state and had been directly although tardily responsible for Master Kung's recall but to the latter he was only a youth who had, like an unruly schoolboy, ignored the precepts of his master.

'He is no follower of mine, my children,' he cried to his disciples when he learned that the illegal tax had been imposed. 'Beat the drum and assail him.'

If the duke and the baron expected the returned philosopher to show any gratitude for his recall by a complaisant attitude towards the way in which they were conducting affairs, they must have been very much disappointed. During his long voluntary exile he had kept an attentive ear on all news from home, had never lost touch with its affairs. Many of his disciples were from Lu, a few were employed there and of those who followed him in his wanderings several made periodical visits to their homes and on their return were able to inform the Master as to everything that was transpiring. Some of those who were serving as officials in Lu made occasional visits to Master Kung, following him to remote places in order to ask his advice on matters of importance. With all these sources of information at his disposal he did not have to spend any time studying the affairs of the state for he was already familiar with it. He had appraised the prominent men just as he had appraised them when he had been in charge of the government of the state, and just as he had recorded an appraisal of the characters of the prominent men in most of the other feudal states. His age and his long and discouraging period of wandering had not soured the natural sweetness of his character, but he had developed the frank outspokenness which is the prerogative of honest old men, and talked to the duke and the barons as he would to his disciples. They were, indeed, children from his point of view. The duke was the third to rule since the death of the duke who had seventy years before sent Kung the Tall his congratulations on the birth of a son. Baron Kang was the grandson of Baron Ping for whom Master Kung, as a young man, had measured the grain and counted the oxen. Most of his old friends and companions were dead and had been replaced by men who in his mind were immature youngsters. Master Kung wasted little unnecessary politeness on them and his remarks were, to put it mildly, not very diplomatic. Duke Gay questioned him in a general way regarding the government and Master Kung said:

'Good government consists in the correct choice of officials.'

This was as direct a criticism of the duke as even a lax interpretation of etiquette would allow, for the duke had followed the precedent established by his weak-kneed predecessors and had left the selection of officials to the coterie of heads of the three families and powerful political schemers who controlled the duchy with little regard for ducal authority. His premier was not, as he should have been, the ablest man he could select but was the corrupt Baron Kang, of limited mentality, who was given the position merely because he was the head of the most powerful of the three great families. Other principal officials were selected in the same arbitrary way and these men, incompetent to carry out their duties, delegated their authority to others of their own selection. The duke not only failed to select his officials wisely; he had not in fact chosen them at all but had left their appointment to the chance fortunes of precedent.

The duke in his inquiries then shifted to safer ground and foolishly asked about the dress of scholars, assuming this would be a matter on which the sage would discourse at length without impinging on embarrassing subjects.

'We wear gowns with wide sleeves and a black cap,' said the scholar. 'In the country, where we have spent most of our time, we just wear loose and comfortable clothing. I don't know whether you would call that a garb for scholars or not.'

The conversation was not flourishing and the duke, in his anxiety to be polite and keep away from embarrassing subjects plunged beyond his depth by asking:

'What constitutes scholarship?'

'Ah! That is quite a different question,' said Master Kung. 'I cannot answer it so quickly. Even if we were to tarry here until your servants all went to sleep and you had to summon a new crew, I would not be able to tell you all that scholarship implies.'

Then he gave the duke in brief outline more information, in all probability, than the limited ducal intelligence could absorb. He stressed the fact that scholarship was neither adherence to conventional forms as in the dress of a scholar nor the blind absorption of facts but was, in the main, a mental discipline which resulted in the building of character.

The philosopher was even more outspoken in reprimanding Baron Kang under whose patronage he had returned. The baron was very much distressed because of the great number of petty thefts by the people of the state and remembering the honesty of the countryside when Master Kung had been at the head of the government asked the latter's advice about how to put a stop to this evil. Baron Kang was, as a matter of fact, the greatest thief of them all. He did not, like the artisans and peasants, steal pigs and goats, odd pots and pans, and other articles of small value but with the aid of his officials he collected unjust taxes from the people so that he might pilfer more generously from the ducal treasury for the benefit of his own account. By reason of his success in these enterprises he was one of the richest men in the country and in his vulgar display of wealth gone far beyond the excesses of his father and grandfather who had assumed rank and privilege to which they were not entitled. He had the supreme effrontery to offer sacrifices to Tao Shan, the great sacred mountain, of such majesty that its influence extended only to kings; and maintained a palace which was superior to any in Loyang. All this was made possible by stolen riches. The philosopher did not sugar-coat the pill of his answer but replied:

'Sir, if you were not so avaricious and did not countenance thefts yourself, the people would not steal, even though you rewarded them for it.'

Not satisfied with this rebuff and probably in order to turn the subject into less embarrassing channels Baron Kang asked:

'What do you say to the idea of executing the wicked for the benefit of the good?'

'Sir,' replied Master Kung, 'in carrying on your government why should you kill anyone at all? Let your evinced desires and your example be for what is good and it will not be necessary to punish anyone. The relation between superiors and inferiors is like that between the wind and the grass. The grass must bend when the wind blows across it.'

Obviously such an outspoken critic of the conduct of his superiors would, if given any official powers, be an embarrassment to the duke and the baron, and would make life very uncomfortable for the lesser dignitaries who might come within the orbit of his power. The latter were, of course, against him with the unanimity and zeal

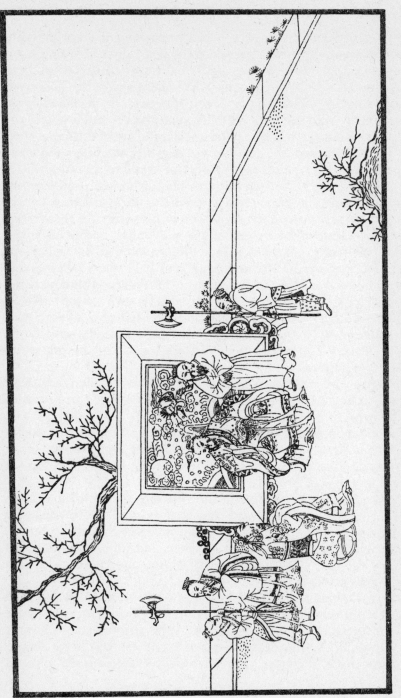

Duke Gay made foolish inquiries of Master Kung regarding the dress a scholar was supposed to wear.

of members of a trades union trying to prevent the employment of a non-union workman. The old stories about his encounter with the fascinating Madam Nan Tze, about his purely mythical friendship with the eunuch of Wei, were furbished, given a new coat of gaudy paint and set out for the edification of the duke, the baron, and the public. They made every effort to spatter his reputation, telling stories of events in distant places which might easily be believed but could not so easily be disproved. Under the circumstances it is not surprising that plans for the employment of the scholar did not prosper. The ruling powers were afraid to give him any authority because it was obvious that his ideas of reform in the state began at the top and as they would be the first to be affected this might have extremely serious consequences. For more than a generation he had received the support of the masses who at this time in the desperation of their sufferings were verging on blind and unreasoning revolt. It was only by holding them in more or less terrified subjection that serious trouble was avoided. The least encouragement from this talented native son might upset the entire political machine and make effective the anarchy which was threatening.

On the other hand it was equally obvious to Master Kung, after his first interviews with the duke and the baron, that he had not been recalled because either of them had any intention of conforming in any way to his ideas and politics, but because they thought he would provide a cheap and highly-efficient vehicle for extricating them from the difficulties into which they had precipitated themselves through their own cowardice, stupidity and avarice. Some time previously Master Kung had expressed his contempt for officials who would accommodate themselves to a policy of this kind and said of them:

'They are only so many pecks and hampers and need not be taken into account.'

To Master Kung an appointment under such terms as were offered him was even more humiliating than his employment had been as collector of tithes fifty years before. There as an employee without authority he was in no way responsible for the injustices which were committed but here matters were on a different footing and it was with the idea of shifting to him the responsibility for their actions that the duke and baron had invited him to return. He did not press any claims he may have had for official preferment and except on the occasion of an unexpected and tragic happening did not attempt in any way to interfere in governmental affairs.

He had been back at home in Lu more than two years when news was received of the murder of the Marquis of Tsi. This was the third ruler of Tsi who had been assassinated since the death of Marquis Ching, less than ten years before. Even at the time of the treacherous peace conference the plotters around Marquis Ching were planning to gain power for themselves through the selection of his successor, a task presenting many interesting possibilities, for his only son by his legitimate wife was dead and there were many sons, the offspring of various concubines. As his years increased the plots multiplied until there was a camp of supporters around each of the numerous sons. One day a minister who was anxious to see which way the wind was blowing, presumed to suggest to the marquis that as he was growing old he should give some thought to the naming of a successor.

'If you have no worries about your duties with the affairs of state,' suggested the marquis with icy politeness, 'why do you not spend your idle time worrying about your own health instead of bothering about mine. You seem to be in good health now but you might fall very seriously ill at any moment. In the meantime enjoy yourself as best you can and don't lose any sleep over the question of who is to be my heir.'

When a few years after this incident the time came to name a successor, the aged marquis followed the precedent which had been established by many other noblemen in their dotage and appointed the son of his youngest and therefore favourite concubine very much against the wishes of his principal ministers. The older sons were exiled but each became a focal point for plots and intrigues which soon resulted in the brutal and callous murder of the son of the young concubine. This was followed by the murder of his elder half-brother, who had taken refuge in Lu, and been affianced to the faithless but apparently fascinating Ki Ki. The successor of this unfortunate heir had now been the third to meet the same fate, being murdered by Chan Hang, a well-known official of the state.

Master Kung, righteously indignant as this evidence of anarchy and insubordination in high places, fasted and bathed as if for a ceremony of sacrifice or some other great occasion. Putting on his old court robes which had been neglected for more than fifteen years

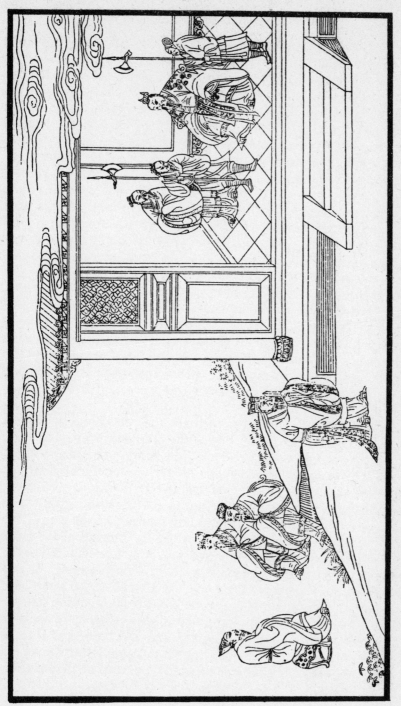

He urged Duke Gay of Lu to punish the murderer of the Marquis of Tsi, but the duke refused to act.

he called on the duke and after the preliminary polite remarks said:

'Chan Hang has slain his sovereign. I beg that you will undertake to punish him.'

The duke argued against any action of this kind not on any grounds of loyalty to his feudal obligations but on the purely utilitarian premise that Tsi was strong whilst Lu was weak and that any attempt to chastise an official of the other state would result in failure and defeat. Master Kung, knowing the uselessness of any other approach to the duke, and with an accurate knowledge of conditions in Tsi adopted a utilitarian argument himself and pointed out that this third political assassination had aroused the indignation of the people of Tsi and said that half of them would come to the support of Lu in any action it might undertake against the assassin. The duke was either unconvinced or did not have courage enough to come to a decision.

'Inform the chiefs of the three families about it,' he finally said, shifting responsibility for taking action in a matter in which he, as the head of a feudal state, should have felt a great deal of personal responsibility.

'As one of the former great officers,' said Master Kung to himself, 'I hardly dared fail to represent such an important matter to him and now all my prince tells me to do is to inform the chiefs of the three families about it!'

He swallowed his pride and did present the matter to Baron Kang and through him to the chiefs of the other two families but, as might have been anticipated, they refused to act.

Aside from his discouragement over his reception by the duke and the baron there was another and perhaps more urgent reason why Master Kung did not in fact push his claims to the appointment he had been invited to accept. With the approach of old age, he found it necessary to amend the schedule of life which he had so rigorously followed. The span of remaining years which he could reasonably expect was not long enough to enable him to carry to a conclusion any administrative reforms which he might now inaugurate. It was obvious that he must leave his uncompleted mission in the hands of the faithful disciples who would survive him, as his day of active life was over and his most important task was now to round off and complete the instruction which he had given to his followers. It was for him a melancholy undertaking. His accomplishments had fallen so far short of his ambitions that he felt his life had been a complete failure and it was now too late to rescue his name from the oblivion into which he was sure it would fall. Though indifferent to personal fame and material rewards, he, like other scholars, was not so indifferent to the more lasting fame which is bestowed by posterity, and was deeply grieved over the conviction that all his work had been transitory and that he would be unknown to future generations.

'The sage suffers because he must leave the world with the conviction that after his death his name will not be mentioned,' he said. 'The path which I have laid out is not travelled and will soon be obscured by weeds and grass. Through what shall I be known to posterity?'

In his modesty and child-like simplicity of mind it never occurred to him that in his teachings to his disciples, as well as in the example of his life, he had set up a standard of ethics and conduct which would be handed down from father to son and from teacher to disciple through many generations. He had no idea that the pure light of his benign influence would fall on countless millions of his countrymen and, after a lapse of more than two thousand years be a potent factor in the lives of the most populous people on the globe.

With the sad conviction that only a few years of life were left to him, he declined to undertake any new responsibilities and devoted his attention to completing his unfinished tasks just as resolutely as his father, Kung the Tall, had set about adjusting his more modest ambitions by procuring a son and heir. His researches had stored in his mind a generous knowledge of many branches of learning which he now felt it to be his duty to revise and classify, and put in orderly and permanent written form through tedious inscription on the clumsy wooden tablets with the aid of his disciples. From early youth and throughout his long lifetime, he had made a profound and thorough study of history, music and the ceremonies, and had encouraged his disciples to make researches under his guidance along similar lines. His vain wandering through various states in search of a ruler who would adopt his ideas had given him an unexampled opportunity to continue and complete these studies. In each of the many places they visited, he studied the music, memorised the poetry and examined the historical data. Each petty court had its own historian who set down facts in such a way as to be pleasing to the local point of view, and it was only by collecting and comparing the chronicles of various states, as he had done on his itineraries that the false could be sifted from the true and an accurate appraisal of history arrived at.

Each state also had its own songs, though many of them were of common origin and differed only in minor detail as to text or tune. The songs, or ballads, constituted the popular literature of the day. Some of them went back to the ancient semi-mythological period, others of stately phrase recounted events in the lives of rulers or provided the musical accompaniment for solemn religious ceremonies. Some were so gripping in their simple humanity that they appear, like the poems of Burns, to have sprung spontaneously into being. In the ballads, the people told their joys and sorrows, their successes and failures and provided a moving and colourful picture of the life of the past as well as of the present. With the zealous aid of his disciples, he now set about making an anthology of the songs of the country and compiling the history of the state of Lu, which by direct reference or inference, told the story of the other states as well. The compilation of the anthology did not present any particular difficulties or take very much time for, as a matter of fact most of the work had already been accomplished and it only remained to do the final editing. In his travels Master Kung had collected more than three thousand of these ballads and many of them he found to be duplicates, with unimportant minor differences in the text. The ballads were only occasionally reduced to written form but were passed from mouth to mouth, county to county and state to state with the differences that might be expected from this method of transmission. Master Kung carefully compared and considered all the different versions of the same song and selected the one which he considered to be the best either from the point of view of literary construction or historical accuracy. In this way he eliminated quite a number of unnecessary duplications, and then he went much farther and despoiled the collection of its rich ribaldry and of every allusion which might bring a blush to a maidenly cheek. When his anthology was completed, a bare 300 selections had survived the process of elimination, but these included touching love-songs and robust narratives of rustic sports,

Among the former may be included the following as translated by
Dr. Herbert A. Giles in *A History of Chinese Literature*:

'You seemed a guileless youth enough,
Offering for silk your woven stuff;
But silk was not required by you;
I was the silk you had in view.
With you I crossed the ford, and while
We wandered on for many a mile
I said, "I do not wish delay,
But friends must fix our wedding-day. . . .
Oh, do not let my words give pain,
But with the autumn come again."

'And then I used to watch and wait
To see you passing through the gate;
And sometimes, when I watched in vain,
My tears would flow like falling rain;
But when I saw my darling boy,
I laughed and cried aloud for joy.
The fortune-tellers, you declared,
Had all pronounced us duly paired;
"Then bring a carriage," I replied,
"And I'll away to be your bride."

'The mulberry-leaf, not yet undone
By autumn chill, shines in the sun.
O tender dove, I would advise,
Beware the fruit that tempts thy eyes!
O maiden fair, not yet a spouse,
List lightly not to lovers' vows!
A man may do this wrong, and time
Will fling its shadow o'er his crime;
A woman who has lost her name
Is doomed to everlasting shame.

'The mulberry-tree upon the ground
Now sheds its yellow leaves around.
Three years have slipped away from me
Since first I shared your poverty;
And now again, alas the day!
Back through the ford I take my way.
My heart is still unchanged, but you
Have uttered words now proved untrue;
And you have left me to deplore
A love that can be mine no more.

'For three long years I was your wife,
And led in truth a toilsome life;
Early to rise and late to bed,
Each day alike passed o'er my head.
I honestly fulfilled my part,
And you – well, you have broke my heart.
The truth my brothers will not know,
So all the more their gibes will flow.
I grieve in silence and repine
That such wretched fate is mine.

'Ah, hand in hand to face old age! –
Instead, I turn a bitter page.
O for the river-banks of yore;
O for the much-loved marshy shore!
The hours of girlhood, with my hair
Ungathered, as we lingered there.
The words we spoke, that seemed so true.
I little thought that I should rue;
I little thought the vows we swore
Would some day bind us two or more.'

By his careful selection of poems which contain no ribaldry or licentiousness Master Kung established a literary standard which has placed all Chinese literature on a plane of its own characterised by an austere morality. His own opinion of the work was expressed as follows:

'The three hundred odes may be summed up in one sentence: thought without depravity.'

The task which he next took up was one on which he thought his future fame might possibly rest. This was the compilation of the history of Lu covering a period of about three centuries and bringing the annals up to two years after his return from Wei. It is entirely possible that this work would, of its own merits, have given him undying scholarly fame such as that of Herodotus, for it was the first sincere and essentially accurate history of his country and provides the starting-point for all historical research. This work, one of the classic books of China is known as *The Spring and Autumn Annals*, which is merely a poetical name for a chronology as spring and autumn marked the turning-point of the seasons. Its bare text is an enigma to the uninitiated, though simple and rather easily understood once the system is grasped. In its method of recording historical events it followed the style of the period, in which the professional historians attached to each petty court or proud family set down in chronological order bald and undigested facts about events of the day, recording with equal brevity the visitation of locusts, the appearance of a comet, the assassination of a duke, or the visit of diplomatic emissaries from another feudal state. If this method of recording history had been in vogue in England in the seventeenth century a certain famous episode would have been chronicled somewhat as follows:

'It was the third year of the reign of his grace King James II.

'In the eleventh month the Prince of Orange paid a visit to us accompanied by his chief military officers.

'In the twelfth month the King went on a visit to the King of France. The Seals of State were lost in the Thames.

'It was the fifth year of the King who was visiting in Ireland.

'On the first day of the seventh month there was a great battle fought on the Boyne River and our troops were successful.

'Prince James left Ireland, returned to France and entered a monastery.

'King William took up his residence in Whitehall.'

Considering their brevity and the cryptic quality of the Chinese chronicles, these official histories managed to embody a surprising amount of propaganda evasion, concealment and clever lies. The historians were, of course, in the employ of the princes, dukes, viscounts, barons and other dignitaries and their histories were necessarily written to meet the historical requirements and ambitions of their patrons. In this frank and non-secretive age it is difficult to visualise the point of view of these ancient notables, many of whom were notorious evil-doers and entirely indifferent to public opinion, but were most meticulous that in the official written records their reputations should be spotless. A few of them did make vain attempts to achieve immortality by construction of imperishable graves and imposing tombs, but the workmen were not skilled enough to produce anything very durable with the result that these monuments usually disintegrated after a few generations. All preferred to repose confidence in an immortality which rested on history – a laudatory history written by their own paid

With the aid of his disciples, Master Kung compiled and edited the history of his native state of Lu.

historians. In order to make sure that the chroniclers performed their duties to the satisfaction of their employers, it was customary to castrate any historian who in his zeal for accuracy strayed from the crooked path of policy into the straight path of truth.

To use a new but vigorous word, Master Kung, in his work 'debunked' the histories compiled by his insincere predecessors, but he did it without departing from the accredited method of cryptic chronology. That he did not suffer the humiliating fate of other honest historians may have been due to the fact that his history did not gain currency until after his death when it was too late to entertain ideas of revenge or punishment. According to some of his most outspoken critics he was not so harsh in his treatment of affairs in Lu as in the case of other states, overlooking or possibly concealing many disgraceful and cowardly episodes and whitewashing the reputations of some of the numerous graceless dukes. They contend that when recording the happenings in the other states, especially states which had treated Lu unkindly, he was not so charitable and held every wicked ruler up to shame. In describing his method one cannot do better than paraphrase and amplify the comments of Sze Ma Chien, the castrated 'father of Chinese history' who wrote a few centuries later:

'The style of Master Kung's text was conservative but the secret meaning could be easily comprehended and was very far-reaching. For example the rulers of the barbarous states of Wu and Chu called themselves "kings" and this term was used in all the annals concerning them. But the falsity of these titles is shown in Master Kung's work by consistently referring to these rulers as "barons". At an assembly of the feudal princes (held in the year 632 B.C.) they had compelled the attendance of the Son of Heaven (the Chow ruler) who was then in their power. This was an act of treasonable insubordination on the part of the princes, and in order to show his disapproval of it Master Kung explains the presence of the ruler of Chow by saying: "The Son of Heaven was hunting north of the Yellow River." By the application of this method, a clue is found to the criticism of men and events of past generations. If some later king comprehends and interprets the meaning of this history and carries out its true significance, then rebellious officials and wicked sons will be terrified.'

The main political lesson Master Kung tried to convey in this history was consistent with all his former teachings, for it was designed to show the advantages of a strong imperial system over the petty state system with its ruinous jealousies and rivalries. The country did not in fact attain any degree of peace and prosperity until, long after his death, this system was finally adopted and the petty feudal courts were wiped out. Almost every page of his annals contained directly or by inference a series of solemn warnings against usurpation of power.

Just as it is impossible for modern theologians to envisage the ideas of that day regarding a future life with its uncertain rewards and punishments so it is difficult if not impossible to comprehend the terror which Master Kung's history inspired in the hearts of wicked rulers, unfaithful sons, rebellious and treacherous officials. As has been noted on an earlier page, the record of their lives and their claim to fame and the praise of posterity had always been in the hands of their own historians with the result that sins were forgotten or glossed over and the pantheon of past heroes offered nothing which future generations could criticise. While they had a hazy or uncertain conception or some very practical doubts as to the immortality of the spirit they had no doubts about the practical immortality of one, the record of whose words or deeds did not die with him.

'Immortality,' said a famous statesman, the one who had caused his laws to be engraved on iron, 'is when a man dies but his words live.'

Now for the first time the true record of their lives was given publicity and set down for the guidance of future generations. Their theory that sins may be washed away by concealment was rudely shown to be false and they were filled with superstitious terror. It was like meeting the Recording Angel face to face!

CHAPTER XXII

During a great hunt in the wilderness near Zigzag Hill a strange beast was slain and Master Kung felt this to presage his early death and the decline of his doctrines. He hastily completed his literary work died and was mourned for three years by his disciples.

IN the spring of the year 481 B.C. the nobles of Lu with their officials and principal retainers conducted, and most of the residents of Lu participated in, a great hunt in the forest wilderness which was then to be found near Zigzag Hill. This was one of the semi-annual drives in which animals were secured for the sacrifices and was a period of boisterous sport and gaiety in which many archery contests and other similar diversions were indulged in. Although hunts like these had a certain remote religious significance, there was nothing austere in their observance for there was a great deal of drinking and hilarity and rough practical jokes. One of the favourite pranks was to organise parties which would steal game from the more fortunate sportsmen, and sometimes enterprises of this sort were carried so far that bad blood was engendered and there were free-for-all fights. As the people of Lu depended on the plentiful supply of game to give variety to their larder every man, it might be said, was a hunter and shot pheasants with arrows or snared rabbits at every opportunity. But the semi-annual hunts provided unequalled opportunities for sportsmen for on these occasions the ducal game preserves were thrown open. The animals, ranging in size and ferocity from rabbits to tigers were driven by beaters toward the archers and spearsmen and in that way they killed a great many animals which would ordinarily escape them including rare beasts which would come out of cover only on these occasions. In this historic hunt, a charioteer attached to one of the baronial families of the state captured and crippled a beast of such strange appearance that its unusual form filled him with superstitious fear, which was shared by his fellows. One of them, being frightened, threw the animal in a rubbish-heap outside the suburbs of the city where it later died. The charioteer's curiosity proved as strong as his fright and he sent a messenger to tell Master Kung about the strange creature and ask what it was. Others had looked at it but as it was new to their experience they could not identify it. Master Kung went at once to the spot where the beast had been thrown. When he saw it he was very much agitated and at once pronounced it to be a *chi lin*, one of those fabulous animals whose appearance was supposed to be an omen of great good. He wiped his eyes with his sleeve while the tears fell on his lapel.

'Why has it come? Why has it come?' he cried to himself.

Disciple Tze Kung asked the Master why he wept and the latter said:

'The *chi lin* comes only when there is an intelligent king. Now it has appeared when it is not the time for it to do so and has been killed. It must mean that my doctrine will decline. That is why I wept.'

The *chi lin* is not mentioned often in Chinese history but its appearance is recorded frequently enough to prove that some rare and peculiar animal of this kind did exist. The vague and romantic descriptions of the beast as given by the Chinese historians and the wholly fanciful way in which it has been depicted by Chinese artists does not give experts an opportunity to identify it though the most generally accepted theory is that it was a small one-horned antelope which has long since become extinct. That it was then very rare and possibly nearing extinction at this time is indicated by the fact that several generations usually elapsed between each appearance. It was such a curious beast and was seen on such rare occasions that the very sight of it came to be classed with those manifestations of nature such as eclipses of the sun and showers of meteors. Master Kung with his sound common sense, ignored the absurd superstitions of the day and seized on many opportunities to prove their fallacy; but in a country where superstition played such a large part in the lives of everyone it would be remarkable if he did not, like all other scholars, attach significance to the appearance of this animal and its death. It will be recalled that a similar strange animal had appeared before Master Kung's mother shortly before his birth and

Master Kung wept when the strange beast was captured and killed for he felt that this event presaged his death, and the failure of his policies.

his interpretation of the appearance, crippling and death of this *chi lin* was that his life had been a failure and that he was about to die. Many fanciful stories have been woven about this episode, as about the supernatural manifestations at the time of his birth. Whether one accepts or doubts or thoroughly disbelieves these stories is not a matter of any particular importance so far as this history is concerned. The current acceptance of the fables by the common people, and their later incorporation in the important historical works of the period show quite clearly and conclusively that they were taken quite seriously then and have not since been questioned by orthodox Chinese scholars. The appearance of the *chi lin* was set down in the historical records of the day by Master Kung himself in a manner to indicate that he looked on it as an event of supreme importance and his appraisal was not questioned by contemporary or future historians. An intelligent examination of the event can record this fact and go no farther.

At about this time one of his favourite disciples, Yen Yuan, died. His excessive grief over the death of this most faithful and talented follower has been referred to in a previous chapter. When on the death of Yen Yuan, he exclaimed 'Heaven is destroying me!' he was not indulging in any hyperbole of speech or the false rhetoric which he detested for he had expected the young man to survive him, to carry on his teachings, and possibly bring about the redemption of his fellow-men and restore the country to the idyllic days of the golden age. In spite of the fact there had been little to give him any encouragement and that wickedness and corruption were to be met with on every hand Master Kung still persisted in his belief that truth would eventually prevail and that the idyllic fairy-tale happiness to which he thought every man entitled would descend on his beloved country. During his life, the times were out of joint, but Yen Yuan was young and should have many more years to live. He was superbly equipped in character and attainments. In a life which was largely made up of griefs and disappointments the saddest blow he received, except for the death of his mother, was occasioned by the death of this beloved son. It appeared to him to constitute the climax of calamities which wrote a definite and conclusive finis to his work, leaving it devoid of present accomplishment and without hope that future generations might carry it on.

I am done for,' he exclaimed, 'no one knows me!'

'What is the meaning of your saying that no one knows you?' inquired one of his disciples solicitously.

'I do not murmur against heaven, I do not grumble against man,' the Master declared. 'I pursue my studies here on earth and am in touch with heaven. It is heaven that knows me. Of those who came before me there were some who did not lower their standards or shut their eyes to corruption, and there were others who did. Still others, unable to countenance the evils of their day, became recluses or hermits and refrained from speaking about the evils they knew existed. In their conduct they conformed to their ideas of purity and in their retirement they maintained their ideals of conduct. But I am different from these men; for me there can be no choice of conduct on my part and no compulsion on the part of others.'

Another blow fell on the old philosopher, for a second faithful disciple Tze Loo died in Wei. The two disciples were as different from each other as any two honest and sincere men could well be. Yen Yuan was a frail young ascetic of phenomenal intelligence and precocious learning. Tze Loo who at the time of his death was almost twice the age of the younger man was at heart a burly soldier, often rude, and always brave and adventuresome. The Master had long ago predicted that Tze Loo, intrepid and always courting danger, would not die a natural death, and his prophecy came true. Tze Loo had been employed for some years by the Duke of Wei as one of his principal military officers and had remained in Wei when Master Kung returned to Lu. During his absence on duty, the city in his command was captured by an enemy who was waiting an opportunity to complete his victory by killing the absent commander. On his return Tze Loo was warned of this but learning that his ducal employer was still in danger he said:

'He who eats a man's food may not abandon him in his hour of peril,' and so went on to what he knew to be certain death. He succeeded in gaining entrance to the city but soon afterwards was mortally wounded by an arrow which displaced his cap. Remarking that a soldier dislikes to die with his helmet off, he calmly replaced his cap, tied the strings and expired.

If after the appearance of the *chi lin* any further indication of his approaching end were required the death of these two disciples supplied it; the Master lost no time about completing the work he had in hand which was his history of the state of Lu. It was practically completed at this time and he had only a few final lines to write. He brought it up-to-date by recording the appearance of the *chi lin* without comment though the fact that he terminated the record in this abrupt way would certainly indicate the importance he attached to the event. He made no further entries though death was not so near at hand as he had thought and he lived two years longer.

These final years he spent in a study of *The Book of Changes*, a curious and puzzling treatise on philosophy, which is generally ascribed to the authorship of the founder of the Chow dynasty. The text of this strange and mystifying book consists of sixty-four brief essays full of symbolism and cryptic comments which no sound scholar of to-day pretends to understand. How far the work approached the perfection with which it was credited no one has, for centuries, been able to express an intelligent opinion but at the time of Master Kung it was credited with being a philosophical treatise so complete as to transcend human intelligence in its perfection. The essays so far as they can be understood are all of a social, moral and political character. Each was designated by a combination of broken and unbroken lines, known as hexagrams, each combination having a symbolic significance which would give an indication of the text and provide hints for further philosophical speculation. These hexagrams with their simple but numerous changes and combinations were early seized upon by the superstitious as a means of foretelling the decisions of the fates and many battles were fought or abandoned and many other important matters decided as the result of the combination which different lengths of broken reed assumed when thrown on the ground or the cracks which developed when the shells of tortoise were burned. Those who were skilled or pretended to be skilled in such matters were accredited with the ability to see in the arrangement of the broken reeds or in the cracks in the burnt tortoise shell a similarity to one or more of the hexagrams and so predestined by the fates. Master Kung had never paid any attention to these superstitious beliefs and did not do so now. On the other hand, he was absorbed by the philosophical speculations of the essays. In his study of this work, he was able, for the first time, to indulge in the luxury of purely scholastic reflection and study, for during his long and busy life of study and scholarship his mind has always been exorcised with practical affairs and melancholy problems. Having through consciousness of the early approach of death found release from the high-minded and unselfish ambitions which had absorbed him for more than a half-century he was now able to find complete relaxation in this abstruse study. The eternal principles of the *Book of Changes* had naught to do with the petty ambitions and chicaneries of dukes, barons and ministers or the wickedness of beautiful Madam Nan Tze and the unfaithful Ki Ki. He now, in fact, became the recluse he had been urged to become many years before and was definitely through with human endeavour though the choice was not his own but had been forced on him through that most inexorable of fates, old age. He studied the book so assiduously that he wore out three sets of leather thongs which bound the wooden pages together.

'Ah!' he cried with a return to the enthusiasm of youth. 'If I had fifty years more to live, I would spend them all in a study of this book!'

The Master fell ill and Tze Kung, the last of the three favourites: asked permission to visit him. He hurried to the appointment as soon as permission was granted but the Master suffering great bodily pain complained querulously:

'Why are you so late?'

With his little remaining energy he pulled himself to his feet and with the support of his staff dragged his body back and forth across the courtyard crooning:

> 'Is the sacred hill decaying?
> Is the roof beam breaking?
> Is the wise man weakening?'

Tze Kung grieved to himself: 'If the great mountain crumbles, to what shall I look up? If the strong beam breaks, what will protect me? If the wise man withers away, on whom shall I lean?'

Master Kung then burst into tears and said to the disciple:

'For a long time the world has been unregulated; no one understands how to follow me. Last night I dreamed that I was sitting before the sacrificial offerings between the pillars where the coffin is placed.'

In this dream as he described it, the altar was arranged in the style which has been followed by one of the most ancient which had fallen so low that it was now entirely extinct and had no one who

'Why are you so late?' demanded Master Kung querulously.

could offer sacrifices to the spirits of the deceased kings. This appeared to him to indicate that he awaited a similar fate.

Seven days later the Master died. This was in the summer of the year 479 B.C. and he was seventy-three years old. Except for his young grandson there was no relative near him but his death-bed was surrounded by faithful disciples who were spiritually more akin to him than mere blood relatives could be. When they heard that he was dangerously ill many former disciples who were living in distant places left their homes, some resigning their employment, to hurry to him and pay their last respects. For some reason his disciples who had charge of the arrangements did not bury him at the ancestral tomb at Fang, the ancestral home he had selected for his father and mother, but near the place of his death.

Duke Gay of Lu hastily ordered his ritualists to compose a song of mourning:

'Merciful Heaven, thou hast no compassion upon me, in that thou hast not left the one venerable man fitted to protect me, the Unique One, during the period of my rule. Full of mourning am I in my painful sorrow. O woe! Now I no longer have anyone who can serve me as a model!'

He followed this by providing a funeral sacrifice in which an extravagant number of animals were displayed on the altar.

Since the duke had never availed himself of the services of the Master and had certainly never used him as a model, either in his official or personal conduct, there was not a little hypocrisy in this obituary tribute and Tze Kung, the one who had attended the Master during his last days was dangerously outspoken about it. The duke, he said, was besotted, had not obtained the goodwill of his people, had not been interested enough to inquire about the welfare of the Master when he was alive and finally had committed a grave breach of decorum, had used unpardonable effrontery, by referring to himself as 'the Unique One' which was the designation of a great king and could not be used by a petty feudal ruler. Tze Kung made a direful prophecy:

'The duke will surely not die a peaceful death in his land of Lu.'

It is not really known whether the duke died a peaceful death or died in Lu for by the time that event occurred a few years later he was such an obscure and powerless refugee that his death was not recorded and no one knows either where or when it occurred.

In contrast with the undoubted hypocrisy and insincerity of the duke was the sincere and heartfelt mourning of the disciples. There is some doubt about the actual number who were in attendance on the Master at the time of his death but the pantheon of accredited disciples has been set down by historians as numbering seventy-two and we may assume that those who surrounded his death-bed were approximately that number including former disciples who had returned to this last sad duty. Many of them who were employed elsewhere came to his sick-bed as they would have come on the serious illness of a father or mother. By common consent they mourned him for three years, which was and is the period of mourning due to a father from a son. In order to show that their grief was no empty display of ceremony they did not put on the usual ritualistic mourning garb but merely wore old clothing and abstained from feasts and amusements. The mourners constituted a motley assortment, old and young, married and single, rich and poor, eminent and obscure. But they were as one in their almost religious devotion to the memory of their master and the intelligent enthusiasm with which they set about making his teachings known to their fellow-countrymen.

During their period of grief the disciples discussed the teachings of their Master and recalled the advice he had given to them and to others usually in the form of terse remarks. Purely by the aid of their memory these sayings were compiled and are now known in their translated form as *The Confucian Analects* though a more correct title would be 'The Conversations of Master Kung'. They form the basis of the Confucian philosophy and have had a profound influence on the lives of his fellow-countrymen. It is very difficult for one who has not lived in China or made a rather thorough study of Chinese life to have any comprehension of the almost universal acceptance of his teachings as embodied in this work. From a period which antedates the birth of Christ every schoolboy has been required to memorise his teachings and every educated man has mastered them with the result that the dry and sketchy comments of the *Analects* are much better known to educated Chinese than the dramatic episodes of the Bible are known to educated residents of Christian countries. It obviously never occurred to Master Kung that his conversations with his disciples would be put in permanent written form; he certainly never

All the disciples mourned the death of the Master for three years and when they departed for their homes Tze Kung built himself a hut and mourned for an additional three years.

dreamed that his fame of which he was so apprehensive would be made secure by this work alone.

At the end of the three-year period of mourning the disciples packed up their baggage and departed for their homes where many of them became masters of philosophy in their own right and taught disciples of their own, who in turn became masters of their own and taught others and so in endless progression down to the present day, a matter of some seventy generations. In many parts of China there are towns whose principal claim to fame is that a disciple of Master Kung once taught there; others are even more famous because of the burial-place of a disciple and while the tombs of kings and princes have been forgotten the honoured resting-places of the disciples have always been kept in good repair. Disciple Tze Kung did not feel that the debt he owed to the Master had been adequately repaid by three years of mourning so when his companions had departed he built a hut by the master's grave and lived there alone for another three years when he also departed.

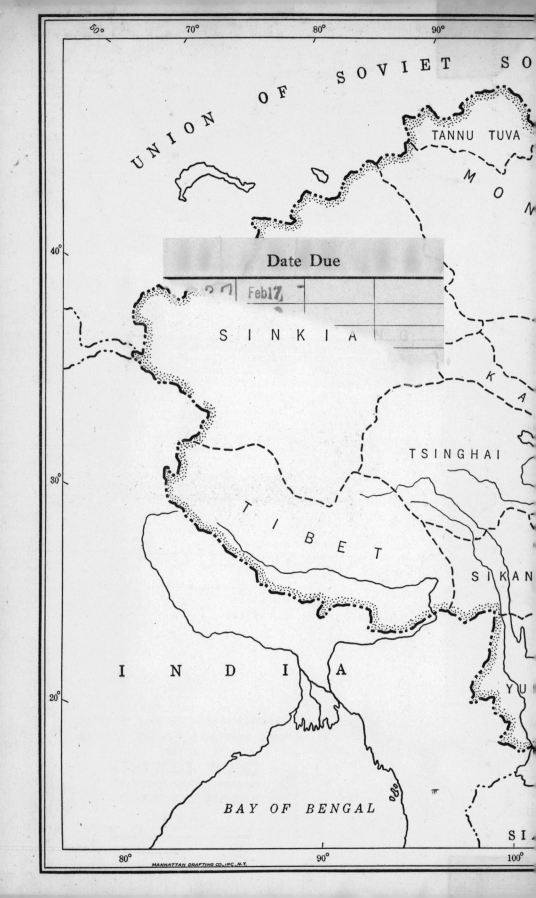